1986

America's
Musical Stage

America's Musical Stage

TWO HUNDRED YEARS OF MUSICAL THEATRE

Julian Mates

CONTRIBUTIONS IN DRAMA AND
THEATRE STUDIES, NUMBER 18

GREENWOOD PRESS
WESTPORT, CONNECTICUT • LONDON, ENGLAND

Library of Congress Cataloging in Publication Data
Mates, Julian, 1927-
America's musical stage.

(Contributions in drama and theatre studies,
ISSN 0163-3821; no. 18)
Bibliography: p.
Includes index.
1. Musical revue, comedy, etc.—United States.
I. Title.   II. Series.
ML1711.M42   1985   782.81'0973   85-935
ISBN 0-313-23948-7

Library of Congress Catalog Card Number: 85-935
ISBN: 0-313-23948-7
ISSN: 0163-3821

First published in 1985

Greenwood Press
A division of Congressional Information Service, Inc.
88 Post Road West
Westport, Connecticut 06881

Printed in the United States of America

The paper used in this book complies with the Permanent Paper Standard
issued by the National Information Standards Organization (Z39.48-1984).

10 9 8 7 6 5 4 3 2 1

This book is for

Barbara

Ethan

Jessica

Karen

Contents

List of Illustrations

Acknowledgments

It is difficult to know where to begin, and when to stop, acknowledging help. If I attempt to list all the names, then I reveal how little is mine and how much is owed to others; if I record few names, I am in danger of omitting outstanding help.

Still, the staffs of some libraries cannot be ignored—those of the Library of Congress, the University of Chicago, Harvard University, Yale University, Columbia University, Long Island University (the C. W. Post Campus), the Museum of the City of New York, the New-York Historical Society, and the New York Public Library, both at 42nd Street and, especially, at the Library of Performing Arts, Lincoln Center.

Three sections of the book were published, in somewhat different form, as articles, and I am grateful to *Theatre Survey* for permission to reprint material on *The Black Crook*; to *Ventures in Research* for permission to reprint material on melodrama; and to *American Music* for permission to reprint material on the first 100 years of American musical theatre.

I am grateful to correspondents and to workers in the field who have found time to talk to me—people who have made suggestions and helped. I am grateful to the outstanding professionals in the field—Stanley Green and Gerald Bordman and William Green, for example—who have offered suggestions or encouragement. Friends and colleagues cannot be thanked properly no matter how hard I try—Richard Griffith who read the manuscript and helped make it readable; David Jasen who generously loaned sheet music for many of the illustrations; and, most of all, Barbara, who was the patient sounding board for the book's ideas.

America's Musical Stage

Overture

SOME HISTORY, AN ANALYSIS, AND A POLEMIC

The musical stage has become so much a part of everyday American life that we hardly notice its presence outside the theatre—at political conventions, sporting events, industrial shows, circuses, and parades. It is performed by touring road companies, dinner theatres, outdoor playhouses, indoor arenas, summer stock companies, community theatres, amateur companies, elementary schools, high schools, and colleges.[1] A critic has noted that, in the United States, the American musical included "the minstrel show, burlesque and extravaganza, comic opera, operetta, vaudeville, revue and musical comedy." It is, in other words, "a large popular genre with many sub-genres, each with its own formulas and conventions and each reflecting American values, tastes and character."[2] Music as used in films and television productions (including commercials) is derived from our musical stage. Our opera houses increasingly add Broadway musicals to their repertories (for example, *Lost in the Stars*, *Candide*, *Song of Norway*, *Sweeney Todd*, and *Porgy and Bess*). All this activity emerges from a history of American musicals that began over 200 years ago. Certainly, the American musical has some claim to be termed indigenous; and, in addition, it is central to America's cultural life.

All this is an explanation for the pages which follow. The history of theatre companies in America demonstrates the way drama came to this country and how it spread. And then the history of the repertory makes clear that the repertory of these companies was always heavily musical in nature. And the history of performers shows the necessity, given the repertory, for performers to act, to sing, and to dance.

Then, with history as a base, various structures are inspected—each an aspect of America's musical stage. When opera (both comic and grand) and operetta have been viewed, their relationship to each other becomes clear; the same analysis is given to the minstrel show and the circus, and they, too, are seen as not only related to each other but to the other forms discussed. Gradually, the pages following add melodrama, dance, burlesque, revues, vaudeville, and musical comedy—all interrelated, all forming a part of what we refer to as the American musical stage.

No other work on the American musical stage has attempted to demonstrate the interrelationship of musical stage forms, and to do so in a context which is both historical and analytical. The point of view is that our musical theatre is both indigenous and our oldest theatrical tradition.

Yet three misapprehensions constantly challenge the American musical stage's right to be considered a serious artistic form.

The first is historical. Trends in our musical theatre, this argument goes, change the nature of musicals approximately every decade, so how can one study them or even take them seriously? Or—and this is merely a variation—musicals are too recent a stage form to have shape, meaning, and aesthetic significance. Historically, artistic genres have not changed in short periods of time or disappeared quickly once established. Tragedy, for example, evolved slowly over 2,000 years ago and is still a viable form. If allegory is no longer written with the verve its medieval audience enjoyed, it still has a place in the literary scene. Relatively new structures such as the novel and the short story have their roots in such forms as the novella, yet despite frequent announcements concerning their deaths, they continue to be written. They do change (a stress is placed

on personae, on point of view, on epistolary or picaresque modes),
but the forms remain.

Yet the musical, this discussion suggests, is a new form,
scarcely worth noting, which began with *Pal Joey*, or *Oklahoma!*, or *45 minutes from Broadway*, or *The Black Crook*, or
In Dahomey, or *Show Boat*, or— .

A close relationship between drama and music, in any case,
is not a recent development. The Greeks used songs and dances
and a chorus and musicians. So did the Romans. Later, in Italy,
a group of composers, the *camarata*, attempted to recreate Greek
tragedy—and invented opera. In fact, someone should write a
startling book, one which shows the last 100 years as an ab-
erration, plays written *without* music. In other words, the history of Western drama was, until recent times, that of a musical
stage, with music playing a greater or lesser role, but never
wholly absent from the theatre.

At the time this land was evolving into a nation, its first
theatre companies sailed here from England. At that period a
large part of England's repertory, thanks to the ballad opera
and comic opera (and to England's peculiar licensing laws),
was musical. Even those plays not specifically considered to be
musicals contained several songs, perhaps a dance or two, and
much musical accompaniment. The eighteenth century's use
of an afterpiece (usually a one-act musical) added to the repertory still more musicals. And no theatre could function without its own orchestra. The first plays performed in America
were quite musical in nature, and wherever our first actors
traveled, they carried with them this musical repertory. In
effect, the musical stage became the only theatre known in
early America.

The historical approach to the musical, then, unless one is
willing to investigate a larger span of time than a decade, and
unless one is willing to recognize the long history of music on
the stage, may not only distort history but may also neglect
an important American heritage.

The second misapprehension concerning the American musical is that it is merely a "popular" art form, unworthy of serious
consideration. Aside from the fact that one generation's popular
art may be another's masterpiece (note, for example, Shake-

speare, Molière, Lope de Vega), the study of America's musicals *is* the study of a serious art form. What is meant when something is called popular? Something is popular, from one point of view, if it attracts many people. The fact that American audiences have flocked to hear musical works on the stage for over 200 years is no guarantee, in itself, that the works are not artistically of the highest aesthetic quality. And who can deny the seriousness of an art form which has attracted over the years in America such composers as Benjamin Carr and Alexander Reinagle, as Stephen Foster and Victor Herbert, as Leonard Bernstein and George Gershwin? An art form in which the best of America's actors, singers, and dancers perform? From our earliest days, the line between serious and popular art was thoroughly blurred not only by the works but by the abilities of the performers appearing in them. Again, a 200-year-old tradition enables our musicals to display performers adept at acting, singing, and dancing, to the incredulity of other countries.

Throughout American history, serious composers have devoted their best efforts to a stage genre; the best actors, singers, and dancers America could produce have performed on the musical stage; and an audience has been willing to attend and to approve even of experiments. All this may be the basis for popular art, but in America it has certainly been the basis for serious art as well.

The final major objection to America's musical theatre has been to the form itself. Drama tends to be taught by English teachers who stress its literary merits. But popular works may have great theatrical merit. And if aesthetic criteria for this most popular of American art forms do not exist, then who teaches, who learns, and how do we pass on a tradition and a heritage? "Hybrid," "bastard," "mixed"—all these contemptuous appellations are used to describe our musical stage. Of course, it is a bit difficult to decide what is a legitimate art form. Is a Beethoven symphony pure? Does it not require an orchestra comprised of many musicians, plus a conductor? What of acoustics and audience? Is the drama pure? Does it, too, not require the collaboration of many people before it can be fully realized, as intended by its author? In a sense, all the arts are hybrid, since they depend upon an interrelationship between the artist, his art (and all the variable media through which the artist must work), its presentation, and its audience. In effect, all the performing arts, especially, require the collaboration of many artists. Brockway and Weinstock refer to the opera, for example, as a form neither pure music nor pure drama, a hybrid with glamour, so much glamour, they claim, that tens of millions are drawn to it, live or via the broadcast media.[3]

The difficulty with this approach to musical theatre, glamour or no, is that music critics find the music wanting, drama critics find the librettos absurd, and few critics are available to see the musical stage work as a whole. For example, in drama two characters cannot speak at the same time, yet on the musical stage they can and do—and each comes clearer as a result. A libretto must be short to allow room for musical development. A silly story may be given profound dimension by the music which underlies it, accompanies it, or exists by itself. Again, perhaps an aesthetic of the musical stage is needed, one that provides the possibility of evaluating a *total* work of art, of viewing each element as a part of a whole rather than in isolation. In opera as well as in operetta, in the minstrel show as well as the circus, in melodrama as well as in dance, in vaudeville and burlesque as well as in the revue, and in the musical, certain basics are at work which tie all musical-stage forms together. The American musical theatre is made up of different genres, but the underlying definition—a dramatic-musical work for the stage—holds throughout.

And if, after all, some critics insist that the musical—the heart of America's stage—is a bastard art form, perhaps we need to answer with Edmund from Shakespeare's *King Lear*: "Now, gods, stand up for bastards."

Act I

HISTORY: THE DEVELOPMENT OF AN INDIGENOUS FORM

SCENE 1

Companies

The changing organization of America's theatre companies was in good part responsible for sustaining a musical-stage tradition. The kinds of dramatic companies and the ways in which they moved across the continent, spreading theatre—musical theatre—across the country, helped shape an appreciation and an audience for the musical stage. For the most part, when Americans in the eighteenth and the nineteenth centuries saw their first dramatic representation, it was musical in nature.

The story begins with scattered amateur performances in the seventeenth century and a few attempts at professional ones early in the eighteenth. Snippets of news in diaries and newspapers about operas and about increasing numbers of productions indicate a burgeoning interest in the drama. The stage in America really came alive when theatre companies arrived and began to have a sustained impact. The first of these companies was that of Murray and Kean; another was that of Robert Upton; finally, a troupe of players arrived that had the greatest influence on our eighteenth-century theatre—the American (later called the Old American) Company.

The Old American Company was initially a sharing company (a tradition going back to Shakespeare's day); that is, the manager received one or more shares, the owner of the property used by the company got several shares (usually this was the manager as well; even his children might, collectively, receive one share if they performed in minor roles), and each of the actors received shares according to ability or reputation.

Lewis Hallam brought the American Company here from England. They arrived in Yorktown in 1752, and they gave their first performance in Williamsburg. In the 1750s they performed in small cities in the South as well as New York, Charleston, Jamaica, and Philadelphia. In the 1760s they added still other cities, including Albany, Alexandria, and Boston. Then Newport, Providence, and Annapolis were visited. In 1775 they opted to sit out the Revolutionary War with a stay in Jamaica until 1782. When the company returned, they brought theatre to other communities. Soon, however, it became unprofitable to travel as far as the South, especially since successful local companies were busily setting up residence there. And so, the end of the 1780s found the Old American Company with a shortened route—New York, Philadelphia, Baltimore, and Annapolis. Large cities enjoyed their own companies in the 1790s; the Old American Company, for example, was based in New York, and Wignell and Reinagle's troupe used Philadelphia as their home.

During the summer, a company might split into two or more units, each of which would visit a different city (Hartford and Providence, for example) with an abbreviated corps, then join together for a larger city (such as Boston) before commencing their regular season in their city of residence.

In some cases, one or two actors might even strike off by themselves in the summer, offering scenes from plays and musicals or concerts and appearing wherever they thought an audience could be brought together. There were few theatres available in these small communities, and any place (usually taverns, or hotels) which held enough people to repay the actors for their labors might serve. Still, pioneer communities with little or no available entertainment must have been delighted at the opportunity to see live performances.

The manager of the full company gradually took a stronger position. As the company changed from sharing to one where the actors were hired for a season on weekly salaries, the manager made all arrangements for leasing theatres, both in the company's home city and on the road. He was responsible for casting (within the limits imposed on him by the actors' contracts) and directing all plays; he served as treasurer and bookkeeper; frequently, he acted as well. And these were but the beginning of his chores. He was responsible for hiring an orchestra leader-composer. He served as stage manager. He supervised doorkeepers, carpenters, property man, box-office manager (who, in addition to tickets, was expected to sell the songs of the operas being presented), callboy, constables, general attendants, and prompter (this position evolved into that of stage manager, thereby freeing the manager from one of his chores). The most important function of all, however, was the manager's responsibility for determining the repertory of his company.

The Old American Company, in the closing years of the eighteenth century, was probably made up of at least fifty people, exclusive of its large orchestra (up to twenty-five players by 1800).[1]

Outside the main cities, much theatrical activity was going on as smaller communities were gradually opened to drama. Normally, the process began with local amateurs (frequently soldiers), who were usually followed by either a circus or a minstrel show. Only then did the professional theatre arrive.[2]

The nineteenth century revealed theatres spreading all through America. A brief geographical survey of the United States shows how the essentially musical stage moved everywhere.

In the northeast, Sol. Smith's company worked its way from Rochester to Cincinnati in 1828, stopping at Lockport, Black Rock, Niagara Falls, Fredonia, Westfield, Mayville, and Jamestown. By the Civil War, theatres had been built in all the larger cities of the South—for example, in Savannah, New Orleans, Mobile (with seven before 1855), Richmond, Wilmington, Atlanta, and Montgomery. Even smaller towns and villages always managed to find some sort of space for traveling entertainment.

Away from the South, amateur performers played in 1790 in Pittsburgh, in 1798 in Detroit, in 1799 in Lexington, Kentucky, in 1801 in Cincinnati, with the preferred work being the comic opera *The Poor Soldier*, usually followed by a musical interlude or brief comic afterpiece. By 1815 the principal towns of the Ohio Valley had seen professional productions—works like the "grand melodramatic opera" *The Devil's Bridge*, performed in St. Louis in 1821. The circus in those days was musical theatre from start to finish—and, in fact, rural Missouri enjoyed over sixty circuses before the Civil War.[3] The circus troupe of Ed and Jerry Mabie toured from Wisconsin to Texas (always accompanied by a minstrel show; the Model Dramatic Troupe toured the same general area in the 1850s).

Chicago heard a variety of opera troupes in the 1850s, and Houston boasted a theatre company in 1838, managed by Henry Corri, a ballet dancer.[4]

West of the Rockies, the pattern held. The earliest recorded performances were by military amateurs (Stevenson's New York Regiment) in minstrel shows. As Douglas McDermott points out, California's northern and central portions were economically and geographically one region, and this affected touring circuits.

In this respect California's theatrical frontier was like the Eastern Seaboard when the Hallams monopolized it; like the Ohio Valley for Samuel Drake; like the Gulf Plains for Noah Ludlow, Sol Smith, and James Caldwell; like the Lake Plains for John Blake Rice, Dean and McKinney, MacKenzie and Jefferson. Like their counterparts on previous frontiers, players in California toured because that was the only way they could reach an audience to support themselves for the entire year.[5]

Thus, California's frontier theatre found stock companies based in a large city, touring smaller settlements and "thereby maintaining the tradition on which the nation's theatre was founded." Los Angeles was late in viewing professionals; not until 1860 did the first professional company, a troupe of minstrels, arrive in that city. But a full decade earlier minstrel shows and circuses began to tour the Willamette Valley of Oregon. Salt Lake City featured an amateur theatre by 1850 (the Old Bowery, with the Desaret Dramatic Association). San Francisco witnessed its first grand opera in 1851, and a variety of itinerant troupes performing French and Italian grand opera appeared in the 1850s. Nevada had eight theatres by 1861 (in which dance was stressed heavily), along with circuses; by 1860 Nevada had seen opera as well as minstrel performances. Portland, Oregon, was treated to amateur productions as early as 1846, a circus in 1852, and minstrels in 1854. Records exist of amateurs performing operatic selections in Seattle in the 1850s. Larry Robert Wolz's work on the theatres in Texas reveals a similar sequence of theatrical events in Austin, San Antonio, Waco, Dallas, Fort Worth, El Paso, and Abilene: first amateur productions, usually musical, then circuses, and either English or grand or comic opera, and melodrama.[6] Wherever people settled, there was musical theatre, amateur and professional, circus, and later, minstrel.

The circus, almost always the first professional theatre to arrive, began its popularity in America in the eighteenth century. The two major circuses were those of Ricketts and Lailson. Ricketts visited at least sixteen cities with his circus. By 1800 both he an Lailson had closed down, but in a few years others came (Victor Pepin and John Breschard arrived in 1807–1808, for example) and began to establish circuses in America. By 1820 over thirty circuses were moving through New England and the Atlantic states alone.

Circus buildings were designed for both equestrian and dramatic performances, with ramps for horses leading from both sides of the stage into the orchestra, forming an oval within which circus acts might be performed. In addition, many theatres were at least temporarily redesigned to make some form of circus possible. The Lion Theatre in Boson was converted, for example, as were the St. Charles in New Orleans, the American Theatre in San Francisco, and Niblo's in New York. Rival circuses began to appear in some cities, each drawing audiences from the other and from the playhouses.[7]

The minstrel show, too, was a tremendous force in spreading theatre across America.[8] Though there was not much theatre in Los Angeles until 1880, a professional minstrel troupe appeared there in 1860. In the 1850s, parts of Oregon began to see minstrel shows, though the territory was too sparsely settled for more elaborate theatre to try the route. In fact, the history of town after town in the United States shows the minstrel show as one of the first available entertainments. In Pittsburgh, during the 1840s alone, the following companies traveled through: the Christy Ethiopian Minstrels, the Original Ethiopian Serenaders, the Harmoneons, the Northern Exquisites, the Original Sable Harmonists, the Tyroleon Singers, the Washington Euterpians, the Ethiopian Warblers, and so forth. Minstrel troupes traveled easily because they carried little equipment, and rural Missouri was treated to them. They rarely gave much advance notice and performed in any space where an audience could be assembled—but the area had virtually no other theatre until the Civil War. In large cities and small communities, the minstrel troupe performed everywhere.

As if the legitimate theatre in the nineteenth century did not have enough competition from circuses and minstrel shows, showboats, too, were a source of diversion. The *Floating Palace*, for example, which in company with at least three other showboats toured the Mississippi in the 1850s and 1860s, was 250 feet long and provided both circus and minstrel show auditoriums. Commercial boats (for example, the line between Fall River and New York City) featured minstrel companies, as did steamboats touring the Ohio, Cumberland, and Tennessee rivers.

Museums also demanded a share of America's theatre-going public. Although they began in the United States in the eighteenth century with a little musical entertainment to complement their exhibits, it was not until the nineteenth century that they really became entertainment centers. In the middle of the nineteenth century, the Providence Museum put the regular theatre out of business by adding a hall for drama to its museum of curiosities. The New York museums of 1839 and 1840 (the American Museum and Peale's) were predecessors of the variety halls of mid-century and of the vaudeville to come. The Chicago Museum in 1864 featured opera. Probably here, as with so many other apsects of American life, the stress was on education. All Puritan scruples might be overcome if the end was educational. In his *Reminiscences*, Henry Clay Barnabee, actor and manager, suggests the appeal of museums. He attended the Boston Museum where he saw the elder Booth as Richard III and found a full string orchestra. The museum, which had opened in 1841, had a hall of curiosities, a music saloon, and a theatre. The reason for its popularity (in Boston as in other cities in America) is suggested by Barnabee: "For years and years many thousands of the good people of that city [Boston] who would never be seen going into a theatre as such, could compromise with their consciences and take it in as a Museum attachment, without violence to their uprightness and religious scruples."[9]

Fighting off all these entertainments—minstrel shows and circuses and showboats and museums—was the legitimate theatre, especially the local stock company, different from the Old American Company of previous years. The star system began. to take over at the turn of the century, and this made a huge difference.

The star system did not necessarily imply one star but rather an act which might be hired by the manager of a resident stock company to perform for a given period of time during the season. The "star" might be an actor, a singer, or a dancer, but might also be a troupe of acrobats, an opera company, or a dance corps.

So, the stock companies in each city (except for such large cities as New York, where many theatres were needed) functioned in two ways. First, they provided continuing theatre between the visits of stars; second, they provided all other roles needed by the star turn. The manager was responsible for renting, hiring, booking, and touring.

Later in the nineteenth century, largely as a result of the efforts of Dion Boucicault, another form of touring company was created, the combination. In this, a successful show was cast, and costumed and sets designed, in New York, and the entire show sent on the road. In many cities, the old stock company was killed because of the superior quality of these packaged shows. The fact that it was not economical for a combination show to appear for only one night also helped kill the repertory system, in which a different show was performed each night.

Still, the stock company existed into the twentieth century, as did the package show and all the other types of theatre spawned by the nineteenth century. Throughout the new land, a great range of theatre development could be found, from those in fully built up cities to those in the most undeveloped parts of the frontier. The result was that all types of theatre companies co-existed, from the sharing company of the eighteenth century through nineteenth-century medicine shows (the latter were prepared to offer, as Nevada Ned, a showman, summarized: "drama, vaudeville, musical comedy, Wild West shows, minstrels, magic, burlesque"[10]). Concert companies (bands with comic and musical acts) were popular along with Uncle Tom's Cabin troupes (sometimes referred to as Tom Shows). Tent rep, sometimes called rep shows or rag opries, with a repertory of plays and accompanying vaudeville large enough to allow for a change of bills for as much as a week flourished; an estimated 400 tent shows were traveling through the United States by the mid-1920s. Something of the fluidity with which companies operated is suggested by Caroline Schaffner, writing recently of her experiences in 1925: "You played in the tent in the summer; you closed on Saturday night in the tent and moved into theatres or opera houses for repertoire in the fall, and then into a town like Marshalltown, Des Moines, or a larger town for stock until summer, when you moved back into the tent."[11] Some types of shows, such as the Wild West exhibitions, the medicine shows, and the chautauquas used music primarily as background, while music and musical acts were crucial to others, such as honky-tonks, burlesque, and, later, vaudeville. In the twentieth century, musical theatre found homes all over the country, including universities. In some cities, theatres were built exclusively for one type of entertainment, such as opera, though for the most part many types of entertainment could be put into any space that had room for entertainers and audience, such as tobacco warehouses in the eighteenth century, or even courthouses, hotel dining rooms, and frequently, taverns.[12] Today, "resident" theatres—six dozen or more, according to Michael Bandler—are spread out across the United States, much like the old stock companies.[13] Actors, composers, and playwrights have new opportunities in an increasingly decentralized theatre.

A great range of theatres and companies spread all across the United States is only significant to the musical stage if the repertory is musical. It is time to look at the repertory of the American theatre.

SCENE 2 ───────────────────────────

Repertory

───────────────────────────

A variety of circumstances conspired to create a musical stage right from the beginning of America's dramatic history. Certainly, the excitement, vitality, and creativity of today's musical theatre must have long roots, and these roots do extend back to the eighteenth century.

Both Puritans and Quakers had strong objections to the drama. The idea of the playhouse as Devil's workshop goes far back in Western civilization. The Bible objected to the artistic depiction of man, which is why no paintings or plays show up in ancient Jewish documents. Except among the Greeks, the reputation of the drama was rarely high, and it was banned from Rome by early Christians. Even in Shakespeare's day, the highest peak of drama anywhere in the world (note such playwrights as Marlowe, Jonson, Marston, Chapman, Dekker, to mention only a few), the public playhouses were for a long time forced outside the boundaries of London. Excuses, other than the supposed immorality of the drama itself, included the possibility of spreading the plague, the possibility of seditious behavior, and the possibility of immoral practices in a crowd. One of the first things the Civil War in England was responsible for was the closing of the theatres in 1642; they did not open again until 1660, and then in very different form.

In America, the Puritan and Quaker objection to drama was

reversed when it came to music. While some objections to music have come to light (witness the publication in 1725 of a sermon entitled "An essay to silence the outcry that has been made in some places against regular singing," or, "Promiscuous singing no divine institution; having neither president [*sic*] nor precept to support it, either from the musical institution of David, or from the gospel dispensation. Therefore it ought to be exploded, as being a humane invention, tending rather to gratify the carnal ears of men than to be acceptable and pleasing worship to God," 1793)—nonetheless, for the most part music was considered to be moral as well as entertaining. After all, the very first book published in the colonies was the *Bay Psalm Book* (1640). Some published writings from the eighteenth century are both amusing and instructive: "Letter Addressed to Young Married Women" (1796) describes music as one of the "most winning accomplishments . . . necessary to preserve the lover in the husband." "Music Physically Considered" (1789) discusses the use of music for medical treatment. Other works include "Power of music over animals and infants" (1794), "Power of sound, or the influence of melody over the human heart; calculated for the advance of public religion" (1786), "Regular and Skillful music in the worship of God . . ." (1774), "The lawfulness, excellency and advantage of instrumental music in the public worship of God" (1763).[1]

Outside the church, music was so much a part of people's lives that studying an instrument was an important element in a young man's or young woman's education. American publishers brought out at least 113 "songsters" (books of popular songs) in the eighteenth century alone.[2] Concert life in America was rich and broadly based. In fact, in order to avoid being either censured or canceled, a theatrical production frequently had to list itself as a concert. Music, then, was a tremendously important part of America's entertainment heritage.

A second factor in developing a musical stage was the very repertory of the eighteenth century as it arrived here from England. In 1660, when Charles II was restored to the English throne, he authorized by letters patent (causing them to be known as patent theatres or Theatres Royal) two companies, those of Thomas Killigrew and Sir William D'Avenant. D'Avenant had been successful in bridging the interregnum between Cromwell's closing the theatre in 1642 and Charles II's opening them by producing operas (*The Siege of Rhodes*, for example, in 1656). Despite the patents, however, many theatres were able to produce plays in England until Parliament passed the Licensing Act of 1737. In an attempt to improve manners and morals, playhouses were theoretically limited to two—Drury Lane and Covent Garden (though, after a while, the Haymarket was given permission to put on summer entertainment). Despite their unofficial status, many other theatres continued to attract audiences, but they were forced to resort to subterfuge (for example, calling a play a concert) or to a heavy use of music. The law was eased in 1788, but not before the repertory of the eighteenth-century English theatre had become heavily musical in nature. (The Theatres Act of 1843 did away with even the pretext of limiting the number of theatres.)

Still more of what was happening in England affected our stage. Nettleton and Case point out, "The eighteenth century was particularly active in developing a musically-enriched theatre, for varied music was an integral part of its way of life. Innumerable ballads were sung on its streets, impressive music was sung in its churches, catches and glees to the tunes played on delicate instruments were sung in the coffee-houses in London and at country houses in the outlying countries."[3] And within even the legitimate theatres music was used to introduce the players and to fill the time between the plays and pauses between the acts.

The repertory, then, as it arrived from England was made up of about 10 percent musicals. By the end of the century, the American repertory was more than half musical. This point is essential. The first plays seen in America were either musicals or heavily dependent upon music.

The core of the musical theatre was the ballad opera. The basic structure of the ballad opera was significant not only to the eighteenth century's productions, and not only to such forms as the minstrel show and the burlesque in the nineteenth century, but also to the very nature of the musical comedy in the twentieth century. Some understanding of the ballad opera, then, is crucial in order to comprehend much of what came later on America's stage.

The first ballad opera—*The Beggar's Opera*—was written by John Gay in 1728. The legend goes that Jonathan Swift suggested to Alexander Pope that Gay write a "Newgate Pastoral," a pastoral drama changed in setting from the country to Newgate Prison. Gay took up the suggestion and wrote a libretto which satirized a good many elements of the English society of his day. First of all, Italian opera was burlesqued (Gay and others felt it was driving away native works); social and political mores as well as actual political figures and events were exposed to ridicule; finally, many of the conventions of the popular drama (excessive sentimentalism, for example) were satirized. Whether it was the satire hitting home or the novelty of the new form, the realism, the excellent acting, or the novel use of music—or all these together—*The Beggar's Opera* was an instant hit. (It was produced by John Rich, and a sort of joke of the period claimed *The Beggar's Opera* made Gay rich and Rich gay.) The audience was delighted to hear long-familiar tunes (no original music was composed for the work) with new lyrics, and to hear the tunes separated by spoken dialogue rather than by recitative. In fact, part of the joy of ballad operas was to hear the original lyrics in the back of one's mind, while listening to new ones set to the original music. Surely, such a popular ballad lyric as

> Oh London is a fine Town,
>   and a gallant City,
> 'Tis Govern'd by the Scarlet Gown,
>   come listen to my Ditty; . . .

must have added a dimension of laughter when the new lyric was sung:

> Our Polly is a sad slut!
>   nor heed what we have taught her.

I wonder any man alive
    will ever rear a daughter![4]

So, ballad operas "may have some new music, but they *must*
have old; they must have spoken dialogue rather than recitative, and a comic rather than a tragic plot; music must hold a
wholly secondary place and must be able to be omitted without
spoiling the plot. Dances may appear frequently and spectacular scenes occasionally. The accompanying dialogue may be
in prose, blank verse, or rime."[5] The story of Macheath, the
highwayman, and his marriage to Polly, had an overture, and
its three acts (operas of the time had three acts; plays had five)
included sixty-nine songs plus incidental music for three different dances.

When ballad opera ceased using primarily popular songs and
moved toward including songs stolen from everywhere (the
pasticcio), it had taken a long step toward its final guise in the
eighteenth century, the comic opera, with music especially
composed for one production by one composer. This resulted in
three different types of musical available to America's earliest
theatrical troupes. A large assortment of other types of musical
were also included in the earliest repertory. Comic operas were
abridged to afterpieces and interludes. Not until well into the
nineteenth century was only one play performed in an evening;
the usual evening was comprised of a main, full-length piece,
interludes or dances between the acts and between the main
work and the second part of the evening, and then the short
afterpiece. Other forms of musical theatre included burlettas,
pantomimes (including speaking pantomimes, serious pantomimes, and pantomime ballets), masques, and extravaganzas.

Even non-musicals—straight dramas—included surprising
amounts of music. Aside from the fact that drama had singing
and dancing and instrumental music before, during, and after
almost all plays, the plays themselves included songs and
dances. And, where the playwright had been so thoughtless or
careless as to omit a sufficient number of songs, someone was
sure to make up for the omission—witness a production of

Shakespeare's *The Tempest* in 1756 containing thirty-two songs and duets.

The musical stage, then, seems to be almost all the American audiences of the eighteenth century were able to see. It is no accident or coincidence that a large number of works for the stage attempted by Americans in the eighteenth and early nineteenth centuries were musicals. At least six by William Dunlap—*Darby's Return* (1789), *The Archers* (1796), *Sterne's Maria* (1799), *The Knight of Guadalquivir* (1800), *The Wild Goose Chace* [*sic*] (1800), and *The Glory of Columbia* (1803)— helped to establish musicals as American products. Some other early American musicals worth noting include Peter Markoe's *The Reconciliation* (1790), Anne Hatton's *Tammany* (1794), Susannah Rowson's *Slaves in Algiers* (1794), Elihu Hubbard Smith's *Edwin and Angelina* (1796), John Minshull's *Rural Felicity* (1801) and *The Sprightly Widow* (1803), William Ioor's *Independence* (1805), L. Beach's *Jonathan Postfree* (1807), J. N. Barker's *Tears and Smiles* (1807) and *The Indian Princess* (1808), Joseph Hutton's *The Wounded Hussar* (1809), S. B. H. Judah's *The Mountain Torrent* (1820) and *The Rose of Arragon* (1822), Charles Talbot's *Paddy's Trip to America* (1822), Samuel Woodworth's *The Deed of Gift* (1822) and *The Forest Rose* (1825), and Micah Hawkins' *The Saw Mill* (1824).

Even when an English or a French or a German work was imported, American musicians frequently wrote original scores (the music to which was sold in the lobbies of theatres) for the piece, even as a sea change was forced on the libretto to make it acceptable to an American audience.

Americans wrote in all of the other musical stage forms: interludes, masques, pantomimes, and the like. And so, American audiences were not only accustomed to performances of musical works, but they were accustomed to these works by American authors.

A flourishing concert life in the colonies also helped in the growth of America's musical stage. Performers from the theatre were always a part of concerts; they were needed to sing and act scenes from the theatre's musicals. These concerts were also America's introduction to grand opera, again through an

assortment of scenes. When the Garcia troupe arrived in 1825, with complete operas in their original tongue, American audiences had been prepared for them through frequent performances of operatic selections in concerts.

As theatres spread from village to village, from city to city, and along the frontier, it soon became apparent that the American repertory was different from that of other countries, and if one expects to find something closely resembling a British repertory, for example, one will be surprised. Perhaps because England's dramatic tradition went back to the *Quem quaeritis* in the tenth century, a tradition which picked up miracle plays, morality plays, and chronicle plays and interludes well before Shakespeare came along, a tradition in which *commedia dell'arte* and romances could be absorbed, perhaps such a long tradition could easily absorb the new musical repertory (or, at least, the new stress on music) without seriously disrupting the basic orientation toward the drama.

But in America, there was no dramatic heritage, no tradition. The first plays seen here were heavily musical, tragedies and comedies, and certainly in the great range and variety of musicals themselves. America's only dramatic heritage was a musical one, and all the theatre traditions were tied intimately to music.

Salem, Massachusetts, for example, had a few theatre performances as early as 1759, and in the period between 1783 and 1823 saw eighty-nine opera performances (twenty-seven operas) by eight composers.[6] As early as 1814, Albany needed a ballet master and a corps of dancers (a Mr. Drummond fulfilled the first need and helped with the second and was indeed an actor with the company as well).[7] If one looks at southwestern Mississippi, one finds that a great range of musical plays in the 1820s and 1830s are performed all over the region. J. M. Free, a historian of the area, notes full-fledged English opera and farces with songs, and comments, "This deluge of vocal music became an outstanding characteristic of the period."[8]

A chronicler of James H. Caldwell's company in New Orleans found its major effort in the 1830s "was toward spectacle and music drama."[9] Caldwell was so successful with opera that he made good singing voices a desideratum for his regular company. And after the success of the fantastically popular dancer Mlle. Celeste, he stressed dance, too. With a company of fifty, an orchestra of thirty, and a separate corps de ballet, he was prepared to enact dramas, operas, and dances by his regular stock company even without the presence of a star.

Alexandre Placide, whose initial reputation was as a dancer, managed the Charleston Theatre (and started the custom of shuttling his company between Charleston and Savannah); later, Charles Gilfert, a musician, managed the Charleston Theatre from 1817 to 1825; and in 1841, W. H. Lathan, a singer, took over the theatre and emphasized the musical side of the company's repertory.[10]

One of the most delightful accounts of our early repertory and the cities which saw it comes from a native-born actor-dancer-manager, John Durang. He speaks at one point of his summer tour, from Baltimore to Hanover, Pennsylvania, in the years 1808–1816.

My plan was to have all the pieces I ment [sic] to play in the season studied in the first town and got up with as much correctness as possible, for I well knew that the performers would not study after they once was in pocession [sic] of money in a nother [sic] town, for I have found them so. Therefore I made my arrangements in the commencement and made a selection for seven or eight nights, the bill affair [sic] of each night new, after the first town. I allways [sic] mentioned the number of nights at the top of my bill; by that means I had the house fill'd every night and could play every night in succession and then off to the next place. And that was the only way to save myself and make anything, tho' the labour was great.

He then proceeds to list all the entertainments he got up during the summer seasons—including fourteen plays (from Shakespeare to Dunlap), five operas, four "Romance Burlettas," twenty-four farces (many musical), seven one-act interludes, seven "Ballettes," seven dances, three pantomimes, and eight transparencies (including shadow plays, which were usually accompanied by music.)[11]

The earliest records in Montgomery, Alabama, show a company with actors and dancers and orchestra members, a circus with tight-rope dancers, and comic operas in the repertory;

Tuscaloosa, Alabama, saw the usual split bill, with a comic opera on at least one half.[12]

Chicago's first opera, Bellini's *La Sonnambula*, was performed in 1850, an Italian opera troupe played there in 1853, and by 1858 the Durand English Opera Troupe had arrived with *La Sonnambula, Daughter of the Regiment, Fra Diavolo, Bohemian Girl, Der Freischütz,* and *Il Trovatore*. Houston's first theatre opened with a musical farce, after which the company gave elaborate musicals, extravaganzas, and dances.[13]

If almost all entertainment outside the regular legitimate theatre was musical, what appeared within the theatre was also largely musical. The stars who visited the stock companies brought opera and dance (little or no distinction was made between a dance troupe and an acrobatic troupe; the famed Ravels, for example, performed both and specialized in extravaganzas and melodramas, as well). Minstrel performers were frequently a star turn, as were concert singers and singing groups and, of course, the stars of the legitimate drama. If no stars were booked, the stock companies' repertory included Shakespeare and those dramas popular in nineteenth-century England as well as here; in America, operas were important— as were extravaganzas, though a large percentage of the repertory consisted of melodramas.

Melodramas were accompanied by music all the way through, and the performance was closer to dancing than to acting. This musical form introduced much of America to the legitimate theatre—in Wisconsin, Missouri, Iowa, Ohio, Mississippi, California, Louisiana. In established theatre cities such as New York melodrama made up a considerable portion of the repertory; and as drama traveled west and south, more and more melodrama made its appearance. For example, in Charleston, in 1850, 32 percent of the repertory was made up of melodrama; in New Orleans and St. Louis, 50 percent.[14]

There is no question of melodrama's popularity in America. It was played wherever there was a troupe to act—aboard showboats, in museums, in sophisticated cities and newly opened territories. And for at least half a century it was almost exclusively a musical form.

Dance productions were a part of most musicals, serving as

frequent *entr'acte* entertainment, and in the early years of the nineteenth century formed a small but significant category in their own right. All stock companies included some dancers and a choreographer, though the dancers were expected to act and sometimes to sing as well. During the eighteenth century, dancers were used primarily between the acts or between the main production and the afterpiece; they were needed as well for the assorted types of pantomime so popular in the 1700s. When romantic ballet came into its own in the nineteenth century, such stars as Mlle. Celeste and Fanny Elssler helped to create a demand, so that each company welcomed dancers and dance companies as stars (again, the resident stock company was expected to fill in minor dance roles). Each resident company made the dance portion of the evening's bill more elaborate, so that melodramas and pantomimes often featured elaborate ballets. Ballet pantomimes (frequently called *ballets d'action*) were especially popular, since they provided plot, spectacle, songs, along with music and dance; in addition, the ballets of popular operas were danced both in the opera and, frequently, as separate ballets.[15]

Variety shows and burlesques also started their journey through time in America's early years, though their influence on America's musical theatre does not become significant until after the Civil War.

Some theatre managers were aware of what was happening, even if they did not like it. "The opera," Sol. Smith said, "has no permanent home in New York, but, broken into fragments, scatters itself into the interior towns and cities, where, with scant orchestra and chorus of eight or ten cracked voices, *Il Trovatore*, *Il Barbiere di Siviglia*, and all the other *Ils* of the Italian repertoire, are given to the worthy citizens of Peoria and Detroit at a dollar admission, children at half price, and no extra charge for securing seats."[16] As American theatre grew in large Eastern Seaboard cities and as it followed the frontier, it became apparent that the musical stage would not be separated from the legitimate repertory. If Smith objected to the *Ils* of opera, his partner Ludlow again and again wrote about being saved by opera. If, after the firm of Warren and Wood broke up, Warren referred to the number of times musicals and dance programs saved the company, then Wood in his recollections spoke of death of stock companies thanks to musicals. William Dunlap was given to more speculative thoughts about the nature of American theatre. He worried about "theatre abandoned to the uneducated, the idle, and the profligate" where "mercenary managers will please their visitors by such ribaldry or folly, or worse, as is attractive to such patrons, and productive of profit to themselves." But he also felt that "No arts can be more effectual for the promotion of good than the dramatic and histrionic. They unite music, poetry, painting, and eloquence."[17]

Perhaps the managers, tending to disapprove of the necessity to provide musicals in order to attract audiences (Joe Cowell wrote of "dancers, mimics, mummers" who "have usurped the claims of poetry and morality and brought the stage to its present [1844] degraded position"),[18] perhaps these managers were too close to the situation to see what was happening. They tended to agree that musicals had a disproportionate share of the repertory. But perhaps it was observers outside the theatre who had the clearest vision. Alexis de Tocqueville said (1835–1840), "The tastes and propensities natural to democratic nations in respect to literature will therefore first be discernible in the drama, and it may be foreseen that they will break out there with vehemence. In written productions the literary canons of aristocracy will be gently, gradually, and, so to speak, legally modified; at the theatre they will be riotously overthrown." Democratic communities "like to see on the stage that medley of conditions, feelings, and opinions that occurs before their eyes. The drama becomes more striking, more vulgar, and more true."[19] Brigham Young, no drama critic, encouraged the drama but disapproved of tragedy—in his community's theatre, dance was stressed.[20]

In fact, the line dividing musicals and legitimate drama in the first 100 years of American theatre was very slight. Inside and outside the legitimate theatre, in older dramatic forms and in new ones, the musical stage was what American audiences demanded and got. Because we lacked any other, the musical stage became our primary dramatic heritage. And for a very few people, the thought was not horrifying. Margaret Fuller in 1846 wrote,

A considerable portion of the hope and energy of this country still turns towards the drama, that greatest achievement when wrought to perfection of human power. For ourselves, we believe the day of the regular drama to be past; and though we recognize the need of some kind of spectacle and dramatic representation to be absolutely coincident with an animated state of the public mind, we have thought that the opera, ballet, pantomime ... would take the place of elaborate tragedy and comedy.[21]

As, for the first 100 years at least, indeed they did.

In short, prior to the Civil War, America's large cities, such as New York, Boston, Philadelphia, and Charleston were able to support more than one theatre, and the repertories of these cities were basically provided by stock companies. By the time of the Civil War, however, these stock companies were used almost exclusively to support stars and to provide occasional performances between the visits of stars. In smaller cities, the stock company was crucial, and while it was expected to support visiting stars, its basic function was to provide continuing entertainment, regular performances. The repertory in both types of situation consisted chiefly of musicals—with comic operas, melodramas, and extravaganzas making up a significant part of the repertory. Added to these were visiting minstrel shows, circuses, ballet troupes, and opera companies to serve as some part of an evening's entertainment. In those areas of the country where theatres were economically unfeasible, amusements were provided by visiting circuses and minstrel shows. And everywhere, one finds evidence of amateur theatre, much of it also musical in nature.

The Civil War provided little break in the development of repertory. That is, although audiences stayed away from theatres for a while, by 1862 theatrical life was flourishing in the North, in New York, Philadelphia, and Boston. The South was harder hit, especially since most southern entertainment moved to the North. Still, the southern theatres (for example, the

Richmond reopened in 1863 after being burned down in 1862) soon began to rebuild during the war, and newly created minstrel companies began to establish new, southern routes. Some new plays were written during the war, and the musical stage continued to find outlets—for example, at the Tremont Temple in Boston was produced a comic opera, *Il Recrutio*, in 1863.[22] Yet, on another level, the Civil War was the dividing line in the development of American theatre, even if the war itself was not the direct cause. "It was an epoch of changing and of disturbed conditions," says one theatre critic, and another noted that after the Civil War there was little respect for the authority of the past and that this impatience with tradition applied with special force to the theatre; the old drama was considered irrelevant, and the old school of acting pompous and artificial; the new generation of serious theatre-goers required realism of effect and relevance of subject and theme.[23]

Yet, old school or new school, the musical drama remained at the core of the American repertory. Deane Root points out,

Plays with music, probably the most pervasive form of American popular stage music during the 1860s and 1870s, were performed before audiences from the lowest to the highest classes, at urban theatres and on stages throughout the United States and its territories. They were given by amateur performers in homes and small-town theatres, and by professionals as part of circuses, minstrel and variety shows and dramatic productions, on riverboats, in tents, variety halls, dramatic theatres, and open houses. They included such varied forms as sketches, farces, burlesques, and full-length plays. Their subject matter ranged from broad comedy to melodrama to ethnic portrayal."[24]

The development of the sustained run during this period exerted a tremendous effect on the repertory. The Boston Museum, for example, in the 1851–1852 season had produced 140 different plays; each New York theatre produced a comparable number. Only twenty-five years later, the Museum was putting on only forty to sixty full-length plays, and the typical New York theatre produced only fifteen to twenty-five. Repertory was still a part of each theatre's wares, but it had to take its turn with a long-running new play.[25] One of the great outlets for the musical theatre had been, from America's first companies on, the musical farce or afterpiece; the afterpiece, too, began to disappear at this time.

The dramatic repertory along the frontier lagged behind changes in the East. California theatres expanded rapidly, so that in its first decade of theatre twenty-two plays by Shakespeare could be seen, in addition to other Jacobean playwrights and a variety of Restoration and eighteenth-century plays; contemporary English plays (Bulwer-Lytton's, for example); farces and afterpieces; Italian opera and other musical attractions. In addition, the usual honky-tonks, variety halls, circuses, and minstrel shows set up shop. Again, the repertory in all stages of America's theatrical development could be seen some place in America.[26]

As the nineteenth century moved to its end, one finds an increasing number of theatres with an increasingly sharp line dividing their offerings. Legitimate theatres might include music as a part of their general ambience, but some theatres began to specialize. While the term "opera house" had been current for many years (as a sop to those for whom attendance at a "theatre" would have been considered immoral), it was only in the late nineteenth century that self-supporting opera houses were able to exist. Variety houses (the term vaudeville was rarely used) vied for customers, offering acts which were primarily musical, or at least employed music in some fashion. Burlesque houses were separate, too, as were structures for circuses. Minstrels, of course, might appear anywhere and in any house, though they, too, increasingly performed only in their own theatres.

Several events of the late nineteenth century helped pave the way for the growth of the musical in the twentieth century. Beginning with the tremendous excitement when the operettas of Gilbert and Sullivan arrived here in the late 1870s, this form became an important part of the American repertory. From Offenbach, Gilbert and Sullivan, and Lecocq through Johann Strauss and Von Suppé, America could see all that was exciting on Europe's musical stages (at first almost entirely in their native tongue and then, as their popularity grew, almost all in English). Soon Americans began to experiment with the form, thanks to such men as John Philip Sousa and Reginald de Koven. In 1867 *The Black Crook*, showing little originality in structure but great inventiveness in publicity, brought its skimpily dressed girls and elaborate settings to national prominence. Lydia Thompson and her British Blondes arrived and with them the beginnings of modern burlesque. Nate Salsbury's *The Brook*, Harrigan and Hart's *Mulligan Guard* plays, and Charles Hoyt's *A Trip to Chinatown* all made contributions to the development of America's musicals. And the musical tradition in opera remained alive with the founding of the Academy of Music (1854) and the Metropolitan Opera (1883) in New York City. Fanny Elssler's worldwide popularity on the stage with ballet helped, too, in providing those events necessary for the burst of excitement with musical theatre in the twentieth century. All these developments will be discussed in appropriate chapters below. Here we need merely to notice the tremendous expansion of the musical repertory just before the dawn of the twentieth century.

By 1900 New York had become the center of all theatrical activity in America. Some cities, such as Boston and Chicago, continued to maintain strong stock companies, but generally the procedure was to try out plays before opening in New York and to send New York hits touring through the rest of the country. Not only the legitimate shows emanated from Broadway; Weber and Fields, for example, sent four or five companies of their Music Hall productions on the road. New York in 1900 had more legitimate theatres—forty-one—than any other city in the world.[27] All legitimate theatres, of course, regardless of whether a musical play was on the bill, had a pit orchestra to play before the show began, during intermissions, and after the show was over. The New York season of 1899–1900 featured eighty-seven productions; the 1900–1901 season saw seventy productions, but these excluded all of the musical activity in seven vaudeville and six burlesque houses, to say nothing of New York's opera houses. As one critic pointed out, "Vaudeville and musical comedy were the natural medium of Broadway before World War I."[28] The number of productions, for comparison, rose to 254 in the season of 1927–1928, sank to eighty-seven in 1950–1951 and to forty-two in 1968–1969. Yet in the 1979–1980 Broadway season, sixty-three shows opened.

The last years of the nineteenth century, then, found the popular theatre especially prosperous. The showboat, for example, which had disappeared from the Mississippi during the Civil War, now returned—the *New Sensation*, the *Floating Palace*, the *Water Queen*—"with all kinds of entertainment from grand opera and Shakespeare to melodrama and minstrelsy." Evidently, even at this late date, Americans made little distinction in their theatre-going habits, indeed in their very preferences, between popular theatre on the one hand and serious art on the other. Perhaps this is the most important point to grasp as we attempt to evaluate the place and the effect of musical theatre on the American stage. With the disappearance of all but seven or eight resident stock companies, theatre was provided on the national level by over 500 road companies. These road companies came from New York and provided the best that Broadway had to offer. And much of what Broadway had to offer was musical theatre. In the 1920s, 444 new musicals of one kind or another opened in New York; in the 1960s there were 144; and in the 1970s, 132. (If the number of musicals suffered a sharp decline in those years, so did the number of legitimate plays. The Broadway of 1946–1947 viewed eighty-seven productions compared to 302 in 1927–1928.)[29]

Still another way of perceiving the musical stage is to look at just one season. The 1919–1920 season, for example, presented 150 offerings to Broadway (including four plays of Shakespeare); of these, approximately one-third were musicals, including (the categories are those the works used for themselves) thirteen revues, sixteen musical comedies, one operetta, one opera, four musical farces, one musical extravaganza, one musical spectacle (which included vaudeville, circus, and musical comedy), three comedies with music, and one ballad play.

The season of 1936–1937 showed a slight decline in the percentage of musicals, now just under one-third, with eleven operettas, three revues, eight musical comedies, three comedies with music, and even "New Sketches" with music. The Off-Broadway theatre added its own musical impact with revues and even foreign language works (for example, the Yiddish Art Theatre presented a musical this season).

The increase in regional theatres in the 1960s provided a

new source for the musical. If Broadway eventually popularized the work, its origin was elsewhere: *Cyrano* from Minneapolis, *Grease* from Chicago, *Raisin* from Washington, D.C., and *Man of La Mancha, Shenandoah*, and *Annie* from East Haddam, Connecticut. New musicals are produced Off Broadway (*Hair, The Fantastics*), in workshops, in university theatre departments, in concert versions (for example, in 1985 New York saw seven different Jerome Kern shows professionally presented in this format) and in new outlets such as touring companies and dinner-theatre houses, where the preference is generally for musicals.[30]

If one speaks of a national repertory, one must include a surge in opera companies and dance companies. The Metropolitan Opera, established in 1883, found itself challenged by Oscar Hammerstein's Manhattan Opera House in 1906. Hammerstein tried to compete with stars and repertory, and he tried to travel to the same cities as the Metropolitan. The Metropolitan bought him out in 1910 (he made additional profit by selling his stage properties to the Chicago Grand Opera Company). When the New York City Opera was created in 1943, New York found itself with two major companies in residence. In New York, too, one finds summer opera companies, experimental ones, a host of individual performances (frequently in concert format) in a given season, plus, again, performances growing out of or especially written for opera programs at universities.

If New York is the center of the nation for opera, one must not ignore the distribution of opera companies throughout the United States. New Orleans' French Opera House provided an almost continuous record of performance through 1919, when it burned down; since then, many companies have made New Orleans a regular stop on their itineraries. During the course of this century, resident opera companies show up in Chicago, San Francisco, Dallas, Boston, Santa Fe, Central City (Colorado), San Antonio, Tulsa, Fort Worth, Houston, Kansas City. By 1946, twenty-eight resident opera companies had ensconced themselves in various cities throughout the United States, and by the 1970s, 845 opera companies existed in the United States, 418 of them associated with colleges and universities. By the late 1950s, over 3,000 opera performances could be counted in a single year, in addition to the tremendous number of performances given in universities throughout the country.[31]

The repertory of American opera companies tends, with some few exceptions, to be primarily European. In this country, New York and Chicago began to emphasize American works, though not with very great success. In the 1930s, opera companies began to reach out for a wider audience. In part, this concern has resulted in radio and television performances, where millions can hear and see opera. One result has been that more Americans have been writing operas and more operas have entered the repertory—Virgil Thomson's *Four Saints in Three Acts*, for example, or Howard Hanson's *Merry Mount*. Some works have found great popular acceptance—Gershwin's *Porgy and Bess* comes to mind—before entering the standard repertory.[32]

The entrance to the repertory of opera companies is increasingly through the Broadway theatre or the university. Many operas of Weill, Menotti, Copland, Moore, Bernstein, Barber, and Thomson have taken this path. Musicals and operettas have increasingly been accepted by opera companies. In short, the musical stage of the twentieth century must include opera houses or be in danger of ignoring one of the prime sources for a view of the American repertory. The line between opera and the musical becomes increasingly blurred, even as the audience for both seems to grow at an astonishing rate.

A similar explosion of interest may be seen in the dance repertory of the twentieth century. Theatre dance has always had a dual function in this country: it has served as handmaiden to a variety of theatrical entertainments, such as opera, melodrama, the circus, and acrobatic troupes; and it has served independently as a separate art form.

No overview of America's musical theatre can afford to ignore the explosion of dance in the twentieth century. No dance had any roots in America (with the possible exception of some folk and ballroom dances) until the twentieth century. Periodic interest in dance was aroused by individual performers such as Fanny Elssler or individual shows such as *The Black Crook*, or even by American performers beginning to gain international reputations. Anna Pavlova started another dance craze, this time in the twentieth century, after her American debut in 1910.

The explosion was probably set off by Isadora Duncan. In her struggle against formal ballet, in her insistence upon self-expression in the dance, she created something of particular appeal to Americans (though her influence extended to Fokine and his reforms in Russia). Others who followed her in attempting this new dance included Ruth St. Denis and Ted Shawn. The school they founded, Denishawn, taught three geniuses of modern dance: Martha Graham, Doris Humphrey, and Charles Weidman. Another generation of dancers, including Merce Cunningham, José Limón, and Paul Taylor, have created works which are now a part of the standard dance repertory.

Possibly the excitement generated by Pavlova might have sufficed to keep formal ballet alive. Possibly the interrelationship with the popular stage helped (for example, Pavlova danced in a Hippodrome revue). Possibly the interest in dance spurred by modern dance helped. Whatever the reason, ballet caught on. Two major ballet companies are now in residence in New York, the New York City Ballet and the American Ballet Theatre. The latter has been particularly important for native dance in that it has added to the dance repertory American-style ballet with American choreographers—*Fancy Free* by Jerome Robbins, Agnes de Mille's *Rodeo*, Eugene Loring's *Billy the Kid*, Michael Kidd's *On Stage!*, and Eliot Feld's *Harbinger*.

Thanks to such companies as the American Dance Machine, it is possible to see the dances of musicals as they were performed in the past. Thanks to video tape development, it is possible to record visually and aurally the dances of current musicals. The repertory's enrichment with specific dances from musicals, then, forms still another means of adding to America's dance repertory. Whether as part of a musical work or as a musical entity by itself, the dance is one of the strong elements making up America's musical stage. And so, in the legitimate theatre, in the opera house, and in theatres featuring dance, the repertory of America's musical stage finds an audience and grows.

SCENE 3

Performers

From the beginning, performers on American stages were forced to be versatile—to act, to sing, to dance, and frequently to be musicians as well. In part, this happened because of the nature of a repertory which included so many musicals and so much music. Later, the repertory itself was shaped by the talents of the performers. And later still, American musicals could be written in a particular style, thanks again to the talents of its performers. But all this begins, as do so many other aspects of America's musical theatre, with the eighteenth century.

The earliest itinerant players were forced to travel with a huge repertory. Thanks to the popularity of *The Beggar's Opera* and its effect on the repertory, actors who had never thought of singing were now forced to make music.

Late in the eighteenth century, when permanent companies were being established in various cities, actors and singers were permitted to specialize again, though each was expected to do some work ouside his area of specialization. That is, actors were expected to sing and singers to act, and the contracts which have come down to us are quite clear on the point.

The parts an actor took were established by his "line" and, to a much lesser degree, by seniority. The line of parts was determined by his particular abilities, and some contracts listed his roles, some the type of part (old men, for example), and some all the parts he was able to take. A contract for an actress in New York in 1798 read:

Mrs. Oldmixon engages for the ensuing season at New York: to play the first line of Opera, or such characters as she has given in a list of, the best of the Comedy Old Women, the best of the Chambermaids, or her choice in Comedies the same as Mrs. Mattock's line of playing: Salary seven Guineas per week—she finding her own Wardrobe, and having a benefit free of the Charges on benefits. Stipulating not to sing chorusses, unless in certain circumstances of the Company she may herself choose so to do.[1]

Mrs. Oldmixon's contract indicates some interesting points in connection with the musical stage. First of all, it is apparent here and elsewhere that many actors on the early American stage signed contracts indicating not one but two lines of parts— one in straight roles and one in singing. The wording of Mrs. Oldmixon's contract is an indication of still another aspect of our musical theatre; even stars were generally expected to sing in the chorus when a large chorus was called for.

The reference to a benefit is also significant. Late in the eighteenth century and early in the nineteenth, some actors demanded and got two benefits in a season. Actors used benefits both as a test of their popularity and, of course, as a means of adding to their income. On an actor's benefit night, he or she paid the evening's expenses in the theatre and collected everything over expenses. A really big name in the theatre might demand, as Mrs. Oldmixon evidently did, to have a benefit "free of Charges." There was the risk of too few people attending, in which case the actor not only made no profit but might take a serious loss after paying for the costs of the house. The actor, in a desperate attempt to fill the house, might resort to all sorts of stratagems, though the one thing that could almost always be counted on was an attempt at some sort of novelty, something not in the regular repertory, something, usually, of a musical nature. And so even benefit nights helped to add to America's musical-stage repertory. Rarely were new works given on benefit nights in England, and here is another way in which America's repertory began to separate itself from England's.

A sidelight on actors' privileges also relates to the musical stage. All songs might be encored. The result was that each actor demanded a share of songs and then a share of encores. Some evenings in the theatre went on and on and on.

Many English stars were tempted by American managers with extremely favorable contracts to cross the ocean, and most stayed once they were here. Some top stars made even more here than they could in England, though the demands on them may have been greater. For example, John Hodgkinson and his wife were hired to perform "in Tragedies, Comedies, Operas, Farces, Interludes, Pantomimes" and John was expected to superintend the musical department as well. Perhaps another word or two about John Hodgkinson may demonstrate something about eighteenth-century American performers. In Charleston, in the 1803–1804 season, Hodgkinson took eighty-eight different parts. When he died, in 1805, someone who had seen him perform commented that he had played "tragedy, genteel and light comedy, opera and pantomime, with almost equal ability," and a fellow actor wrote of him that "his voice could be compared to nothing but a many-stringed instrument which his passion played upon at pleasure."

If a person's primary ability lay in singing, his vocal line was divided in much the same fashion as the dramatic; that is, the singer might be hired for the first or second line of opera in addition to some line or lines of drama. Singers were expected to sing comic opera songs as well as those in French and Italian opera, ballads (from ballad operas as well as popular), patter songs, duets, catches, and glees. They frequently commissioned songs that they could interpolate into their performances in the theatre. A manager of the time commented about singers: "As most of the operas had been composed with a view to the peculiar powers and voices of some original representative, it frequently happened that these pieces were not suited to the ability of later singers, and it became necessary to omit much of the composer's music, substituting such popular and approved aires as were most certain of obtaining applause."

The leading male singer for many years with the Old American Company was Stephen Woolls. He had studied under Dr.

Arne in England; he starred in musicals here (Macheath in *The Beggar's Opera*, for example), but handled secondary straight roles, such as Northumberland and Douglas in Shakespeare's *Henry IV*.

Singers in early America also found employment in teaching and in church performances. One of the chief sources of income, outside the theatre, was in the flourishing concert life of the time, where entire scenes from operas and comic operas might be performed.

Each American company in the 1700s was also expected to have some dancers. Aside from the fact that the earliest repertory included pantomimes, audiences had come to expect dances between the acts of plays as well as between play and afterpiece. Troupes of French dancers began to tour the colonies with a strange blend of entertainment which added to the dance some French opera, some tightrope and slack-rope dancing, some acrobatics and tumbling, and some juggling for good measure. The French company would be hired by the local company, with the locals filling out parts in French dances and the dancers helping to fill out casts in the regular company's productions.

Even if no French company of dancers happened to pass through, each city's resident troupe included a few dancers, mostly French, though Americans began to turn to the dance, too. John Durang, for example, was one of the first Americans to become a professional dancer. His career illustrates the lot of a dancer at the beginning of American theatre. He was a member of the Old American Company in 1785. He

became a prominent member of the first American circus troupe; and was certainly the first to play Shakespearean leads in Pennsylvania Dutch ... he painted scenery, built playhouses, performed acrobatic and equestrian feats, constructed a puppet show, developed summer amusement parks, organized and directed acting companies, founded a short-lived theatrical dynasty, devised transparencies, pyrotechnic displays, and pantomimes, and played minor roles in the legitimate drama.[2]

When he performed with the circus in Philadelphia, Durang wrote of his duties there: "I was the clown in the ring, the

Harlequin on the stage. All the pantomimes and ballets got up and under my direction, I made all the fireworks, rode the Tailor [a standard equestrian act of the time] . . . [performed on] slack rope and wire, songs and dances."[3]

Dancers also appeared in concerts, and led the ball which inevitably followed each concert. The children of dancers were used to fill out small parts in ballets and dramas. John Durang used his own family on the stage, and his son Charles commented that early companies, rather than hire extras, used the children of the performers, who were thus taught dancing and music.

Finally, the dancers, even the minor ones, were frequently called upon to arrange the choreography for various productions. Some of the leading dancers of the time, such as Alexandre Placide, began their own theatre dynasties; Placide was one of the best-known and most respected managers of the nineteenth century.

Still another reason for the acceptance of musical theatre in America was the fact that the earliest and best orchestras in America were the theatre bands. The first companies used amateurs to play in their bands wherever they performed; after a while, professional musicians were hired, though they were frequently expected to dance and sing. The early orchestra leaders, too, were expected to sing, dance, act, and arrange the music for ballad operas and comic operas; outside the theatre they played at concerts, ran music and dancing schools and music stores, and many went into publishing, too. The orchestra leader was expected to gather a band together in whatever city his acting company visited. By the end of the eighteenth century, most original American musicals had been composed by the leaders of orchestras, such men as Alexander Reinagle and George Everdell; in fact, almost all secular music in eighteenth-century America was by a man who played in the theatre orchestra of some city. A strong thread also connected orchestra pit and stage: even well-known actors frequently played in the pit, and, even more commonly, musicians were to be found on stage, acting, singing, and dancing. Especially in the early days, all dancers with the company were expected to play in the orchestra when not on stage.

The number of musicians in a given theatre band toward 1800 ranged from nine in smaller cities such as Savannah through thirteen in Charleston through fourteen in New York in 1798 and probably twenty-five by 1800. A steady stream of comments by visitors from abroad indicates the high quality of these theatre bands.

James Hewitt, violinist and conductor, wrote accompaniments, incidental music, and the occasional musical, such as *Tammany*. Victor Pelissier, French-horn player, composer, and arranger, was responsible for incidental music for eighteen plays, farces, harlequinades, ballets, and an assortment of comic operas (*Sterne's Maria* is an example) as well. Alexander Reinagle played the harpsichord, piano, and violin, and he was a theatre manager in Philadelphia as well as one of the most prolific composers of stage music. Raynor Taylor was a singer, organist, and harpsichordist, and he wrote and performed his own extravaganzas on the American stage as well as writing many pieces for the stage in Baltimore, Annapolis, Philadelphia, and Boston. Benjamin Carr sang in comic operas with the Old American Company and wrote musicals for them—five operas, thirty songs, seven pantomimes, four overtures, and accompaniments to fourteen operas. At least a dozen other composers, men who were active in theatre bands, played and wrote for the American musical stage in the eighteenth century.

The growth of the star system changed the performer's position in the theatre, and most of nineteenth-century America saw great actors rather than great plays, at least until well after the Civil War.[4]

Tremendous versatility and tremendous energy were the chief requirements for nineteenth-century American actors. In their regular acting roles, they kept to fairly rigid parts. Anna Cora Mowatt noted in the 1850s that

Every actor is, of course, engaged for a separate "line of business". The "first old man" does not trench on the rights of the "low comedian," nor the "light comedian" interfere with the "heavy man," (or villain of the theatre), nor the "leading juvenile" jostle against the "walking gentleman," nor the "first old woman" come in the way of the "second old woman," nor the "leading lady" of the "singing chambermaid" and "page," etc. The members of a company, in a well-organized theatre, resemble the men on a chess board. Each has his appointed place, and fights his battle for distinction in a fixed direction.[5]

But outside a regular dramatic "line," versatility was the key. Most actors worked in the resident stock companies of various cities. Their basic job was twofold: to support the stars who came by and to provide continuing performances between the visits of stars. If the visiting star were a Shakespearean actor like Macready, then the company had quickly to learn Macready's version of the play and support him, often being given less than a day to learn revised parts and Macready's unique stage business. Anna Cora Mowatt commented with some surprise that "The day before my debut, it was necessary that I should rehearse with the company."[6] A standard opera company might feature only four singers (the Seguin Opera Company, for example), in which case the actors in the stock company sang all the remaining parts in a given opera in addition to filling out the chorus.[7] The stock company was expected to do the same with the visiting star ballet companies. In Charleston's 1851–1852 season, the stock company worked with two ballet troupes and three opera companies in the first three months of the season!

The sort of energy required of actors may be illustrated by William Warren of the Boston Museum, who performed 577 parts in thirty-six years. And William B. Wood kept aside roles he played in musicals such as melodramas, operas, and pantomimes, and still figured that in straight plays alone he took 340 different parts in his career.[8] Two other examples: Miss Petrie made 128 appearances in eighty-one roles in the 1837 season in St. Louis. And Edwin Forrest, noted for his phenomenal energy, at sixty-six covered 5,000 miles all across America, in 156 nights of performing.

They worked hard and they traveled far. The usual dramatic fare (as differentiated from minstrel and circus performances) along the frontier was musical farces and melodramas. So nineteenth-century actors, like their eighteenth-century counterparts, were forced to include in their training some singing and dancing. All actors might take more than one role in a play, appear in the afterpiece, provide *entr'acte* entertainment, and perform with visiting star companies. All this is true not only for members of the stock companies but for stars as well.[9] The greatest actress on the American stage in the 1800s was unquestionably Charlotte Cushman; yet she had trained as an opera singer, and for part of her career played the banjo and sang between the acts.[10] Forrest, Booth, Jefferson, Brougham—all the names that have come down to us as American stars—all sang and danced as wandering minstrels for a part of their careers or as musical performers when the play called for singing and dancing as, in the nineteenth century, it so frequently did. In fact, many actors got their first exposure on the stage in music halls and in melodeons. Ths melodeon provided raucus entertainment, mostly for men, for a small fee. It did, however, provide excellent training for would-be entertainers. David Dempsey and Raymond Baldwin, Lotta Crabtree's biographers, speak of the versatility demanded in melodeons: "Members of the cast were expected to sing, dance, act in the skits, play at least one musical instrument, and provide a personal cheering section to whoop things up during the grand olio."[11] One of the ways the American stage broke from the English was in the creation of American types, parts no English actor could perform here with credibility; yet in this instance, too, the musical stage came to the fore, since music was a part of the creation of new characters: the songs, as well as the jokes, of such stage Yankees as James Hackett and George Hill, were remembered.

All actors were expected to dance, especially since the very acting style of the nineteenth century was like a dance, stylized and reminiscent of ballet. Melodrama in particular depended upon movements somewhere between pantomime and ballet.[12] Some performers specialized in the dance, however, and were used mostly in ballet, pantomimes, and tumbling. Even the smallest company of actors hired them: the first professional company in Alabama, for example, employed two regular dancers, and the Houston Theatre started in 1838 with one dancer in the company plus the manager, who was himself a dancer. Dancers were expected to do the choreography for their company (in addition, again, to acting and to providing *entr'acte* entertainment). Since circuses featured ballets and pantomimes, dancers were needed with them, too. Sometimes they traveled as individual stars; when they arrived at a theatre, the entire stock company might be needed as corps de ballet. Mrs. Gilbert, in her *Reminiscences*, recalls dancing in ballets, dancing between plays, and taking small parts.[13] This rosy picture of multi-talented performers working together like so many "singing masons building roofs of gold" is destroyed when one notes that women ballet dancers were looked down upon by everyone, actors and audiences alike: "Ballet girls, in general, are a despised, persecuted, and often misjudged race. . . . They are looked down upon by the acting members of the company as though they belonged to a different order of things."[14]

The nineteenth century continued the practice of interjecting songs into straight dramas (one of the more ludicrous examples found Fanny Kemble introducing a minstrel-show song and dance into a performance of *School for Scandal*).[15] As long as afterpieces were on the bill, songs continued to be needed between the main offering and the afterpiece. The afterpiece itself was usually musical. And the company always included many musicals in one form or another in its repertory. All of these were reasons for companies to hire some performers who were primarily singers, though, as always, they were expected to act and to dance as well. Sol. Smith, with many years of experience as a manager behind him, felt that a good male ballad-singing voice helped in the acting of farces and melodramas.[16]

The nature of the repertory continued to force great versatility upon performers. Lydia Kelly, for example, handled many roles in one season, but four of them may suffice to demonstrate the point: she starred as Rosalind in *As You Like It* and Beatrice in *Much Ado About Nothing*; she sang Susannah in *The Marriage of Figaro* and Bertha in *Der Freischütz*.[17] Singers were featured members of companies and performed as stars, and they, too, traveled as soloists bringing their repertories with them. These repertories were frequently extraordinarily varied; Blanche Chapman, for example, carried seventy-two leading light opera roles. Every performer on the American stage was expected to be musically competent.

The musicians continued, in the nineteenth century, to play an important role in America's musical stage. Both English

visitors and native Americans noted the close continuing relationship between audiences and musicians, further proof of
the importance of the orchestra to America's nineteenth-century repertory. When a company returned to its home base,
the citizenry welcomed members of the band, frequently by
name, as they welcomed the actors themselves. All theatres
had bands. A troupe in Annapolis in 1802, for example, traveled
with eight actors, five actresses, and three musicians; by 1838,
the Providence Theatre had an orchestra of eleven. Noah Ludlow could only get together four or five musicans for his St.
Louis company in 1819 and feared his productions would suffer;
indeed, the failure of an entire season in St. Louis in the 1820s
was thought to be the result of a poor orchestra. When Montana
opened its first theatre, only a military band was available, so
a military band was used—but theatre without a band was
simply not possible. New York in the 1820s had several theatres and each boasted its own band: the Richmond Hill Theatre, for example, had an orchestra of eighteen, and the Park
Theatre, thirty. In mid-century, an opera performance in New
York might have up to forty musicians in the pit.[18]

These theatre bands continued, as they had in the eighteenth
century, to provide the basis for concert life in the United States.
But the theatre is where most musicians found employment—
in museums, honky-tonks, circuses, and the like. In the theatre,
musicians were still called upon to act and to compose music
for the various entertainments. Many nineteenth-century theatre managers were musicians. For most of the century the
conductors were responsible for finding their musicians; later
in the century, concert masters performed this function. In fact,
the composer-conductor was kept busy in a variety of ways:
since all melodramas included music cues, he had to compose
appropriate music and orchestrate it; he adapted music for the
company and the band as each star or star troupe came by;
almost all incidental music, dance music, and songs were his
responsibility; and he supplied patriotic and popular tunes between the acts and between the plays. Occasionally he doubled
as scenic artist or as dancer, and, as Sol. Smith reminds us, as
performer: a musician-actor "who frequently played two or three
parts in one play, and, after being killed in the last scene [of

Pizarro] was obliged *to fall far enough off the stage to play slow music as the curtain descended!*"[19] For all this, he received the highest salary in the entire company. Typical salaries, which reflect the importance of music to the nineteenth-century American stage, may be observed in the Ludlow and Smith Company of St. Louis for 1838: top actor's salary, $30.00 per week; Mueller, the conductor, $40.00; total salary of all the actors, $291.00 per week; total salary of the musicians, including the conductor, $188.50.

Outside the legitimate theatre, the talents of performers had to be even more varied. In the early years of the minstrel show, and to a lesser degree later on, all performers were their own singers and musicians. And all minstrel companies were too small to admit anyone who could not perform *all* these functions, in addition to handling women's characters, or "wench" roles, since no women appeared in minstrel shows.

Stock companies managed to survive into the twentieth century, though road companies carrying Broadway hits predominated. Other opportunities for performers continued to be melodramas, ten-twent'-thirt's (though the melodrama was no longer an especially musical form), minstrel shows, and circuses. Theatres were still available on showboats. And a large number of vaudeville and burlesque houses added further opportunities for the musical performer. Add to all these the growth of successful opera houses, and the twentieth century looked like a lively era for the musical stage performer.

But the basic condition for the stage is change, and vast changes have occurred in entertainment in the eighty-odd years of the 1900s. One of the most important changes is the specialization of the arts, so that, for example, opera tore itself off from the standard stock company repertory; later in the century, dance did, too. In fact, flux begins the century, and the standardization of performance seems likely to end it. In the late nineteenth and early twentieth centuries, the opera singer might appear in any of the available theatres, from beer hall through vaudeville house through Broadway playhouse through opera house; all were also available to the dancer and to the straight actor. The major difference was that now one could not find a person who was expected to do all—act, sing, and dance—except in the theatre of comic opera. That tradition has never died. The wildly popular world of Harrigan and Hart in the late nineteenth century found Harrigan and Hart doing all three, as had minstrels and comic opera artists all through American history.

Blacks started to make a name in the theatre primarily as minstrels, continuing the grotesque, distorted image so popular since the early days of minstrelsy. Soon, however, thanks to such performers as Bert Williams and George Walker, genuine black characteristics began to show up in the theatre, and the way was open for black contributions to the musical stage. Williams and Walker were singers, actors, dancers, writers, producers; they carried on the tradition of versatility in our musical theatre.

And while opera singers were now thoroughly specialized, one still finds opera stars crossing over to operetta early in the century, as Fritzi Scheff and Emma Trantini did in Victor Herbert operettas, and as Robert Rounseville (*Man of La Mancha*), Helen Traubel (*Pipe Dreams*), Ezio Pinza (*South Pacific* and *Fanny*), Robert Weede (*Most Happy Fella*), for example, did later in the century. Specialists in dance, whether ballet or modern, found themselves on the musical stage, at first in vaudeville (Ruth St. Denis and Martha Graham and the Castles are good examples here), then later both performing in musicals (Vera Zorina, Ray Bolger) and choreographing them (Jerome Robbins, Agnes DeMille) as dancing became more and more important in musical comedy.

A long line of superb comic performers brought their specialties to the musical stage (Bobby Clark, Jimmy Durante, Ed Wynn), mostly via burlesque and vaudeville. Such singing actors as Al Jolson and Eddy Cantor and Helen Morgan followed the same route.[20]

And composers for the musical stage, free from the necessity of conducting and performing, were now permitted to specialize, too. The revues that were so popular early in the century might use several composers, but later, one composer per show became the rule. But here, too, one finds composers breaking boundaries between forms, writing works neither pure opera nor pure musical, but something slowly evolving into a unique shape of its own. Kurt Weill, for example, in *Down in the Valley*, *Lady in the Dark*, and *Lost in the Stars*, pushed the limits of the musical, as did George Gershwin (*Porgy and Bess*), Frank Loesser (*Most Happy Fella*), Leonard Bernstein (*West Side Story*, *Candide*), and Stephen Sondheim (*Company, Pacific Overtures, Sweeney Todd, Sunday in the Park with George*).

The point here is that a long tradition of performers and musicians, a tradition going back at least as far as the eighteenth century, has helped to establish a form in which American audiences have come to anticipate experimentation and versatility. One American critic complains: "Just as public taste now demands a super-market range of variety in the actors, so it did in our early theatre."[21] Yet most Europeans are amazed at the demands our musicals place on performers, demands encompassing the need to act, to sing, and to dance. Whether praise or denigration is the proper attitude, the fact is that American composers and librettists can count on a pool of talented performers. As far as the creators' imaginations can stretch, so far can American performers take them. The 200–year-old tradition among performers has unquestionably helped to keep the musical stage alive and thriving.

Act II

AN ANALYSIS OF THE INTERRELATIONSHIPS AMONG MUSICAL STAGE FORMS

American Opera: Comic, Grand, and Operetta

For the most part, grand opera was confined to concert halls in eighteenth-century America. Scenes from operas could be counted on at all concerts, and they were always performed by members of the local theatre company, singing, acting, dancing, and playing in the orchestras. The dependence of the musical life of the country on the theatre was thus established quite early in our history. Purcell, Haydn, Gluck, and Mozart were performed in this manner. Occasionally, puppet shows were used to present scenes from opera. Opera had never really caught on in England, at least among composers, so the masque, carried over from Shakespeare's day, with elaborate dances and heavy allegory, was the only real part of the opera tradition on the English stage. The English attitude toward foreign opera was clear: they found it absolute nonsense (though it held the stage for quite a few years in the early eighteenth century). And that attitude was taken over by some Englishmen transplanted in America: "A true-bred Englishman laughs at all this, or yawns."[1] Fortunately, America featured fewer and fewer "true-bred Englishmen," with the result that European operatic activity was reflected here, even in the eighteenth century.

Serious operas, then, showed up in concert halls, though their music was frequently purloined for pantomimes and ballets and pasticcios (that is, ballad operas with music taken from the best sources rather than actual ballads). Some French *op-éras comiques* (Grétry, Monsigny, Philidor) were performed here, in translation, and with the music altered and adapted to the needs of individual American companies.[2] And, still before 1800, some French actors sang the operas of Cimarosa and Paisiello. New Orleans and Charleston started the first permanent French theatres in this country, so French operas, sung in French, were presented there. Even in New York and Baltimore one finds evidence of French opera before 1800.

But there is little evidence that American composers attempted this exotic form. The basic democratic attitude seemed to be that of a Bostonian, William Aliburton, in 1792: "banished forever, should be all unintelligible Italian airs, trills, affected squeaks and quavers."[3] Francis Hopkinson's *The Temple of Minerva* (1781) has some claim to be the first American grand opera. All of its dialogue was either sung or delivered in recitative; however, its short, allegorical book is weak, and the loss of its score make the claim a bit dubious. In fact, some of the music has been identified, though it is probably by other composers. If we do not accept *The Temple of Minerva* as America's first opera, then we have to wait until 1845 for that event.

In the meantime, Americans were enjoying opera, even if it was not of the home-grown variety. The Garcia troupe made its debut in New York on November 29, 1825, with *Il Barbiere di Siviglia*, and opera was truly launched in America. During the first season here, the Garcia troupe performed at the Park Theatre, where the management interrupted the regular stock company and allowed them about two performances each week, or about seventy-nine the first year. Their company was comprised of three leading females, five males, and an orchestra of twenty-six. Besides *Il Barbiere*, the Garcia troupe presented *La Cenerentola, Tancredi, Otello, Il Turco in Italia* (all by Rossini), Zingarelli's *Romeo e Giulietta*, Mozart's *Don Giovanni*, and two concoctions by Garcia himself.[4]

As opera became more and more popular, it adapted itself to its new environs. In *Music in the New World*, Charles Hamm describes what happened. Operas of Mozart and Rossini were mounted in adaptations, so that Americans saw not merely translations into English but other elements changed. Recitative was largely replaced by spoken dialogue; complex ensembles and finales were transformed into strophic airs and simpler, homophonic choruses. "These and other 'Englished' Italian operas became the most popular musical fare on the American stage in the 1820s, '30s, and into the '40s."[5]

By 1833 New York had constructed its first theatre intended exclusively for opera, the Italian Opera House; it lasted for two years, failed, and it was a while before another opera house was attempted in New York. But meanwhile, two much more important means of presenting opera began to be available to Americans. First was visiting foreign opera companies. A tremendous influx of them toured all over the United States wherever there was a stock company to support them, since the visiting company was usually small and counted on the resident company to fill in parts and chorus. The second means of presenting opera was through the stock company itself as a part of its regular repertory. Admittedly, the operas were adapted either to the traveling star company or to the resident company, but operas they were. Even the terrible custom of taking bits and pieces of various operas and weaving them together into a more or less coherent whole had the effect of providing some opera, and even scrupulous companies and discriminating audiences seemed to enjoy these bastard operas. Most often, however, serious operas were presented, as far as it is possible to tell from this distance in time, with a strong influence from comic opera.

While serious opera, grand opera, was struggling to make itself a permanent institution in America, comic opera was thriving. Probably no single work exerted so great an influence as the first specimen of the form: *The Beggar's Opera*, in 1728. Although the original intent was to use only traditional songs which everyone in the audience knew, the principle was soon violated (indeed, was violated in *The Beggar's Opera* itself, since the March from Handel's opera *Rinaldo* was used for the chorus of Macheath's gang). Songs began to be stolen from everywhere, and the logical next step was taken quickly—one person composing all the music for a show. These changes resulted in some loss—that is, the effect of hearing the words to an old song in the back of one's head, against the new words to the same tune, could not be achieved with new music. (The effect was revived with the minstrel show, however, and later with the rash of burlesques.) Other effects of the new form were permanent. Among them was the novel idea of including songs in a comedy, where the music took second place to the plot. The dialogue was spoken rather than sung or chanted in recitative; the opportunity for dialogue, for a reasonably complex plot with real characters, all derive from this aspect of the new form. Even the stress on realism in *The Beggar's Opera* brought back an element long missing from the stage.

Still, Americans tended to mistrust formal speech, elaborate language, as seeming to indicate strong foreign influence. Perhaps this is why music continued to be such an important element in America's theatre, since it provided a means of communicating other than through speech, a means of adding to the drama a quality lost as reliance on words weakened.

And if, as we have seen, all American performers sang and danced, so all comic operas written in America reflected national elements in form and content. The form tended to slide toward burlesque and parody, so attempts at comic opera were frequently followed by a satire of the attempt—*Zampa, the Red Corsair*, for example, satirized as *Sam Parr and His Red Coarse Hair*. Americans wanted to explode pretentiousness, but the line separating this from good manners was unclear, so both were hit in American comic operas. As Americans began to write more and more musicals in the first quarter of the nineteenth century (works such as *The Forest Rose*, *The Saw-Mill*, and *The Indian Princess*), the content of the musicals began to reflect American experience. Democratic communities, said de Tocqueville, "want to hear something that concerns themselves, and the delineation of the present age is what they demand."[6] Farces played in melodeons in California used local themes and coloring and then satirized even these. Contemporary events, local and national, were immediately dramatized in America's theatres; comic opera, using local characters and situations, provided parts for native actors. Through comic opera, American drama and American acting developed together.

The songs of comic opera, never especially relevant to the

plots or characters, were significant in other ways. "It was in the songs more than in the plays that the patriotic feeling of the times found expression in the theatre."[7] Fashions and politics were good subject matter for American comic operas and tended to set off American from English musicals. J. N. B. Barker's *Indian Princess* (1808) ties its various plot elements together in its final song.[8] The reprise, repeated three times, demonstrates the comic opera's focus:

> Freedom, on the western shore
>   Float thy banner o'er the brave;
> Plenty, here thy blessings pour;
>   Peace, thy olive sceptre wave!

So little distinction was made in America between comic opera and grand opera that one constantly finds singers who specialized in one, singing the other. For example, Signorina Garcia (later the internationally famed Madame Malibran) opened New York to grand opera with her father's troupe in 1825. Two seasons later, her farewell performances, besides opera, included such comic operas as *The Devil's Bridge* and *Love in a Village*. Visiting opera companies came by with both opera and comic opera—though English troupes stressed the latter, and all others stressed the former—and stock companies were expected to handle both, in addition to their regular chores.

A sort of hodge-podge is probably the best way to describe most early opera productions. Sol. Smith, manager, recalled an 1833 production of *Cinderella* in the Southwest; it was "made up of Rossini's original work of that name, and *other* productions of that composer, *William Tell* being largely drawn upon."[9] Another good example is a popular opera called *The Libertine* in some places and *Don Giovanni* in others; it contained some of Mozart's music, arranged by Bishop, and was sung by the regular resident stock acting company.

In the mid-nineteenth century, grand opera began to achieve a certain snob value and started to split off from comic opera in terms of its audience appeal (not obviously, as a form; it had always been different there). Philip Hone, in 1846, ruminated about opera and found it to be "a refined amusement, creditable to the taste of its proprietors and patrons; a beautiful parterre in which our young ladies, the flowers of New York society, are planted to expand in a congenial soil, under the sunshine of admiration; and here also our young men may be initiated into the habits and forms of elegant social intercourse, and learn to acquire a taste for a science of the most refined and elegant nature."[10] A British visitor said, "Although the traveller considered the opera and theatre in the same breath, there seemed to be a subtle distinction in the minds of the natives which purified opera attendance, even for the ladies."[11] When one compares this sort of ideal with the behavior observed by Mrs. Trollope during the early 1800s in the American theatre (smoking, spitting, men's hats on, legs dangling over rails),[12] one sees grand opera becoming a cultivated art even as America's musical stage, the comic opera, becomes a popular one.

Serious opera in America, then, tended to slip in on the coattails of comic opera. For example, in 1841 in St. Louis a piece called *Quasimodo, the Bell Ringer of Notre Dame* was introduced; the music was selected and adapted by a local musician from various operas of Weber.[13] Even so discriminating an opera lover as Philip Hone, on viewing a "new" opera called *Rokeby* (based on Scott's poem) with music from various composers, found it to be "very fine."[14] Opera remained a part of the regular theatre's offerings until mid-century, but the 1830s saw opera houses being built, with the consequent separation of opera from the popular theatre.

New Orleans had an opera house from early in the nineteenth century. New York built its first permanent opera house in 1833, then the Astor Place Opera House and, with greater success, the Academy of Music in 1854; the Metropolitan House in 1883 led New York Opera into the twentieth century, when the Metropolitan got a new house at Lincoln Center as did the New York City Opera. Columbus, Ohio, built its first opera house in 1864; it was opened by the Italian Company of Associated Artists Troupe with such favorites as *Il Trovatore*, *Norma*, *Favorita*, *Rigoletto*, and *Don Giovanni*. By 1863, three separate opera companies were performing in Chicago, and in 1865 a theatre devoted to opera was built there, the Crosby Opera House; Peck's Auditorium Building, for opera, was erected in Chicago in 1889. San Francisco built its Grand Opera House in 1873. But city after city welcomed opera in its regular theatre, and by the twentieth century most large American cities had constructed their own opera houses.

Despite the increasing number of opera houses, it was the rare one that was able to support its own company. For the most part, opera companies toured the country, presenting their repertory in a city and moving on. The names of many of these companies have come down to us, and a list of a very few of them suggests their range and their source: The Italian Company of the Associated Artists Troupe, the Seguin Opera Troupe, Signor and Signora Pellegrini's troupe, the German Opera Troupe, the New Orleans Opera Troupe, the Grau Italian Company, the Italian Grand Opera Company, the Tedesco Opera Company, the Havana Italian Opera Company, the Boston Museum Company, and so on.[15]

Perhaps the most popular of these early opera companies was that run by the Seguins, and it is both interesting and helpful to an understanding of early opera in America to look at the way in which they worked.[16] They arrived in America in 1838 with a company comprised of four singers: Mr. and Mrs. Seguin, Mr. Frazer, and Mr. Andrews. They would normally go to a city where a stock company already existed; all minor roles and choruses were sung by the stock company. After three rehearsals, they were ready to go on. They had a fairly extensive repertory, which included such works as *La Sonnambu a*, *La Gazza Ladra*, *The Marriage of Figaro*, and *The Barber of Seville*. The number of cities they visited in their many years in America is nearly incredible, though perhaps the best way of envisioning their performances is embodied in a letter Sol. Smith wrote from New Orleans in 1845:

The Bohemian Girl was got up with entirely new Scenery, painted from the drawings and sketches you sent—and we had 18 men and 10 ladies for the Peasants, Gipsies as required, and were all on as ladies and gentlemen in the third act. The truth is, (between ourselves) Seguin and wife were the only persons acknowledged here as Singers—Frazer was so *uneven* in his singing that he could not satisfy the most easily pleased. ... Andrews, tho' a gentlemen, and a very excel-

lent man I doubt not, was not *Archer* ... and Miss Coad, who was
selected by Mr. S[eguin] for the Queen, was just—nobody! How the
d___l *could* an opera succeed with such a lack of material? I forgot to
mention that the orchestra consisted of twenty-two musicians, led by
Mueller.[17]

But the quality soon improved in great strides. After the Civil
War, according to John Tasker Howard, "To a rich opera tradition would be added the growth of fine orchestras, and American singers and instrumental virtuosi would compete with any
in the world."[18]

Under constantly bettering conditions, American singers
found training and audiences; by the twentieth century, the
fact of being an American was no longer a deterrent to success,
either here or abroad, with the result that American opera
stars now perform everywhere in the world. Whether Adelaide
Phillips or Lillian Nordica or Emma Eames in the nineteenth
century, or Lawrence Tibbett, Helen Traubel, or Roberta Peters
in the twentieth, American singers prove the fascination of
Americans with musical theatre.

Only in the writing of grand opera is there a weakness. If
Francis Hopkinson's eighteenth-century *The Temple of Minerva* is discounted, then William Henry Fry's *Leonora* (1845)
must have priority as the first grand opera written by an American to reach the stage. And even here a cavil must be expressed, since Fry's brother had to take over the management
of the Astor Place Opera House in order for *Leonora* to be
produced. Ten years passed before the appearance of another
American opera, George Frederick Bristow's *Rip Van Winkle*.
And then came a long hiatus, possibly the result of the Civil
War, before the next American opera saw light, Walter Damrosch's *The Scarlet Letter*, in 1896, with a libretto by George
Parsons Lathrop, Hawthorne's son-in-law.[19]

An outstanding historian of opera noted, "In a word, American opera remains, until well into the twentieth century, simply a longed-for but unrealized ideal."[20] Yet, in the twentieth
century, well over 150 American composers have seen one or
more of their operas on the stage, either in opera houses or on
Broadway or in university workshops.

Probably the great breakthrough came at the Metropolitan under the aegis of Giulio Gatti-Cassazza. In 1908 he began a long reign at the Met, a reign which featured many attempts to stage operas by Americans. The first American opera at the Metropolitan was Frederick Converse's *The Pipe of Desire* in 1910 (though the opera's premiere had been given in Boston in 1906). After the event, a curious pattern emerged for a number of years: while the rest of the country was content with operas from the European repertory, New York and Chicago were beginning to emphasize native American works, with original operas emerging from any other city only rarely. The experimentation with new American compositions in the early years of the twentieth century proved not very successful. Most of the names of operas and of composers are mere footnotes in histories (Walter Damrosch's *The Man Without a Country* or Charles Wakefield Cadman's *A Witch of Salem* are good examples). Perhaps the best of these early operatic composers was Deems Taylor, whose *The King's Henchman* and *Peter Ibbetson* received not only critical praise but even an occasional revival.[21]

In the 1930s the nature of American opera began to change, and it began to reach out for the wider audience it had known in its first years in America. To some extent, the libretti had always been concerned with American themes, with Indians or American literature or American history (one critic has counted no less than thirty-two operas entitled *Columbus*),[22] but their music tended to be couched in the idioms of European operas. Now, however, the themes became more experimental, and the music relied more heavily on indigenous material— jazz and folk songs, for example.

A few composers have managed to write works that show every promise of becoming a regular part of our operatic repertory: Virgil Thomson, for example, with his *Four Saints in Three Acts*, with libretto by Gertrude Stein. It was performed first in Hartford in 1934 with an all-black cast. Note, too, Thomson's *The Mother of Us All*, written in 1947 and performed first at Columbia University. Louis Gruenberg's *The Emperor Jones* made its premiere at the Metropolitan in the 1932–1933 season, and his 1930 *Jack and the Beanstalk* found an audience in 1930 at the Juilliard School of Music. One must pay attention, also, to such works as Howard Hanson's *Merry Mount*, George Gershwin's *Porgy and Bess*, and Marc Blitzstein's *The Cradle Will Rock* and *Regina*. More and more, Broadway or universities are the places where original operas are given their first exposures before assuming a place in the regular operatic repertory. George Gershwin, Kurt Weill, and Gian-Carlo Menotti's operas tended to be produced first on Broadway, while most of the others first saw their works in production either in an opera house or on the stage of a university opera workshop. Douglas Moore (*The Devil and Daniel Webster*), Aaron Copland (*The Tender Land*), William Schuman (*The Mighty Casey*), Lukas Foss (*The Jumping Frog of Calaveras County*), Leonard Bernstein (*Trouble in Tahiti*), and Jack Beeson (*Hello, Out There*) are a very few of the many composers who have achieved success with their operas and have concentrated on works with specifically American themes.

Something of the new stress on American operas may be seen in the forty American operas performed at the New York City Opera between 1948 and 1971. Or, even better, the new interest may be seen in the explosion of new opera workshops in colleges and universities across the country. These workshops seem to have taken over the role of the eighteenth-century patron of the arts, and new works by a good many American composers were first seen in academic environs: those of, for example, Jack Beeson, Robert Russell Bennett, Lukas Foss, Douglas Moore, and Virgil Thomson.[23] This use of university theatre for opera seems to be peculiarly American and seems to be growing constantly—another instance of America's fascination with the musical theatre. As far back as 1952, one could count over 100 opera workshops in the colleges and universities of thirty-four states; the number has increased since. Further, about 4,000 performances of opera were given at the turn of the 1960s, divided among a total of 700 different organizations designed specifically to produce opera. Of these 4,000 productions, more than half were written after 1925, and of this half, most were by American composers. The figures become even more surprising as we move into the 1980s. In 1980–1981, for example, United States companies performed

3,653 presentations of American operas—something like 38 percent of the total number of operatic works put on the stage![24]

The American musical stage, through a sort of cross fertilization among its various forms, has been able to take an essentially foreign genre and turn it into a popular one. Of course, the long-running radio series from the Metropolitan plus the rise of opera on television have helped considerably. Whatever the reason, American composers have not been frightened away from opera, or at least something very like opera. Critical discussions about whether *Porgy and Bess*, *The Most Happy Fella*, *Lost in the Stars*, *Amahl and the Night Visitors*, *Song of Norway*, and *Sweeney Todd* are really operas or musicals are constantly surfacing, and the very critical confusion is an indication of the closeness of American opera to the American musical. American opera, regardless of how close it comes to the American musical, has begun to find its own way and is making a significant contribution to our musical theatre.

Before looking at the rise of comic opera and its absorption into other forms, we must look at a peculiar sort of mixed form. The pasticcio was born in the eighteenth century, though it refused to die then. It was a way station on the road from the ballad opera to the comic opera; the plot remained comic, with the music subservient to the book. But instead of using songs that everyone knew, it brought together the works of two or more composers. In Italy, the form was "a mixture of heterogeneous ingredients, an operatic pie, made up of airs from different works by different composers, composed at different times for different cities."[25] A libretto by Metastasio might use bits and pieces of Zeno, Goldoni, and other writers plus music by Gluck, Ciampi, Galuppi, Cocchi, Jommelli, Handel, and others.

In comic opera, the English pasticcio used the same devices as the Italian, though not quite so formally. A good example is Bickerstaffe and Arne's *Love in a Village* (1762). Bickerstaffe received credit for the book, though at least three other authors' words may be discerned; Arne's score was put together from an overture by Abel, thirteen of Arne's songs from other works plus six new ones, and some music of Handel, Boyce, Howard, Baildon, Festing, Geminiani, Galuppi, Giardini, Paradies, Abos,

Agus, Gardiner, Carey, and Weldon! These pasticcios made their proud boast that their music was "compiled from the most eminent masters."

Love in a Village quickly found its way to America, where its popularity assured imitations. One of the first of these was by Royall Tyler, *May Day in Town, or New York in an Uproar,* and it opened in New York in 1787, with music "from the most eminent Masters."[26]

Apparently, both in the opera house and in the popular theatre, these pasticcios continued to be written and enjoyed in America. For example, *Rokeby,* an operatic piece which was first produced at the Park Theatre in 1830, had music selected and arranged by F. H. F. Berkeley; even musically sophisticated audiences seemed to enjoy these conglomerations of the famous works of Italian, French, and German composers. A great specialist in making "arrangements" of masters into new works was C. E. Horn, the first regular conductor of the Handel and Haydn Society of Boston, and a conductor of music in English and American theatres. Even the twentieth century features these strange works. William Dodd Chenery, for example, after selecting melodies and choruses from operas, oratorios, and other standard works, "and by suitable modulations, interludes and connecting harmonies, has woven them into a composite whole which has been scored for full orchestra." He wrote his own libretti for these. His first, *Egypta,* was produced in Illinois in 1893 and received a tremendous number of performances thereafter; as late as 1910 it found an audience every night for seven weeks in Indiana. Chenery's dramatization of *Elijah* was produced in Boston as late as 1924 and in Springfield, Illinois, in 1927. Other pasticcios (it is difficult to know what else to call them) assembled by Chenery include *Joseph* in 1911 and *Xerxes* in 1912.[27]

The pasticcio's history on the popular stage continued for a while, too. In fact, one could make a case that *The Black Crook,* usually accorded, for the convenience of the critic, the reputation of "the first American musical comedy," was no more— and probably a good deal less—than a pasticcio. Though the score for *The Black Crook*'s first production in 1866 (at Niblo's Garden in New York) was largely by Operti, it also contained songs and ballet music by Thomas Baker, Jacobi, Lothian, Frederic Clay, G. Blackwell, Mons. Ronzani, and others. And additional music was thrown in whenever and wherever the piece was performed. The twentieth century continued the custom, in a way, since stars were permitted to interpolate songs when they wanted, and later, producers added songs by many composers to add excitement to a show. A good example is Julian Edward's *The Girl and the Wizard* (1909), which contained six songs of Edwards plus eight interpolations representing five other composers.[28] Deems Taylor referred to a 1911 musical, *The Echo*, produced by Charles Dillingham; Taylor wrote the original score, and Jerome Kern and others were asked to add songs. Taylor says that on opening night, Bruce Edwards (Dillingham's manager) turned to Kern and said "I hope your show goes well tonight, old man." Fourteen men said, "Thanks."[29] If the tone of the show was destroyed by various musical styles, no one seems to have minded. The pasticcio has managed to stay alive, in one shape or another, for a very long time.

The heart of America's musical theatre, however, was neither in opera nor in the pasticcio. Comic opera sustained the thread of lyric theatre through much of the nineteenth century in America. Comic opera was, basically, a play with lots of songs interspersed. The play had to be a comedy, though some of the eighteenth-century comic operas, particularly those of William Dunlap, tended to stress patriotism so heavily as almost to subsume the comedy.

Early American comic operas did not attempt to make the music relevant (or even appropriate) to the action. Music did not necessarily grow out of the action; it did not attempt to illustrate or deepen character. It might deal with an aspect of the plot, or it might not. It might set mood and tone, but it usually did not. Only rarely did it have the effect of thrusting the plot forward.

Americans, as mentioned above, tended to mistrust elaborate speech as an indication of an aristocratic or a foreign influence, and so the language of comic opera tended in the 1800s to be as simple as possible. But some sort of communication was necessary, and music—songs—provided the means to communicate other than through speech. In short, as the dialogue went down, the music went up. And so the form and content of comic operas in the nineteenth century tended to shape the developing American drama. The songs themselves were significant in another way as they tended to reflect the concerns of the time, the development of the nation.

Even in the eighteenth century many American musical stage works were produced, from ballad operas (*The Disappointment*, for example) to pasticcios (*May Day in Town*, for example) to full-fledged comic operas. Many composers were extremely prolific, among them Victor Pellissier, who wrote twenty-eight pieces for the American stage, and Benjamin Carr, who listed under his works five operas and the accompaniments to fourteen others. Composers of comic operas were generally the conductors at the theatres, though a few of them were peripatetic and composed when they could make some money from a local company.

The level of humor in the eighteenth-century works may be seen in some lines from the comic opera *The Archers* (1796). This story of William Tell, with book by William Dunlap and music by Benjamin Carr, was written years before either Schiller or Rossini touched the story; its comic underplot features Conrad and Cecily (a seller of wooden wares and a basket woman respectively), who discuss going off to war.

Conrad: Aye, but a soldier is never allow'd to carry any other beast of burden with him but his wife. Of wives he generally takes care to have enough.

Cecily: You are an impudent good-natured rogue, and I don't care if I do. But you don't think I'll go without you marry me?

Conrad: Certainly not! You don't suppose I would think of leading the beast without the halter?

At this point, they swing into a duet which begins—Conrad: "If a man would a faithful follower have,/ O! there's nothing in truth like a wife." The tone of the main plot may be suggested by these words of William Tell:

> Already are our charters violated;
> Already Gesler, in despite of laws,
> However sacred, grinds our peasantry;
> And adds to injury, unmanly insult.
> O Switzerland, my country, we *must* rouze![30]

The political relevance was presumably not lost on Americans.

The nineteenth century saw a large number of Americans writing comic operas. The tone changed so that some of the high moral stance eased; the characters were a little more true-to-life and a bit more clearly identifiable as Americans. True, the bastardization of standard works continued, so that grand operas found themselves turned into comic operas as each performer substituted popular songs for the original arias, and singers who could handle grand opera frequently did the reverse, substituting arias for popular songs. A good example is the Don Juan story, which appeared on the Philadelphia stage in the 1813–1814 season in drama, opera, and pantomime, for a total of six different versions. Performing companies, recognizing the overlap between comic and grand opera as late as the last decade of the nineteenth century, frequently attempted to produce both. The Bostonians' repertory, for example, included Gilbert and Sullivan, von Suppé, and Offenbach, as well as such operatic works as Flotow's *Marta*, Donizetti's *Elixir of Love*, and Mozart's *Marriage of Figaro*. Companies producing musicals of all types continued to exist into the twentieth century, some traveling all over the United States, some remaining regional. Even when a foreign work was imported, American musicians frequently wrote original scores for the pieces, and American writers changed the libretti to suit American taste.

But Americans were continuing to write in the comic opera form, whatever foreign influences came about. Some outstanding examples include J. N. Barker's *Indian Princess* (1808), S. B. H. Judah's *Mountain Torrent* (1820), Samuel Woodworth's *Forest Rose* (1823), and Micah Hawkins' *The Saw-Mill* (1824). A look at one of these will help demonstrate the nature of American comic opera in the first half of the nineteenth century.

Micah Hawkins wrote both libretto and music for *The Saw-Mill; or, A Yankee Trick*, and James Hewitt did the orchestrations.[31] This comic opera achieved a number of performances and seems to have been reasonably popular. A triple plot tells of two friends, each in love with a girl, plus the story of their servant and his love. The setting is upstate New York and involves a trick (switching building plots) conceived by the friends in order to win the hands of their respective young women. The comic opera is in two acts. The influence of melodrama may be noted in the number of music cues to accompany the action, for example "Exit Elna. (Music No. 9)" or "Appropriate music (No. 15)." There are solos, duets, trios, quartets, and chorus work—for a total of sixteen songs plus several dances. The quality of the prose and use of song may be ascertained from the opening moments. At the curtain's rise we are in Bloom's house in Rome, New York, and Bloom is reading a newspaper. His servant, Jacob, enters singing:

> Richard Bloom, Esquire,
>   I do desire—
>   I come
> To know if, this bright day all through,
>   Thou'rt home
> To all who may inquire for you?

Bloom asks, "What, Jacob?" and Jacob responds: "Richard Bloom, Esquire, of Rome, Oneida County, and state of New-York, A man without, I think would speak with thee." Bloom: "Admit him." Jacob: "He shall come—while I do go—So, he advances and I retrograde—Thus, of quick comes and goes, this life is made." And he exits to the second musical theme. A heavy stress on patriotism remains the hallmark of our early comic operas. At one point Count Phlegm, a heavily satirized "foreigner," says, "Infernal leveller—fell Democracy!"—and much that was awkward and heavy-handed is in his words.

Comic operas were subject to regular spurts of enthusiasm, as the works of William Dimond were produced here and as an occasional hit induced imitations. For the most part, however, the music was played down and the comedy played up—a path similar to that trod by melodrama. Still, ballad operas, the progenitors of comic opera, continued popular in the minstrel show and in burlesque. And the comic opera itself retained some audience as late as the 1920s, when each season found a few works listed as "comedies with music."

Whether American operetta was a "logical outgrowth of the extravaganza and burlesque"[32] or an immediate response to some European imports hardly matters. The fact is, that musicals have always fascinated American audiences and American audiences, in turn, have been willing to sit through experiments and innovations in musical theatre that they would not suffer on the legitimate stage.

After the Civil War, the first powerful importations to the American musical theatre were the *opéra-bouffes* of Jacques Offenbach. The Offenbach vogue began with his *La Grand Duchesse de Gerolstein* in 1867 and continued in full flower for about ten years. His works were mostly presented in French, so that Americans lost much of the wit and satire—probably a good thing, since some loss of popularity occurred when Americans were informed that much of the wit was based on sexual innuendo.

Offenbach's works were enjoyed, for the most part, by the same audiences which attended Italian opera. His operettas were genuine opera but with dialogue; their music was somewhat more easily accessible than that of grand opera. Many of these *opéra-bouffes* were increasingly popular here, especially Offenbach's *La Belle Hélène* in 1868, *La Vie Parisienne* and *La Perichole* (most recently performed at the Metropolitan Opera) in 1869, *Barbe-bleue* in 1870; also popular were Lecoq's *Giroflé-Girofla* in 1875 and *Les Cloches de Corneville* in 1877.

The next major foreign impact on American musical theatre came from the works of Gilbert and Sullivan. The Boston Museum presented *H.M.S. Pinafore* on November 25, 1878, and the flood began: by August, Boston had seen 241 presentations by assorted companies, even including a children's troupe. *Pinafore* took the country by storm, though Gilbert and Sullivan, thanks to the lack of a copyright agreement between England and the United States, received nothing from its extensive performances. They brought the D'Oyly Carte Opera Company to New York in 1878, to show the authentic *Pinafore* with Sullivan's orchestrations, and then gave New York the premiere performance of *The Pirates of Penzance* in 1879. For decades thereafter (and to some extent even today) Gilbert and Sullivan operettas were popular all over America. Part of the joy in these works lies in the musical satire of grand opera, though part is in the delight with the music itself, as Sullivan had it both ways. Certainly the ease with which audiences could come to the music separated it from opera. The wit, the satire, the absurd plots and nonsensical moments all contributed to the popularity both of *opéra-bouffes* and the operettas of Gilbert and Sullivan.[33]

With the addition of sentimentality and glamour and romance and exotic locales peopled by royalty, a kind of "well-bred artificiality," the operetta was ready for an even wider audience. Franz von Suppé's *Fantinitza* came to New York in 1879, and with it the Viennese tradition of operetta. Even so, operetta seemed in the minds of most Americans as fit company for opera. The Boston Ideal Opera Company (later known as the Bostonians) was in existence for twenty-five years, and during that time its repertory included the major works of Gilbert and Sullivan, Offenbach, and von Suppé, but also of Flotow, Donizetti, and Mozart.

The Casino Theatre in New York opened in 1882 as a home for musicals, and in the next seven years presented thirty-five European operettas. No question, these helped to spark the popularity of operettas here. Johann Strauss, though not really popular in America till the twentieth century, was nonetheless instrumental in carrying on operetta's traditions here; his *The Queen's Lace Handkerchief*, for example, showed up at the Casino. Operetta was by this time firmly established in America. In one year, 1894–1895, as a case in point, fourteen companies toured the United States with European operettas.[34]

The first decade of the twentieth century found importations outnumbering native operettas—no great surprise when one considers that operetta was in no sense a native genre. But Americans had begun to experiment with the form before that, and several of them made names for themselves in operetta.

When Offenbach came to America for a series of concerts in 1876, the concert master of his New York orchestra was John

Philip Sousa.[35] Perhaps it was the influence of Offenbach that stirred Sousa to compose one of America's first operettas, *The Smugglers* in 1879, the very year that *The Pirates of Penzance* was first presented here by Gilbert and Sullivan. Sousa's most successful operetta was *El Capitan*, in 1896, and although his current reputation rests with his marches, he was responsible for composing nineteen operettas for the American stage. Willard Spencer's *The Little Tycoon* (Spencer wrote both words and music) in 1886 had an extraordinarily long run for the time— 500 performances, a box-office record that lasted for years— and is considered by many to be "truly the first American operetta." While many other American operetta composers achieved some degree of success—for example, Gustave Kerker, Karl Hoschna (with eight operettas to his credit), Gustave Luders (thirteen operettas, the best known of which was *The Prince of Pilsen*, first produced in 1903)—only two others carried major reputations from the nineteenth into the twentieth century: Reginald De Koven and Victor Herbert.

De Koven was born in Connecticut in the same year as Victor Herbert, 1859. His first operetta was an attempt to cash in on the popularity of *The Mikado* and was called *The Begum* (1887); perhaps something of its quality may be inferred from the names of two of its characters, Howja-Dhu and Klahm-Chowdee. Probably his best-known work was *Robin Hood* (1890), the show which featured "Oh Promise Me." He continued to write operettas until 1913.[36]

But it was Victor Herbert who made the American operetta famous and whose name and works remain with us today. He was in no sense an innovator. He was content to take and to work with all the conventions of the form, the impossible lands of make-believe, complete with intrigues, with the black-and-white morality of melodrama, where virtue wins out as the hero and heroine are united and the villain punished, the lands of sentiment and romance where songs are tossed in without any relevance and dances for the same reason. If his music remained primarily European in identity—one critic said it was "essentially Irish in the sentiment and sweetness of melody, essentially German in harmonic idiom and orchestration"—he did add an incredibly fecund gift for song. Some fifty works show up in the list of Victor Herbert operettas, and he wrote pieces as well for orchestra and songs for those editions of the *Ziegfeld Follies* that fell between 1918 and 1923. His first operetta was written in 1895, though his first success, *The Fortune Teller*, did not come until three years later. Some of his operettas are still performed, despite their dated librettos, their ludicrous stage business, and their silly sentimentalism, because of their incredible lyricism; these include *Babes in Toyland* (1903), *Mlle. Modiste* (1905), *The Red Mill* (1906), and *Naughty Marietta* (1910). Rousing choruses, songs in three-quarter time, dances from the ballroom (waltzes, galops)—these were the hallmarks of operetta and of Victor Herbert. By the time he died in 1924, two other Americans had taken over the operetta form, Rudolf Friml and Sigmund Romberg.[37]

European operettas had continued to rule the realm of operetta (though not musicals in general, where American musical comedy retained its dominant hold on audiences). Franz Lehar's *The Merry Widow* arrived here in 1907 and was tremendously popular. Oscar Strauss's *A Waltz Dream* (the title alone seems to summarize both operetta's techniques and its aspirations) in 1908 and *The Chocolate Soldier* in 1909 helped considerably, and the renewed popularity of Johann Strauss's works (especially *Die Fledermaus*) all made operetta the place for an American composer to go. Rudolf Friml took advantage with *The Firefly* in 1912; he wrote it for an opera star (on several occasions, Victor Herbert did, too), in this case Emma Trentini. Between 1912 and 1928 Friml wrote his most popular and most enduring operettas: *The Firefly*, *The Vagabond King*, *Rose Marie*, and *The Three Musketeers*. While he wrote both for stage and movies after 1930, his later works never achieved any popularity.

The operettas of Sigmund Romberg followed a similar pattern. His "best music is essentially Viennese," said one critic, though he wrote hundreds of songs for close to fifty Shubert Brothers musicals and revues. His songs are still sung, possibly one of the criteria for including him in any book dealing with America's musical theatre—songs from such shows as *Maytime* (1917), *Blossom Time* (1921), *The Student Prince* (1924), *The Desert Song* (1926), and *The New Moon* (1928). Romberg, in an attempt to get away from Vienna, composed *Up in Central Park* in 1945, though by this time he was near the end of his career; he died in 1951.[38]

For the most part, 1930 may be considered the end of operetta in America. While the works of Victor Herbert, Rudolf Friml, and Sigmund Romberg are still played, no American operetta of significance has been composed since 1930, although Stephen Sondheim's *A Little Night Music* (1973) can make a strong claim to be a delightful revival of the genre. The form served for a while to permit American audiences to hear what was being written in Europe with the resulting infusion of ideas, literary and musical. These ideas might be accepted by our writers of musical comedy, or they might be rejected, but they were not strong enough in tradition to stand in America by themselves. The broad range demanded of voices, the exciting jumps, the embellishments of opera and operetta, the three-quarter rhythms (as opposed to the four-four time of most American songs) all served to enrich our musical theatre for a while. The American musical stage is indebted to the operetta as one of many streams feeding it, but for the most part the American musical, despite the brief popularity of operetta, continued to go its own way.

Minstrel Show and Circus

The minstrel show and the circus were heavy contributors to the growth and development of a native musical theatre. The minstrel show gave us an indigenous form, and the circus helped it traverse the country.

The minstrel show's origins can be found in classic times, in eighteenth-century English plays, in performers (both black and white) around the time of the American Revolution, and, of course, on the plantations of the South, where many African elements found their way to this country.

But all of this, while indicating an interest in black drama and preparing the way for the minstrel show, makes little real progress toward the new form. A giant step was taken by Thomas Dartmouth Rice, who put on ragged clothes (not the exaggerated clothing later affected by the minstrel shows) in order to imitate a song and dance he had heard and seen performed by a crippled black man. Imitation of a real man and even authenticity of dress are the crucial points here. Rice seems to have been a competent actor and was noted for his *entr'acte* songs and dances. He introduced his new number, "Jump, Jim Crow," in *The Rifle* by Solon Robinson, in which he played a "Kentucky cornfield Negro." The audience began to call for "Jim Crow," and the management was forced to have it repeated. Not only did the song establish Rice as one of the leading entertainers of the period, but, more important, his was the first great success as imitator and interpreter of black Americans. And most important, the 1820s and 1830s found the main styles of black impersonation being set; Rice's portrait of the southern plantation black helped establish a character who was to be as important to American folklore as any other legendary type.

Rice made a career of Jim Crow, and he brought Jim Crow again and again to an astonishing variety of places. He showed up constantly in the late 1820s and 1830s in New York, Louisville, Pittsburgh, Cincinnati, and a host of small Ohio towns; he played in Washington, Baltimore, Philadelphia, Natchez, Charleston, and London.[1]

The lyrics to "Jim Crow" give some indication of the flexibility with which Rice was able to add humor, local color, and politics to his performance. Between each stanza was repeated a chorus, with an imitation of a black man's dance which he had observed:

> So I wheel about,
> I turn about,
> I do just so,
> And ebery time I wheel about,
> I jump Jim Crow.

The stanzas helped him to create, in song and dance, the first minstrel character. He visits New York:

> Broadway is a pretty place
>   And de Battery has de bench
> All for to commodate
>   De hansome nigger wench.

Several stanzas attempt to show the different dances he has noted in his travels; for example:

> This is the style of Alabama,
>   What dey hab in Mobile,
> And dis is Louisiana,
>   Whaar dey track upon de heel.

He visits the president in Washington and reflects the pre-
vailing American attitude toward taxation:

> And after I had treated him,
>   To a smaller of de best,
> I went count my money,
>   And found a quarter left.

And his boasting puts him firmly in the tradition of such American folk heroes as the river boat man and the Yankee:

> Oh Jim Crow struck a man,
>   His name I forgot,
> But dar was nothing left,
>   But a little grease spot.[2]

Rice went directly to his sources and as a result of his refusal
to distort the original was considered the most accurate por-
trayer of blacks in his day. And this was crucial in the origin
of the minstrel show. Noah Ludlow, in whose theatre Rice got
his start, commented later that Rice's talent "consisted in his
great fidelity in imitating the broad and prominent peculiar-
ities of other persons, as was evident in his close delineations
of the corn-field negro, drawn from real life, and for which he
was greatly celebrated."[3]

Black influence on the American theatre came about, then,
not directly, since many years would have to pass before blacks
could perform with any regularity on the stage here. Rather,
it came indirectly, through imitation, through a stress on authenticity, when whites brought to the stage black songs and
dance.

Rice earned the title "the father of minstrelsy" in still another way. Through the creation of other black characters, he
began to write "extravaganzas" for the stage, and these, in
effect, were small ballad operas, similar in every way to those
ballad operas which helped to launch the American drama in
the eighteenth century. Rice may not have been the first to
attempt a play in blackface, but he helped to set the form and
to popularize it. These productions were, at the start, short
skits, sometimes merely the expansion of a popular Negro song;

a small number of blackface comedians danced and sang in them. Soon the play grew into miniature ballad operas with all of the characteristics of the form—spoken dialogue, dance, and music, the latter, well-known Negro songs, were frequently used as settings for new words. Rice began to collect Negro melodies and to weave them together in these "Ethiopian operas." In 1833 he introduced his *Long Island Juba, or, Love by the Bushel* (Juba was a well-known black entertainer who danced on the stage for many years); over the next few years, some of his Ethiopian operas included *Bone Squash, The Virginia Mummy, Oh! Hush! or, The Wirginny Cupids*, and *Bone Squash Diavolo*. And he took advantage of his great character creation by adding him to these musicals: *Jim Crow in London* and *Jim Crow in Foreign Service*. Others began to compose Ethiopian operas, and many of these have come down to us: *Old Zip Coon*, for example.[4]

A visitor to the United States, George Moore, wrote an account of his journey, published in 1845: "In the evening visited the Chatham Theatre, a regular Yankee place, to see the original Mr. Rice perform a burlesque *Othello!* and the farce *Here's a Go!*"[5] This operatic *Othello* was quite popular and keeps cropping up in accounts of the American theatre.[6] It is typical of the extravaganza which was to form part of the minstrel show. It is in one act (with seven scenes), and a note at the end of the manuscript indicates that performance time was one hour and twenty minutes. Each song lists the tune which is to be used and to which the new words are set (for example, "Sitting on a Rail," sung by the Chorus of Senators in scene 3: "The council we have met tonight/ Like men to do the thing that's right/ And beat the foe that's now in sight/ For Venice shall be free"). Music serves as a background to the entrance of various characters, a technique transferred from melodrama. The dialogue is rhymed throughout. Othello is asked to defend himself against the charge of stealing away Brabantio's daughter. He begins with a recitative in black dialect but modeled on Shakespeare's words, and then, to the tune of "Ginger Blue," sings:

> Her fader lub'd me well
> And he say to me one day

Otello won't you come wid me and dine.
As I whar rader sharp set
Why, berry well I say
I'll be up to de trough Sar, in time.
We had terrapins, Chicken Stew
And nice punking Pie
And a dish filled with nice Maccaroni
And last not least come de fried Sassingers
All cooked by de fair Desdemona.

Later, Iago sings one of his songs to the tune of "Yankee Doodle" and Othello one of his to "The Girl I Left Behind Me." At the end, Desdemona pops up, unmurdered, and the Ethiopian opera ends with a dance by all the characters. When one notes that a raccoon-hide towel is substituted for Othello's handkerchief and that Desdemona was played by a man (as were all female parts in the minstrel show; these "wench" roles, that is, women's parts played by men, were especially sought after), some additional humor shows through. Not only, then, can we clearly see a type of minstrel entertainment in Rice's *Othello*, but a clear way station on the road from ballad opera to musical comedy.

Some actors were content to perform Rice's works, and other blackface comedians added to the repertory. Regular members of the stock companies in each city acted in these mock operas. The immediate importance of Rice's work is that these musicals became an important part of the minstrel show when that form was finally born.

But the actual basis for the minstrel show was the attempt to emulate the dress, the manners, the speech, the song, and the dance of blacks from various parts of the United States.[7] This point cannot be stressed too heavily. Later, the attempt was to caricature blacks and still later to ignore them altogether (or combine a presentation of the stage Negro with the stage Irishman or the stage Indian). But at the beginning, the appeal of the minstrel show was (aside, of course, from its entertainment value) the "educational" experience. From the beginning, Americans insisted that theatre be an educational experience, partly as a means of placating the Puritan conscience. The minstrel show was to entertain and to educate, the latter through the accurate presentation of blacks in song and dance. And it was precisely this attempt at accuracy which helped lead to all the indigenous elements the minstrel show offered to the American theatre.

Most visitors to America commented on the songs and dances of the blacks. John Bernard, actor, observed in 1800 that "The negroes have always been proverbial for their homage to St. Vitus, being known to walk five or six miles after a hard day's work to enjoy the pleasure of flinging about their hands, heads, and legs to the music of a banjo, in a manner that threatened each limb with dislocation."[8] Another actor, William C. Macready, in his *Reminiscences* (1849) remembered that "The Negroes sang in their wild, fantastic yet harmonious chorus, which, in the night, passing the various lights from shore and boats, had a very pleasing effect."[9] Another writer speaks of "The crooning melodies sung to the accompaniment of guitar or banjo by the plantation blacks, and their peculiar shuffling dances," and remarks that "Negroes sang in the streets of New York, Philadelphia, and other Eastern cities, probably to banjo accompaniment, as early as the American Revolution and were well established by the early nineteenth century as popular street entertainers."[10] Mrs. Trollope, too, commented with delight on the chants of Negro boatmen. Dance combined with song was what blacks did at corn-shuckings; the jawbone was a favorite instrument; the slaves tended to play their unique instruments in small groups; and the southern plantations probably preferred offbeats in their music, offbeats of African origin—and all of these factors assured a "constant musical intercourse between the slave and the white society."[11]

Rice collected those Negro melodies he had heard and wove them into his extravaganzas, and the earliest minstrel shows leaned heavily on authentic black music. The seeming authenticity of their imitations was one of the strongest elements of their appeal. The source of their original pattern "was the singing of the slaves on the plantations and waterways of the South and Southwest." Some writers admit the imitation but suggest other sources: "The negro minstrel show started as a frank imitation, and oddly enough, in New York state. Negroes sang in the New York City street years before the Revolution."

One approach to the minstrel show goes even further. Insisting that the origins are as obscure as any other folk creation, this school says the plantation blacks' impromptu shows "proved so popular that occasionally a troupe was invited to the big house to entertain the master's guests. Sometimes such groups would travel from plantation to plantation for that purpose." Indeed, even the early blackface companies were "imitating the bands of Negro plantation players."[12]

Visitors to America were impressed by the phenomenon: "The songs, and jokes, and eccentricities of the negro race are the growth of the soil, and the hyperbole and extravagance which mark the performances of their stage representatives, are the distinguishing characteristics of native humor"; and another: "Christy's Minstrels are amusing enough. They are a set of apparently black men . . . who impersonate the 'darkies;' talk as they talk, sing as they sing"; another, writing of Sanford's minstrel troupe: Sanford "is careful in discrimination of the blacks of various states." And when the Ethiopian Serenaders visited England in the late 1840s, the English commented especially on the portrayal: an article in an English newspaper noted "the Americans' avowed purpose of affording an accurate notion of Negro character and melody. . . . They have been provided with letters of recommendation from President Polk, and some leading personages in America, who must be better able to appreciate the accuracy of their African delineations than Europeans."[13] Just as Jim Crow was a frank though broad imitation of the southern plantation black, so "Zip Coon" came to be recognized as the dandy (he was sometimes called "Dandy Jim"), the northern, urban black, in his long-tailed blue coat; this character, too, was modeled on reality. A survey of playbills (the Harvard University Theatre Collection alone has thousands of playbills for over 400 different minstrel companies before 1900) indicates the stress placed on authenticity in the early years: the Florida, the Georgia, the Kentucky, the Virginia Minstrels attempted to portray the subtleties of accent, song, and dance of a given region. Even late in the century when minstrel shows began to decline in popularity, they continued to stress their authenticity, though this verisimilitude now showed up on only a small part of the program. Even the dialectal distinction between the black field worker and the plantation house servant was observed at the beginning.

Certainly those who were responsible for launching the minstrel show were aware of what they were doing. Daniel Decatur Emmett said, for example, "In the composition of the walk-around I have always strictly confined myself to the habit and crude ideas of the slaves of the South." E. P. Christy insisted that his company portrayed "Negro dandyism" and "the broad humors of plantation life." And articles in the United States in the 1840s were quite clear about the early shows: The minstrels "sing the songs of the plantation slaves of the South, dance their plantation jigs and imitate the language of the real Virginia Negro."[14] As the minstrel show grew, it came to lean more heavily on some aspects of black people's lives and less heavily on others, particularly as caricature became a dominant mode; yet there was always an association with real blacks. And the result was indigenous elements added to the American stage and a style and type of acting that, for the first time, could best be acted by Americans rather than imported Englishmen.

If Rice was father of the American minstrel, then Emmett was father of the American minstrel show. Playbills show pictures of Rice in his ragged Jim Crow costume, appearing as between-the-acts entertainment. His extravaganzas might be used between the acts or as an afterpiece. Small combinations of men singing and dancing became popular in the 1830s and 1840s, but Emmett provided the formula, the pattern which gave life to the form. He had teamed with Frank Brower (comedian, singer, bone player, dancer) in New York in 1842. The bone player used real bones held between the fingers of each hand, producing individual, rhythmic clicks or rolls of clicks; later, of course, Mr. Bones, one of the end men, derived his name from his occupation: playing the bones. Soon they added two others (Bill Whitlock and Dick Pelham) "in a venture which was to open up a new chapter in the history of the American popular theatre." They opened in January 1843 in New York with a new kind of ensemble: violin (Emmett), bones (Brower), banjo (Whitlock), and tambourine (Pelham). They called themselves the "Virginia Minstrels," and they sang, played their instruments, danced (all these both in ensemble and in solos and duets), and in addition used some of those "operas" popularized earlier by Rice. Their first programs were in two parts, though each part featured the same type of entertainment. "The novel feature of the Virginia Minstrels was the association of four entertainers in a coordinated team, dressed in distinctive costumes, each assigned a specific role in the ensemble, each playing a characteristic instrument, and putting on a complete, self-contained show."[15] Soon, however, additional patterns became clear: the stress on exclusively musical entertainment, the singing and playing at the same time, the songs linked with (even interrupted by) dialect conversation. (This was to result in the "stump speech," a lecture on some current topic delivered in dialect and filled with puns and malaprops). E. P. Christy, too, claimed to have founded the first minstrel show; certainly, Christy's Ethiopian Minstrels helped with the wild popularity of the minstrel show. Richard Moody points out that they opened at Mechanics' Hall on Broadway: "They planned to run for a few weeks, and stayed for nine years and eleven months."[16] But Emmett's Virginia Minstrels, with their ensemble at the heart of their entertainment, with Negro acts as crucial, with the popularity which accrued to them, probably earned the name of the first minstrel show, at least as the form came to be accepted and to dominate the American theatre for forty years and to influence it for many years beyond that.

The 1840s saw a minstrel troupe made up of four to six men. The program began to feature a "walk-around" (where the entire troupe sang and clapped hands, after which each member stepped out of the semi-circle and performed his specialty in the center) as the traditional end of the first act. The first act gradually evolved into an attempt to show the "dandyism of the Northern States," and the second half displayed the "Ethiopians of the Southern States." By the 1850s the form shifted again, into a three-part structure, one which remained fairly standard: sentimental songs in Part I, an olio (a mixture; each performer displaying his versatility) with musical specialty numbers in Part II, and an attempt to portray genuine black characteristics in Part III. The walk-around, which had been a dance executed by soloists in the 1840s, became in the 1850s an ensemble number, and by the 1860s was both danced and sung. It evolved into two sections of equal length: the first sung with solos and chorus, and the second competitive dancing in a circle. But by this time, the minstrel show had changed into something which looked much more like vaudeville.

E. P. Christy and his minstrels brought to the form other elements: the semi-circular line-up of performers with the tambourine at one end and the bones at the other; he was the first to give the interlocutor (in the early days known as the middle man) a central position. Christy also claimed credit for the first loud-colored suits; Mark Twain helped us to see these:

Their clothing was a loud and extravagant burlesque of the clothing worn by the plantation slave of the time . . . it was the form and color of his dress that was burlesqued. Standing collars were in fashion in that day, and the minstrel appeared in a collar which engulfed and hid the half of his head and projected so far forward that he could hardly see sideways over its points. His coat was sometimes made of calico with a swallowtail that hung nearly to his heels and had buttons as big as a blacking box. His shoes were rusty and clumsy and cumbersome, and five or six sizes too large for him.[17]

Christy also asserted that his were the first street parades and his the variety acts of the olio. Other elements were featured as minstrel shows proliferated and traveled all over the country. A burlesque of grand opera became important to the performance. The careful accuracy of imitations continued to be insisted upon; for example, an Englishman, writing of Sanford's minstrel company, noted that Sanford is "careful in his discrimination of the blacks of different states."[18] Finally in 1865 a black man, Charles Hicks, organized the first successful all-black company, the Georgia Minstrels, and before long, many blacks began to appear in their own companies.

In fact, by the 1860s one can discern many trends in the minstrel show. The music became more elaborate, and a band played outside the theatre before the performance began. A good many companies featured both a brass band and an orchestra. The Arlington Minstrels, for example, boasted "over 75 First-Class Artists" plus a ten-piece concert band plus a "matchless orchestra." Harry Bloodgood's Minstrels listed the names of the ten men in their orchestra plus the fourteen men in their brass band. Pictures on the playbills reveal the musicians seated either in the pit or ranged behind the semi-circle of performers. The performers still hold banjo, tambourine, and bones, but they are no longer, obviously, providing the main music of the evening.

More and more companies listed themselves as Minstrel and Burlesque Opera Companies (for example, Carncross and Sharpley's Minstrel and Burlesque Opera Troupe; Leavitt and Curran's Burlesque Opera Troupe, Mammoth Minstrel Organization and Brass Band; Parker's Ethiopian Operatic Troupe) and for burlesque opera something more sophisticated by way of singers and musicians was called for. The kind of happy irreverence that permitted minstrel shows to burlesque black customs and dress extended itself gradually to cover every aspect of American life. Grand opera was probably the hardest-hit victim, though the singing, even in burlesque, was probably good. Mrs. Sarah Maury commented in 1848, "at Palmo's we witnessed several times the grotesque representations and caricature imitations of the Italian opera, and their chief performers. The actors of this singular travestie did not disguise their voices; they (sang) six very fairly; but they were painted ebony with burnt corks, and their dialogue was the lowest dialect of negro language."[19] Buckley's Serenaders stressed the fact in their bills that "The Music executed by the Buckley's in the rendition of their BURLESQUE OPERAS, is the GENUINE MUSIC of the Operas Travestied, with Negro interpolations and intercullations, which drive away the dullness of a too close observance of the original text." *La Sonnambula, Il Trovatore, Il Barbiere di Siviglia*, and *Lucia di Lammamoor* (*Lucy Did Lam Her Moor*) were evidently special favorites, judging by the number of times they appeared on playbills.

Aside from the extravaganzas, from the brass bands and orchestras, from the burlesque operas, from the songs and dances, the playbills reveal the general dissolution of the minstrel show as it grew unwieldly in size, as it stressed variety (and moved thereby toward vaudeville), and as it began to look for gimmicks to attract rather than keeping to the musical heart which had kept it alive for so long. In the 1880s, though the minstrel show had many years left to run, the end, mastodonitis, could be seen in the companies of over one hundred or in, for example, a playbill in the Harvard University Theatre Collection for Haverly's United-Mastodon Minstrels which shows forty men in blackface on stage, fifteen in back playing instruments, and twenty-five arranged in a double row for minstrel acts and dances. The text says the company is "original in Conception and Stupendous in Magnitude, rejecting the Old-fashioned, Old Fogy Ideas, and presenting the Choicest Repertoire of Select Minstrel specialties in quadruple form."

The major advantage of early minstrel companies had been the ease with which they could travel, bringing their entertainment to every part of the United States. Now, however, their size precluded travel, and another unique feature of the minstrel show disappeared.

Still another indigenous aspect of the minstrel show was its music. It was not until the early 1840s that the native content of minstrelsy extended itself to original song.

From the beginning of the forties on, the publication of minstrel songs proceeded at an ever increasing rate. Aside from adaptations of texts to well-known tunes, taken even from operas, there appeared within one decade about two dozen songs which constitute the most indigenous American music, apart from somewhat earlier southern folk hymns and the New England hymn tunes and their settings of the late eighteenth century.[20]

Other critics find still other native sources: There is "a general family resemblance in the basic melodic materials of the three main popular traditions of vocal music that developed in the United States during the first half of the nineteenth century: the revival hymns of the whites, the Negro spirituals and work songs, and the so-called 'plantation' or 'Ethiopian' melodies." This exploitation of black music in the 1840s employed the simplicity of children's songs blended with "the rigidity and rhythmic persistence of ethnically primitive music." Again, the "preference for offbeats is of African origin, and undoubtedly existed on the southern plantation.... If, finally, we consider that the relentless repetition of brief motives and downward direction of melodies are characteristic of primitive music, we can safely conclude that the minstrel banjo style is very similar to what slaves played on their banjos and fiddles." While songs of the 1820s and 1830s used foreign sources, strong evidence suggests that by the 1840s the work songs of cattle drivers, wagoners, and boatmen were interwoven in plantation songs and spirituals—all meshed together to give some taste of the American scene, a type of music which would lead to ragtime and to jazz.[21]

The very form of the minstrel show led to still another type of song; the first part of the show, which had come to present the northern dandy, gradually gave way to sentimental ballads. To some extent, the harmonizing of the black songs (said to have begun with Buckley's Serenaders about 1852) and the use of operatic music as burlesque material helped to transform the kind of music being performed. Chief among the writers of this new type of song was, of course, Stephen Foster.

Whether his source was black work songs heard in Pittsburgh or the fact that spirituals "were a source material for Foster, and he spent much time at Negro camp meetings to better understand Negro rhythms and melodies," Foster became the chief composer for a series of distinctly American songs: "Oh! Susanna," "Camptown Races," "My Old Kentucky Home," and "Old Black Joe" are good examples. Emmett, too, made a name for himself with minstrel songs (for example, "Dixie," written for Bryant's Minstrels) and dances.[22] And a black man, James A. Bland, later wrote some of the best of them: "Carry Me Back to Old Virginny," "In the Evening by the Moonlight," and "Oh, Dem Golden Slippers." Most of the songs presented by any given minstrel troupe were composed especially for it. Again, the minstrel show was an active influence in the creation of a distinctly American music.

It is impossible to talk about indigenous music without considering dance as well, especially since the "prancing walk-arounds and the shuffling shouts were motivated by an identical impulse and resulted from the same traditional concept of 'hot' rhythm in the indissoluble union of song and dance." The early jigs and clogs of the black stage were mixtures of

Irish and Scots dances, though the walk-around was patterned on black dances.[23] There were authentic dance patterns on the plantations and in the North: Juba, for example, a Long Island black, did much to preserve authentic black dance patterns. Later, through the minstrel show, his name became attached to a dance, the Juba, which was fast, requiring plentiful energetic movements and much tossing about of arms and legs. Any minstrel dance in black style came to be called a "breakdown," though these were frequently dances with comic jumps and heel-and-toe techniques which anticipated tap dancing. They began by combining Irish and Scottish jigs with black rhythms and gestures. Soft shoe dances were invented by minstrels, and the term "jigs" referred to banjo tunes for dancing rather than to the music itself. While the southern blacks were an excellent source for much of minstrel dance movement, minstrels used folk dances from other countries as well, embellishing these with black characteristics; but the stage demanded more form than the loosely organized, improvised dances of blacks, and the tradition of theatrical dancing itself became a dominant factor in shaping the dances of the minstrel shows.

All these elements formed part of an unbelievably popular genre. The minstrel show was the backbone of American popular entertainment for over half a century. Certainly it brought musical theatre to every corner of the United States, often along with the first pioneers. Frequently the very first entertainment seen by a new community was the minstrel show, whether performed by professionals or by amateurs. For example, during the Mexican War, in 1847, the men of Colonel J. D. Stevenson's Seventh Regiment of New York Volunteers, in Monterrey, put on minstrel shows; soldiers put on minstrel shows in San Francisco, in Sonoma, and in Santa Barbara.[24]

But professional minstrels broke the ground in most places, as we have seen in an earlier chapter. As one follows the history of town after town in the United States, one is constantly faced with the minstrel show, not only as precursor of more serious drama, but as introducer of a form with music and characters and dance, and even format, with roots in the soil it traversed. The professional theatre came to depend on the popularity of the minstrel show. St. Louis, with a going theatre, used the brand new theatre form initially as afterpiece (for example, the Columbia Minstrels in 1844 followed *Much Ado About Nothing* on the same bill) and then as star turn on the St. Louis–New Orleans–Mobile circuit of Ludlow and Smith. Charleston used minstrels in much the same way, as did Providence and other well-established theatre cities. New York, already the theatre capital of the United States, provided more minstrel shows than anywhere else: there were three minstrel troupes in the city at the same time in 1848, and by 1856 New York had five minstrel companies, each in its own house. Soon after it had ten theatres playing only minstrel shows.

But it was not so much in the larger cities that the minstrel show made its presence felt as along the frontier, bringing with it the basis for a peculiarly American theatre. Chicago, which had a population of only 400 in 1833, nevertheless by the 1840s found minstrel shows were as "enthusiastically attended as they were frequent." Boise, Idaho, whose saloons had songs and dances in 1863, welcomed a minstrel show in 1864. In Virginia City, Montana, minstrels arrived almost simultaneously with the first gold seekers. Galveston, Texas, had minstrels in 1856 and Houston in 1858. Washoe (later Nevada) had minstrels in 1861 and Seattle in 1863 (in fact, every year but seven from 1864 to 1880 found at least one minstrel company visiting Seattle). In San Francisco, the gambling saloons presented minstrel shows in the 1840s, and by the summer of 1855 that city boasted five different minstrel troupes.

It is interesting that throughout the Confederacy during the Civil War, theatre activity went on, and heading the list was, again, the minstrel show. In fact, the minstrel show was frequently the *only* theatre activity in many southern cities. Most stars went north at the beginning of the war, and the South had to build its own companies and form its own routes. Johnson's Minstrels, for example, in 1862, played Mobile, Montgomery, Columbus, Atlanta, Augusta, Savannah, Charleston, and Columbia.

Still other aspects of the minstrel show's influence on American musical theatre can be traced. During the eighteenth century, American museums featured entertainment, and it was the minstrel show which carried this tradition through the

1800s. The circus had always been closely allied with the musical stage in America, and again it was the minstrel show which sustained the connection. Showboats, too, became associated with the minstrel show. The *Floating Palace*, for example, which in company with at least three other showboats toured the Mississippi in the 1850s and 1860s, was 250-feet long, and provided both circus ring and auditorium for the minstrel show. Commercial boats also featured minstrel companies (for example, the line between Fall River and New York City ran two boats with minstrel companies), and one finds steamboats with minstrel companies touring the Ohio, Cumberland, and Tennessee rivers. The tremendous growth of variety shows in the late 1850s and early 1860s, directly descended from the variety sections of the minstrel show, soon metamorphosed into vaudeville shows, and so, on this too the minstrel show made its long-term impress.

Minstrels were associated with other aspects of theatre life. Even the theatre's star system was emulated, witness Billy Emerson who skipped from minstrel troupe to minstrel troupe for over thirty years.[25] When *tableaux vivants* became popular, the minstrel shows were quick to parody them as they had grand opera. As summer gardens, such as Vauxhall in New York, continued their musical-theatrical traditions, minstrel songs provided much of the entertainment. And these same minstrel songs, sometimes with new lyrics, accompanied pioneers and gold seekers as they traveled over the continent. Indeed, most songs of the gold-rush period were written by members of minstrel companies. It was hard to tear loose from minstrels anywhere. The actor Henry Clay Barnabee recalled sitting in church and listening to Dr. John P. Ordway in Boston: "Often he would freeze my young blood by playing that hard-shelled orthodox Baptist congregation out of church with a crazy combination of 'Old Hundred,' executed with the left hand and pedals, and 'Sweet Ham Bone' or 'Climbin' up dem Golden Stairs'... harmonized and deftly embroidered in with the right."[26]

Despite their pervasive influence, minstrel shows will probably never be seen again. There is no doubt that much of their popularity derived from their apology for slavery, or, at a minimum, from the picture of blacks as content with their lot, simple-minded, funny, and irresponsible. Over and over again the playbills show minstrel companies featuring the extravaganza "Happy Uncle Tom." When Walter Thornbury, a British traveler, looked about him, he noted that the leader of a minstrel troupe received a valuable silver service from the students of a southern university for "defending their institutions and showing the slaves in their proper light"—that is, good-humored, merry, and contented.[27] Even the covers of sheet music showed the switch, by the 1880s, to wild caricature. This grotesque stereotype of blacks lasted well into the next century.

But, for a while, the minstrel show provided what the playbill so often advertised, a "unique and chaste performance," one with a basis in American music and song and dance. The minstrel, at the heart of American entertainment for over half a century, provided the American composer with a place to be heard and a subject matter. Listen to Stephen Foster, for example:

I had the intention of omitting my name on my Ethiopian songs, owing to the prejudice against them by some, which might injure my reputation as a writer of another style of music, but I find that by my efforts I have done a great deal to build up a taste for the Ethiopian songs among refined people by making the words suitable to their taste, instead of the trashy and really offensive words which belong to songs of that order. Therefore I have concluded to reinstate my name on my songs and to pursue the Ethiopian business without fear or shame and lend all my energies to make the business live, at the same time that I will wish to establish my name as the best Ethiopian song-writer.[28]

And Foster exemplified what the other composers were doing, too. "The minstrel show took the savagery out of his [that is, the black American's] merriment, making him a harmless figure of fun: while at the same time it related the Negro's homesickness, his sense of oppression, to the frustration and nostalgia inherent in every man, whatever the colour of his skin—and especially in man in a raw industrial society that knew but obscurely where it was going."[29]

And so, the minstrel show, in its wide range geographically

as well as dramatically, was in a position to adapt the forms of the eighteenth century. In its concern with opera, it was able to integrate aspects of the serious musical stage. In its concern with ideas of the time, it remained viable. In its admixture of forms it summed up the past and made the future possible. Indigenous in both form and content, it provided the vitality, the willingness to experiment, the mixture of dance, music, song, and acting—those large elements which are the basis for the American musical of today.

Minstrel shows were carried by circuses, not surprisingly, since the circus, almost from the beginning in America, had served as a vehicle for the musical stage.

The first circuses were performed in America in the 1770s, in Boston, Philadelphia, and New York.[30] These early circuses featured little more than trick horsemanship, with a clown and occasionally some fireworks thrown in for good measure. By the 1780s a band had been added, though it was not until the 1790s that a new form of the circus began to emerge. In England, Philip Astley had added other sorts of entertainment to the basic equestrian show, and it was in this expanded form that the circus made its first real impact on the world of entertainment in America.

John B. Ricketts offered an "equestrian pantomime" here in 1793, and with its success he offered more and more of them. Singing, dancing, and tumbling were important to his tours, and non-equestrian acts began to be featured. By 1794 Ricketts' circus included a small band, a popular stage interlude, and pony races. "The role of music...increased with the growing importance of spectacle."

In 1794 Ricketts built a circus in New York with a stage and another stage with circus ring in Philadelphia in 1795. The circus building was topped with a dome, and underneath were the usual boxes, pit, and gallery, but the boxes were arranged in such a way that platforms from either side of the stage could extend into the pit in front of the boxes, in a circular arrangement. Enclosed within the circle made by stage and platforms was space for the orchestra. In these larger structures, housing audiences from 1,000 to 1,500 people, the fierce competition between Ricketts and his chief competitor, Philip Lailson, or between circus and theatre, was waged.

Some of Ricketts' acts bridged circus ring and stage, but many were entirely on the stage—musicals. Gradually, the circus evening was divided so that the format alternated between stage and ring; circus and theatrical entertainments were equally divided in time. In the final years of the century, pantomimes with song and dance plus other entertainment (rope dancing, tumbling, fireworks, Italian shades—that is, shadow plays—painting exhibitions, interludes, and concertos) made up the larger part of an evening at the circus. The three hours running time of Ricketts' circus at the end of the 1790s was made up of a huge repertory of stage pieces to complement the equestrian part of the evening.

John Durang was ballet master and dancer with Ricketts; he helps us to see the circus as purveyor of musical theatre: in Philadelphia, aside from horesemanship, there were presented "dramatic burlettes [sic], farces, operas, pantomimes, and ballet dancing."[31] The circus, then, was forced to hire two troupes, though the two overlapped in function: in 1795, Ricketts' company employed seven equestrian performers, four theatrical, two painters, two carpenters, and a full orchestra under a Mr. Lubier.[32] The legitimate theatre itself was threatened by a circus which insisted on presenting musicals. One desperate theatre manager suggested buying up all circuses, to which his partner replied: "If *these* [Ricketts' and Lailson's circuses] were ours, cannot others be built?"[33]

Although America's first circuses featured fifes and drums and fiddles, Thomas Parkinson claims the Kent, or keyed bugle, was responsible for a major change. Ned Kendall was famous for his keyed bugle and led brass bands with the Purdy and Welsh Circus in 1837 before showing up with at least three other circuses.[34]

And so, although both Ricketts and Lailson had left America by 1800, the circus continued to provide musicals for its audiences for many years to come. Buildings in New York, Philadelphia, and Boston added stages to their circus rings, and through the 1830s the entertainment continued to be equestrian arts combined with ballet and musical farces and, in some circuses, melodramas as well. By 1820 there were over thirty rolling shows in New England and the Atlantic states, each featuring show parades and bands of music and most offering brief musicals along with circus acts. Gradually, circuses reached the West Coast (by mid-century) as well as river towns and plantation landings. In fact, the decade before the Civil War has been called the golden age of the boat circus, with a boat towing a barge on which were presented circus and minstrel performances. In the 1840s when minstrel shows became popular, it was frequently the circuses which brought them to audiences throughout the country. Some melodramas managed to combine themselves with circus acts, and these horse operas helped continue the tradition of a musical stage in the circus. Such equestrian melodramas as *Mazeppa or the Wild Horse of Tartary*, *The Forty Thieves*, *El Hyder*, *Timour the Tartar*, and *The Cataract of the Ganges* were especially popular.

Gradually, circuses began to give up stage musicals, though as late as 1856 in Tallahassee one finds an ad for a circus with men and horses, clowns, band, a pantomime, a ballet, dancing, and a comic afterpiece.[35]

Whereas before the Civil War, troupes had regularly stressed their dramatic corps, after the Civil War only the band and ballet girls remained. But even here, a cavil must be expressed. The association between circus and musical entertainment continued through the twentieth century, in pleasure gardens or Wild West shows or such a theatre as the Hippodrome in New York. This theatre opened in 1905 with *A Yankee Circus on Mars*, featuring circus acts in an elaborate production complete with book, score, ballet, and songs.[36] Circuses about 1900 began to feature musical compositions written expressly for them, by such men as Karl King, J. J. Richards, Fred Jewell, and others mentioned by Thomas Parkinson.[37] Circus compositions were meant to accompany specific elements of the circus, such as the Grand Entry. For the first forty years of the twentieth century, circus bands gave brief performances of classical music as well. These bands were typically made up of twelve to twenty-four musicians, though some might feature as many as fifty.

The clowns in the 1860s to 1870s were frequently singers, accustomed to plugging songs and printing their own clown "songsters"—thereby allying themselves with one of the worst abuses, in times to come, of the vaudeville and revue stage.[38]

Despite all these musical elements, the circus and the musical theatre have long been separated, though for almost one hundred years the circus brought the musical stage to many parts of the United States where no other entertainment had ever been seen. George Chindahl gives a partial listing of American circuses and finds, through 1956, over 1,100 of them—enough, certainly, to be a strong factor in any history of America's musical stage.

SCENE 3 _____

Melodrama and Dance

_____

Circuses and minstrel shows, however musical, were normally performed outside the legitimate theatre. They brought the musical stage to large sections of the country where legitimate theatre could not go. When legitimate theatres did arrive, they brought with them a repertory heavily musical, and nowhere was this more evident than in the melodrama.

There is something about the word melodrama that causes us to smile. Perhaps the imagination is piqued at the thought of a heroine neatly strapped across railroad tracks while we wait for the train to run over her or the hero to rescue her— and that seems, today, to be funny; or we picture the villain twirling his black mustache, and that too seems reasonably funny. Yet these amusing elements show up quite late in melodrama's history. In the beginning, a particular kind of plot, action, acting, and, especially, music shaped a new form of musical theatre.

The elements that comprise melodrama go far back in time, though the form itself was late in developing. Melodrama's flat character, for example, who does not develop at all and who has only one characteristic, can be found at many points in history. Shakespeare's Richard III limps onto the stage, his body twisted, the personification of evil, and from the moment that he proclaims, with contempt, "Now is the winter of our discontent made glorious summer by this son of York," he never changes—the perfect melodramatic villain. Music is still another element of melodrama. Roman comedy used music not only for songs but in the background, to provide atmosphere. Early opera, about 1600, used music primarily to surround, to describe the dialogue. Melodrama had still more uses for music, as will be seen below.

But if the individual characteristics of melodrama are ancient, three relatively recent men combined them into the new structure: a German, a Frenchman, and an Englishman. Just before the work of these men arrived in America, another popular form helped pave the way, the so-called serious pantomime. It featured a blend of ballet and pantomime, a continuous flow of music, and spectacular scenic effects. A good example is *La Forêt Noire; or, Maternal Affection*, a serious pantomime presented in various American cities in 1794 and thereafter.[1] The first act is in sixteen scenes: Lucille conceals her marriage to an officer (and her child as well). Her father, who wants her to marry L'Abbe, discovers the child and sends it out to be killed. In the second act, the child is saved, Lucille is captured by robbers, and so forth. Scenery includes woods, a mountain, a grotto, and the like. And a typical scene, Act I, scene v, reads like this:

[Lucille's father has just exited in a rage, and she and L'Abbe are alone on stage.] She looks at him with disdain; he attempts to make his court; she turns her back. He offers her his bouquet; she refuses. He offers her some cakes; she refuses. He consoles himself by eating some of them; he takes his snuff box and offers snuff. Lucille vexed, strikes it out of his hand. He menaces to tell her father, and *Exit in a rage.*

That is the entire scene—not a line of dialogue, the whole thing done in pantomime, dance, and a strong musical background. The entire performance is extraordinarily close to the coming melodrama.

Now the three gentlemen mentioned earlier make their appearance. The German was a playwright named August von Kotzebue, who was very popular. He introduced some of the major elements that led into melodrama, for example, chaste women—what Maurice Disher referred to as a "cosmic partiality for the virginal."[2] Another important element of his was the theme that learning is unnecessary to the man of pure heart, a theme dear to pioneer Americans whose lives on the frontier tended to make them suspicious of learning. No fewer than thirty-one of Kotzebue's plays were popular in America all through the late eighteenth and nineteenth centuries. William Dunlap, for example, was translating his plays for eighteenth-century American audiences even before the plays were seen in England; the result was an audience prepared for melodrama and ready for the new form.

The actual father of melodrama was a Frenchman, Guilbert de Pixérécourt. All the elements of melodrama came together in Pixérécourt's works. For the first time, with his fifty plays, the name *melodrama* and the form came together. Probably his most successful melodrama was his first, *Coelina* (1800). An Englishman, Thomas Holcroft, translated *Coelina* as *A Tale of Mystery*, and in this form it arrived in America. The interesting point here is that all of the writers who were working with melodrama in England, France, Germany, and America were writing at about the same time. "Within one year of the appearance of *A Tale of Mystery* from Pixérécourt on the Covent-Garden boards," says Elbridge Colby, "no less than four editions of the London version stolen from France were in turn stolen from England and on sale in the bookshops of New York and Boston."[3] In other words, no country can lay particular claim to the development of the form; other dramatic *genres* came to America after a long history in other countries, but melodrama arrived here at about the same time it was developing elsewhere. So, melodrama went its own way in America and is as close to being indigenous as any dramatic form we can find.

As melodrama developed, as audiences were more and more drawn to it, its writers and producers attempted to increase its popularity by combining it with other dramatic areas. For example, equestrian melodrama became a staple of the circus.

The non-musical aspects of melodrama are easily discerned. Certain themes appear constantly (virtue is always opposed to vice, for example), and some appear more often in particular countries (patriotism tended to show up more often in America, for example, than in England, France, or Germany).

Melodrama featured many incidents, an episodic plot, much sentimentalism, realistic settings, and poetic justice—that is, virtue was always rewarded, even as evil was always punished. Predictability was important and helps to separate melodrama from earlier, similar forms such as tragic comedy. The latter, especially in its seventeenth-century guise, was designed to titillate through unexpected situations and unpredictable characters. But in melodrama, completely predictable outcomes and characters were the law. In fact, the characters were always stereotyped, and as a result found an interesting and immediate place in the American theatre. Melodrama's characters included a hero, a heroine, a villain, a comic man and woman, a comic old man and woman, and a character actor who was given whatever parts were necessary when character variations occurred.

A word about American stock companies helps tie melodramas to American drama. In the nineteenth century, every important city in the United States had its own stock company; each member of the stock company had his own "line" of roles, that is, the type of part he was expected to play. Interestingly these lines coincided almost perfectly with the melodramatic parts mentioned above. When Noah M. Ludlow joined James Caldwell's troupe in New Orleans in 1821, he noted the makeup of the company:

Mr. James H. Caldwell, manager and leading actor in tragedy and comedy...N. M. Ludlow, juvenile tragedy and first genteel comedy, when not played by the manager; Richard Russell, stage-manager and low-comedy actor; Thomas Burke, first old man and a portion of low comedy...Jackson Gray, principal old man in some instances, and second in others...Mrs. Cornelia Burke, principal singer and first comedy "romps"...Miss Eliza Tilden...juvenile tragedy and sentimental comedy lady.[4]

An American stock company of the nineteenth century, then, was well suited to handle any melodrama that came by, because the actors who were there were competent in the specific kinds of parts called for by melodrama.

Still, the most important aspect of early melodrama was not any of these elements, but its music. First, there was dance. At the beginning, melodrama was performed very largely in dumb show, in much the same way that silent films were later acted, including holding up a placard bearing words to replace spoken dialogue. Early dramatic roles were played by dancers. When, for example, Mlle. Celeste, who later made her name as one of the most popular dancers of the century, arrived here, her early billing listed her as the "celebrated melodramatic actress." The Ravel troupe of acrobats and dancers was known early in the century for its performances of melodrama. In short, early melodrama was largely danced, and an entire style of acting emerged to accommodate the new form. No real distinction was made among the acrobat, the dancer, and the performer of melodramas.

The music itself was crucial to melodrama's form. It stressed the emotions and, as David Mayer suggests, probably masked "the improbabilities that we so often recognize in melodrama" and maintained "momentum of the play's headlong rush from sensation to sensation, from crisis to emotional crisis." In melodrama, he goes on, the "need for music never varied, for it was music that helped to focus attention on the stage. Music vividly and explicitly described aurally the visible action of scenes, identified characters for audiences through recognisable themes, and coaxed an extra measure of emotional acquiescence from rapt spectators."[5] The point is that, as its name implies, melodrama was a part of the musical theatre. Larry Robert Wolz defines it as "dialogue opera with much longer stretches of dialogue between the songs"; in fact, he claims, American authors of the nineteenth century wrote both melodramas and operas and made no differentiation between the two.[6] Music did not merely supplement words; frequently, it superseded them.[7] The actors even attempted to synchronize their speech to the music. The modern reader who picks up the script for a melodrama can no more understand what is happening from the words alone than the peruser of an opera libretto can tell what effect its performance will evoke. When the script for a melodrama and the music were put together, something magical happened. Melodrama began the practice (quickly adopted by opera—not the other way around) of using certain instruments and certain themes to identify certain characters and situations. Early melodramas listed the name of the composer as well as the author of the play. All through the play were directions as to how and when the music was to be used.

An example from the very first melodrama is Holcroft's *Tale of Mystery*,[8] based on Pixérécourt's *Coelina*: first, "Confused music," and then "Enter Montano (Music plays alarmingly, but piano when he enters, and while he says) *Montano*: I beg pardon good sir, but—(Music loud and discordant at the moment the eye of Montano catches the figure of Romaldi; at which Montano starts with terror and indignation. He then assumes the eye and attitude of menace; which Romaldi returns. The music ceases)." Six words of dialogue to an intolerable deal of description! The music described, thrust the character forward, told what was happening, delineated character.

Another good example of the centrality of music in melodrama is an American effort. James Nelson Barker wrote the *Indian Princess* in 1808, and it is one of the earliest examples of a play on an Indian theme.[9] (The music for this and for other melodramas, incidentally, was published and sold separately.) The third scene is set in the royal village of Powhatan: "Indian girls arranging ornaments for a bridal dress. Music...Music as Pocahontas enters." She speaks, then, "Distant hunting horn. Music. They place themselves in an attitude of listening. Hunting horn nearer." Then John Smith enters to music "expressive of his situation." Imagine the tremendous confidence the author had in his composer with that direction! Smith then speaks eighteen lines of dialogue with music cues all along the way, and the scene ends with a tableau followed by a chorus singing about freedom. An entire chorus singing—and this is melodrama, not opera or musical comedy.

One more example of an American melodrama, this one a bit later, shows the direction melodrama took. Nathaniel H. Bannister's *Putnam, or the Iron Son of '76* was written in 1845 and ran for seventy-eight nights at the Bowery Theatre in New

York.[10] This extended run shows something of melodrama's influence on our stage. All early acting companies throughout the United States were repertory companies, and only rarely was a production given on two successive nights. But melodrama demanded elaborate sets and created a tremendous audience demand, with the result that the long-run show began to replace the repertory system. Here is an excerpt, which serves to illustrate the direction of melodrama, of part of the Prologue to *Putnam*:

Music changes. Eagle ascends and lion descends. Goddesses dance around moving wands. Goddesses of Liberty and Mars point to clouds. Clouds ascend and draw off. Lights up. The signers of the Declaration of Independence discovered. Ben Franklin at head of table. Music changes.

Though the music is still present, the stress has obviously shifted to elaborate stage effects. This new stage realism was very different from what had gone before; it tended to subsume music and transform melodrama into a new dimension. Yet, for a long time, the effect of this musical stage form was crucial to the American theatre.

In fact, much of this country was introduced to the theatre through melodrama. In Wisconsin, Missouri, Iowa, Ohio, Mississippi, California, and Louisiana melodrama for most of the nineteenth century constituted the largest part of the repertory. Of 1,598 dramatic entertainments in Cincinnati from 1845 to 1861, approximately 700 were melodramas. In Charleston, as mentioned earlier, about 1850, 32 percent of the repertory was melodrama; in Philadelphia, 52 percent; in New Orleans and St. Louis, 50 percent. In other words, a repertory which contained comedy, tragedy, musical comedy, and opera nonetheless was over half melodrama.[11]

Melodramatic acting evolved out of the rhythms of its music and the rhythms of its dance; a patterned quality in speech and gesture emerged. In fact, a case might be made for our native drama emerging from melodrama—a drama which was largely non-verbal, with serious characters pulling away from flat stereotypes, with realism providing settings and themes.

Melodrama, a musical form, became an important source of America's serious drama. The serious dramatic productions in America in the nineteenth century were melodramas. Those things that one finds appealing in our greatest twentieth-century playwrights—Eugene O'Neill, Arthur Miller, Tennessee Williams—in their non-verbal, realistic styles are precisely the direct descendents of melodrama. In effect, America's serious drama is an extension of melodrama, and any study of our modern theatre that ignores the point is in danger of losing both our heritage and our understanding of where our drama is—and where it may be going.

The pantomimical movements in melodrama were as much dancing as acting. In fact, the American approach to dance nomenclature, distinguishing among kinds of dance, had been rather vague all along. Eighteenth-century Americans had a full share of social dances (boleros, gavottes, cotillions, galops, waltzes, and so forth) and a wild profusion of theatrical dances. Playbills from various parts of the country referred to "serious pantomimes," "ballet pantomimes," "operatic ballets," "ballet operas," "tragic pantomimes," "ballets d'action," "dance dramas," "grand serious pantomime ballets" (Polonius himself might have devised this one), "pantomimical dances," "speaking pantomimes," and "pantomime ballets."

Theatrical dance in America began as acrobatics—usually atop either a high wire or a horse. Slack-rope dancing was popular all through the eighteenth century. Yet no matter how far dance developed as an abstract form, it never completely cut itself off from the musical-dramatic theatre. All eighteenth-century concerts were followed by dances. Most dancing teachers worked in the theatre as well. It was almost impossible to separate dancers from actors and singers, since most performers were expected to do all three, precursors of the twentieth-century musical-comedy performers who are still expected to act, to sing, and to dance.

The earliest companies to arrive in America were able to put on pantomimes in addition to comic operas and plays. Dancing tended to precede the drama in many places, so when the drama arrived, it seemed natural to include dances in the repertory, to stuff them into plays, and to use them as *entr'acte* entertainment.[12]

Troupes of French dancers arrived in the colonies fairly early. In addition to training American dancers, they were accustomed to dance, to sing French opera, to perform on the tight-rope, and to excel in acrobatics and tumbling. Fine French companies of dancers complemented the regular theatre company in New York, for example, using the American Company to flesh out their ranks and, in turn, participating in the acting company's normal repertory, laden with musicals as it was. A few French dancers might remain behind after their company left, thereby seeing to it that a part of every company was proficient in dance. Dancers were expected to be choreographers as well, and minor members of the company danced in addition to stars. One of the stage children of this period noted, "The very minor business, and the ballet performances, were executed, principally, by the sons and daughters of the performers, who had received a suitable education in all of these requirements.... The children, thus employed, were taught dancing and music, and the accomplishments necessary to a theatrical education."[13]

John Durang was one of the first Americans to make a name in the dance, though his other accomplishments included acting, miming, singing, clowning, choreographing, tightrope, and acrobatic performing. He spent most of his life touring and performing either in his own companies or in those of others (including circuses) and carrying theatrical dance all over the young country.[14]

When one adds the slack and tightrope dancing at the circus to the acrobatics expected of dancers, one sees not only the varied talents necessary for the dancer but in addition the confusion as to dance forms and as to dance itself in eighteenth- and early nineteenth-century America. Pantomime alone drew into itself spoken and unspoken action, the singing of solos and duets, dancing, acrobatics, and special scenic effects.

The hornpipe was popular in the 1780s. It is considered to be an ancestor of tap dancing, and John Durang was noted for dancing a hornpipe created especially for him.[15]

Playbills of the time sometimes make clear how important

and how elaborate dance was in our early theatres. For example, a Spanish Fandango was advertised between play and
afterpiece in 1796; three actors are mentioned plus four dancers
and five singers.[16]

The 1790s saw real ballet introduced here by the company
of Alexander Placide in 1792. He called his productions "Dancing Ballets" or "Pantomime Ballets," and he introduced to the
United States ballets from popular French operas as well as
some elaborate rope dancing.

Probably the most significant dance form in our early theatre
was the "serious pantomime." It was, as far as we can ascertain,
a perfect blend of ballet, pantomime, and melodrama. Of the
many serious pantomimes performed all over the country, only
one survives: *La Forêt Noire*.[17] It was a precursor of melodrama,
as noted above. It is in three acts and has over twenty-five
parts. A typical scene shows our early musical stage, dance
division, in action:

> The father enters in a rage, takes his daughter by the hand, brings
> her to the front, tells her she must resolve to take the Abbe for her
> husband. She persists in refusing the father: The father is very much
> enraged against her; she seeks to appease him and throws herself on
> her knees; he will not hear her and is going; she runs after him, seizes
> his arms and falls at his feet. Her father pushes her off rudely and
> she falls at her length on the stage; he makes a motion to help her,
> but a transport of fury seizing him, he goes off in a rage.

The lead role in *La Forêt Noire* was danced by the best dancer
with the American Company, Mme. Gardie, whom Lillian Moore
called the "first real ballet star to perform in the United States."

The nature of theatrical dancing changed throughout the
eighteenth and nineteenth centuries. Certain patterns were
clear, however, almost from the beginning. For one thing, the
children of the actors were expected to take children's parts
and to fill out the corps during elaborate dances—as Joseph
Jefferson and his sister did, for example. Henry Clay Barnabee,
famous as actor and as manager, said, "When beginners ask
my advice about studying for the stage, whether lyric or dramatic, I always urge them to go in for dancing and fencing,

the first thing."[18] For another, almost no distinction was made among melodramatic acting, pantomime, or ballet (indeed, tight- and slack-rope performances were considered part of dance in eighteenth-century America). Further, although all stock com- panies' performers were expected to act, to sing, and to dance, nonetheless each company hired at least one or two whose specialty was both dancing and arranging dances, whatever their other duties might be. For example, Noah Ludlow's com- pany in Montgomery in 1825 featured two dancers. The St. Louis company hired one M. Tatin to serve as ballet master and principal dancer. The first theatre troupe in Houston in the 1830s featured dancers in their stock company. By 1850 a typical Boston stock company might feature sixteen to twenty male performers, eight to twelve female performers, and eight or ten ballet girls. The arrangement was similar elsewhere.[19]

As melodrama became more and more popular, dancers be- came more and more important to the stock companies. The reason is fairly obvious: the acting of melodrama was primarily pantomimic—dance-like—in nature. Also, audiences liked to be entertained with dances as one of the evening's major pro- ductions, or between the acts of plays, or between the play and the afterpiece. If an actor were especially good at dancing, he might simply add to his evening's role a dance he was good at. Still, dancers were low on the theatrical totem pole. They re- ceived the lowest salaries in the theatre, and, as noted by Olive Logan in 1870, Americans had never, to that point, accepted dance as a serious art.[20] Despite this attitude, dance was taught throughout the country and was included in the curriculum of most schools. Even West Point added dance classes for cadets. Formal balls included the steps used in ballet and stage danc- ing.[21] Still, professional American ballet dancers were hard to come by; Joe Cowell, actor and manager, remarked on the "poor half-undressed supernumerary women, made, for the first time in their lives, to stand upon one leg, bashfully tottering, and looking as foolish, and about as graceful, as a plucked goose in the same position."[22]

A good part of America's difficulty with dancers was the brevity of costumes necessarily worn. Mrs. Trollope noted, in Cincinnati, in 1833, that "everyone agreed that the morals of the Western world would never recover from the shock." Ladies left the theatre, gentlemen muttered, and "the clergy denounced them from the pulpit."[23] William B. Wood commented that Signora Aria, on a stop in Baltimore during the 1815–1816 season, had a similar effect: "Her first night produced $861, and so divided were the audience as to the decency of the exhibition, that at the close of the evening a strong remonstrance was forwarded to the managers against a repetition of the performance."[24] A clear distinction was made between art and lewdness, as William Dunlap at one point made clear: Miss Rock "danced elegantly, not as a dancer, but as a lady."[25] A supernumerary in the Boston theatre commented, "If a woman can become such a magnet of attraction, such an idol of the people, by elevating her nether extremities to an angle of 45°, or by standing as long on one toe as a barn-yard fowl, or by showing her almost nude figure to the gaze of all, big and little, rude and polished, what must be the feelings of an educated, beautiful, and virtuous woman, when she is deserted, for such an exhibition, such revolting scenes and performances . . . ?"[26]

Despite this disapproval, dancers and dance companies had been welcomed from the beginning. *La Forêt Noire*, an obvious ancestor of melodrama, was performed by the best dancer of the Old American Company, Mme. Gardie. The first American-born dancer, John Durang, was also accomplished as a clown, rope walker, and actor. Some dance companies, however, made names for themselves as separate entities, though even here playbills listed their abilities in dance, in pantomime, in acrobatics, and in melodrama. So, not only did all stock companies have a corps, however small, of dancers, but dance companies traveled in much the same fashion as did other stars, some with an entire family, and some as a small unit. A few of the names of these peripatetic troupes are interesting and give some idea of the scope of the dance: Christine Zovistowski with her ballet and dramatic troupe; the LeComte company (six dancers) in ballet pantomimes and operatic ballets; the Wells family with complete ballets; the Llorentes family; the Lehman family of acrobats and dancers; Mme. Augusta's Ballet Troupe; Mlle. Celestine French's Ballet Troupe; Mme. Weisse and her troupe of forty-eight child dancers. In fact, wherever one looks at local theatre history, one finds additional names of dance troupes going back to the beginning of entertainment in that community. Even in the seventeenth century, dance was considered to be an important accomplishment for a gentleman, and when the theatre arrived here, performers offered dance lessons wherever their company appeared.

The history of American dance is always tied to the musical theatre. A mid-nineteenth-century critic noted that "Some of our best actresses began their career as ballet-girls, and even one or two of our favorite lyric artists commenced in the same way."[27] The relationship between dance and the rest of our musical stage can be seen in the happy state of confusion all through the eighteenth and nineteenth centuries. The Ravel Company is an excellent case in point. Wherever they appeared, audiences raved. But the descriptions one finds vary from writer to writer. They are referred to as pantomimists, acrobats, and dancers. By the time they showed up in Galveston in 1859, for example, they had been popular all over America for nearly thirty years. In the beginning they were known for their rope dancing, and rope dancing had been considered a legitimate form of dance for many years. They also liked to stress their "Herculean feats" and their artistic ability in "Pantomime Ballets." And all these were probably useful when they added a full complement of melodramas to their repertory. The Ravel Company varied in size over the years, from three to four brothers to a fairly large aggregation of brothers, sisters, and special acts by their children. Later, the company divided, with some Ravel brothers in one company and some in the other; an amusing theatrical footnote finds the brothers occasionally booking each half of their company in the same city at the same time. For most of their history, the Ravels traveled as stars appearing in stock companies everywhere—and frequently the resident stock company was forced to fill up the stage around the Ravels for one of their more elaborate productions.

Probably the best way to envision a Ravel performance is from actual descriptions of the time. In 1837 Philip Hone saw them in New York: "The rope dancing and other performances of the Ravel family, consisting of eight or ten of the most as-

tonishing performers in their line of work who have ever appeared in this city."[28] A playbill of 1840 offers the following
promise of goodies to come in the *Green Monster*:

a Sorcerer's Cave, with incantation of witches, the appearance of the
genii, a dance of witches, and the flight of the Bottle Imp. In the next
scene—a garden—Rosalie dreams, the Bottle Imp appears, and promises fulfillment of her dream. Thereupon a bouquet changes to Harlequin (Gabriel Ravel), and the Bottle Imp flies away. In the palace
of Miroque, three knights arrive, to contest for the hand of Rosalie,
whereupon we change to a grand combat in the arena, with the White
Knight (Antoine Ravel) triumphant. Alas, Harlequin defeats the White
Knight! Balloon Ascension! Tableau! The balloon, next scene, descends
in the country; arrival of Miroque and the White Knight, in a carriage
drawn by a real charger!

The thing goes on and on until the tenth scene, at the Golden
Lake, with the White Knight swallowed up by the Green Monster, and a final Grand Tableau bringing the performance to
its end.[29]

Noah Ludlow, as manager, was delighted whenever he could
book the Ravels in any of his theatres. They were, he says,
"undoubtedly the best company in their style of performers that
has ever been seen in the United States up to the present time.
...Every pantomime produced by them was most judiciously
selected and admirably performed, without halting or fail-
ing."[30] Pantomime? Melodrama? Ballet? The answer is probably all three.

Other sorts of performance were also a strange mixture of
forms. One of the most popular productions by local stock companies, albeit one of the most expensive, was *Cherry and Fair
Star*.[31] Although it was originally imported from England, each
company in America added to it and revised it. It was popular
in the 1820s through the 1850s in Cincinnati, Louisville, Nash-
ville, Natchez, St. Louis, and as far west as San Francisco. The
piece depended upon spectacular scenic effects—its ten scenes
range from such places as a palace and the open sea to the
fairy home on the shells of the deep (this scene contained a
"grand fairy ballet"), a hut, the "luminous forest," a desert,
and frozen rocks—much music and song and dreadful puns in

the rhymed dialogue (Cherry: "We've noble blood in every vein I know." Fair Star: " 'Tis very vain of you in saying so.") The plot is too silly to recount, and the whole ends with a pantomime and a grand transformation scene. Again, the combination of melodrama, pantomime, and ballet seemed to be what Americans wanted in the theatre. Add a full orchestra and lots of songs, and the strange amalgam seems to be moving, or rather dancing, in the direction of musical comedy.

Yet something closer to a ballet tradition can be dimly perceived. Probably, it began with Mlle. Celeste. Her first performance here listed her as a pantomimist, though before long she was known primarily as a danseuse. She was born in Paris and first appeared in America in 1827; her debut was in New York. Two years later she and her sister toured the western and southern United States, and before leaving America in 1865 she had appeared in almost every theatre America had to offer. Descriptions of her performances indicate a specialization somewhere between ballet and pantomime. She frequently took two or three roles in the pieces she (or her company) performed. A critic raved:

She has the powers of animation which we did not believe belonged to the human body. In fact, she frequently appears as if closely allied to some celestial or fairy existence, for every motion, whirl, bend, posture, and exhibition is coupled with a grace and ease that robs it of every grosser appearance. The fastidious might look upon her exhibitions without a blush.[32]

Ludlow, too, was enthralled. He found her:

the most gifted lady in her particular line of stage performances, that to this day has been seen in the United States... she did some very admirable dancing, that quite surprised the Louisville people, especially that had not witnessed any French dancing; yet it was rather repulsive to the staid ladies who had not been in the habit of seeing females kick up their heels quite so high in their dancing.[33]

The reaction to Mlle. Celeste, wherever she went, forced stock companies to keep one or more trained dancers as a regular part of their personnel.

Other dancers arrived here from Europe, most notably Francisque Hutin, the Achilles, the Renzi-Vestrises, Augusta, Mariana Petipa, and Paul and Amalia Taglioni. The greatest impact on the American dance in the nineteenth century, however, came from one of the greatest dancers of the century, Fanny Elssler.[34] Though she spent only two years in this country, she demonstrated to America the finest of European ballet, and in the process she completely changed the course of American dance. Incidentally, she was very little help to the managers of the day, since her terms were $500.00 per night plus a benefit. William B. Wood brought her to Baltimore where he claimed she nearly ruined the management by her high contract demands. Still, she traveled all over America and brought with her an entirely new conception of what ballet might be. She was a good actress, and an excellent pantomimist, witness this description of her in "La Tarantule":

> This ballet, which concerned itself with the effect of the bite of the tarantula, required in the chief character the manifestation of every variety of passion, which was effectively executed in the pantomime of Fanny Elssler.... The effects of the tarantula bite, the shuddering of the whole frame, broken by wild attempts at dancing, was a masterpiece of pantomimic acting.[35]

Ludlow, his managerial proclivities coming to the fore, declared her avaricious and without a soul, but even he was forced to acknowledge that "Her dancing was magnificent; she seemed to move in the air, without touching the stage." Philip Hone, too, was enraptured:

> Many and many a night has passed since the walls of the Park [Theatre, New York] have witnessed such a scene. Fanny Elssler, the bright star whose rising in our firmament has been anxiously looked for by the fashionable astronomers since its transit across the ocean was announced, shone forth in all its brilliancy this evening.... On her first appearance, in a *pas seul* called *La Cracovienne*, which was admirably adapted to set off her fine figure to advantage, the pit rose in a mass.... The dance was succeeded by a farce, and then came the ballet "La Tarantule," in which the Elssler established her claim to be considered by far the best dancer we have ever seen in this country.[36]

She arrived here with James Sylvain as her dance and ballet partner (his early reputation was as a pantomimist). The Park Theatre, New York, had, in 1840, a corps of eight men and eight women, and she carried eight of this company with her except when a theatre insisted on using its own (for example, in Boston) or where distance (for example, in Havana) made the large number of travelers too difficult. Her normal repertory involved three ballets, three character dances, and a hornpipe for Sylvain. She was such a hit that a brief list of items named for her in America included boats, horses, boots, stockings, garters, corsets, shawls, parasols, fans, boot polish, and even cigars and shaving soap. New York, Philadelphia, Washington, Baltimore, Boston, Richmond, Charleston, Havana, New Orleans, Providence—she enchanted all these cities with 208 appearances in a little over two years. Perhaps the best story of her dancing is quoted by Barnabee in his memoirs. He says that she hypnotized Boston and that Emerson turned to Margaret Fuller and whispered, "Margaret, this is poetry"; she responded soulfully, "Ralph, it is religion."[37]

Still other forms of dance and other dancers made their way across the stages of nineteenth-century America. The influence of minstrel dance has already been seen. Circuses and showboats were constant purveyors of one form of dance or another. Melodramas helped, too, especially in the West. Hurdy-gurdy girls danced in saloons. And satires of serious dances became popular. Lola Montez, for example, specialized in a parody of Elssler's *Tarantula* called the Spider Dance: "To slow but provocative music—based upon a mixture of the polka, waltz, mazurka, and jig—Lola dramatized the plight of a woman attacked by spiders." She taught another famous personality of the century to dance and sing—Lotta Crabtree. When Lola showed up in New York, she could dance a breakdown as well as any member of a minstrel company.

Probably *The Black Crook* in 1866 changed the direction of American dance for the rest of the nineteenth century. One of the most elaborate ballet companies ever seen in America was used in the production, and the pattern was set not only for future musicals but for ballet through the end of the century. But the ballet introduced by *The Black Crook* soon proved to be deceptive in its seeming progress. Lillian Moore, one of the foremost writers on American dance history, noted, "the full pageant of theatrical dance as it changed from the simple English style...through the exquisite art of Fanny Elssler...to the dry, technical acrobatics of the Italian ballerinas who held the stage after the production of *The Black Crook* in 1866."[38] In fact, other critics have demonstrated that from 1866 to 1909, there were no real ballet companies in America with the exception of the Metropolitan Opera (founded in 1883) *corps de ballet*, so *The Black Crook* was originator, continuum, and a sort of dead end, all in one.

The nineteenth century, as has been shown, saw America invaded by foreign dancers; still, one could produce quite a reputable list of the home-grown variety: Mary Ann Lee (the first American dancer to attain nationwide fame as an exponent of the classic ballet), Julia Turnbull, George Washington Smith, Augusta Maywood (Maywood, indeed, was the first American to be engaged as *première danseuse* at the Paris Opera, our first great internationally famous prima ballerina.)[39]

As vaudeville began to grow in the late 1800s, variety in dance became more and more in demand, thereby proving once more the importance of dance to our theatres, not only as a contributor to other kinds of entertainment but as an independent art form.

The dance, both as a part of other musical stage types and as a form in its own right, made a significant contribution to America's musical stage in the twentieth century. Only folk dancing and ballroom dancing seemed to have any roots here before 1900. But in the twentieth century, American dance came into its own—an explosion with repercussions all over the world.

The easiest approach to this American dance explosion is via the division between "Russian ballet" and "modern dance." The distinction does not hold for very long, but it helps in viewing dance's relationship to the popular stage.

Modern dance begins with Isadora Duncan.[40] The Delsarte System of Exercise, based on exercises that stressed relaxation, became popular in the nineteenth century and had a great influence on the modern dance movement. Still, it was Duncan who began a revolution in the dance, coming at a time when ballet was nearly dormant here and so revitalizing dance that her effect is still felt in our musical theatre. Her earliest performances were in Augustin Daly's company in 1897, where she was featured in those very pantomimes which were at the heart of the stock companies' repertories. She danced in *A Midsummer Night's Dream, The Tempest,* and *Much Ado About Nothing.* She traveled over much of Europe, then returned to New York in 1908, and soon began a tour of the United States.

Duncan appeared in a Greek costume; it was as if she were saying, "Throw out recent traditions of the past and return to the Greeks for the spontaneity of movement, the freedom of the body that they had." Later, she denied that her dances were derived from the Greeks and claimed that they were American in spirit. Whatever the country of origin, she had the effect of freeing the body from the formal movements of ballet. Her most frequently quoted statement was, "To express what is most moral, healthful, and beautiful in art—this is the mission of the dancer, and to this I dedicate my life."[41] In her struggle against ballet she helped the twentieth-century dancer to discover his body; it was the body which was to express one's thoughts and feelings. Her movements, she claimed, were drawn from nature (thereby putting herself solidly in line with a string of American romantics), and then other gestures were organically related. This freedom, this extemporaneous quality, this self-expression burst upon the dance world, and it has never been the same since.

But Isadora Duncan left no school in America or work on which to base the new dance. That was left for other Americans, most notably Ruth St. Denis and Ted Shawn. Ruth St. Denis danced with the Dubarry company of David Belasco in 1904, even as Isadora Duncan had begun with a theatrical troupe, and both made early names for themselves as pantomimists. Pantomime, as a part of dancers' training, continued to serve them in melodrama as in an alternative to serious dance. St. Denis soon worked out her own form of dance, drawing heavily on dances of the Far East; her major contribution here was *Rahda* (1906), with music from the opera *Lakmé.* She toured the United States, and she appeared occasionally in vaudeville.

Here again, the interaction among the various forms of the American musical stage is clear. Almost all serious American dancers of the twentieth century served their apprenticeships in vaudeville.

In 1914 Ted Shawn married Ruth St. Denis; he had studied for the ministry and was also interested in the religious possibilities of dance. Largely in the 1910s and 1920s, Shawn created about sixty original dances for the stage, many on American themes—*Boston Fancy*, *Cowboy Tommy*, and *Dance Américaine*, for example. Together, St. Denis and Shawn created the Denishawn School (and Company) in 1915, a school which had the greatest possible influence on the future of dance and dancers in America. Dancing with bare feet, building on the freedom of movement of Duncan, adding ethnic dances of cultures other than Far Eastern, establishing the right, through training and discipline, to rebel against the formal ballet, Denishawn lay the base for modern dance in America. Most of the next generation of dancers took their early training in Los Angeles at Denishawn. Shawn himself left the school in 1931; in 1933 he formed an all-male group of dancers, and in his works for them he helped the male dancer to find a place for himself, to find recognition as something other than a mere support for the women dancers.[42]

Three geniuses of modern dance emerged from Denishawn: Martha Graham, Doris Humphrey, and Charles Weidman. Like Duncan and St. Denis, Graham ignored conventional ballet techniques and took off on her own. She wanted to express themes other than those stressed at Denishawn; for her, dance was the means, and the end was an attempt to express her beliefs, her inner self, in physical form. She enlivened the popular theatre, as for two years she danced in a revue, the *Greenwich Village Follies*; she spent a long career in teaching (at the Eastman School in Rochester, New York), in dancing, in creating dances, and in nurturing a troupe of dancers. Some of their best-known creations attempt to reveal the spirit of America and include the solo dances *Revolt* (1927), *Immigration*, *Steerage*, *Strike* (1928), and those she devised for her group (which made its debut in 1929)—*American Provincials* (1934), *Frontier* (1935), *Horizons* (1936), *Every Soul Is a Circus* (1939), and *Appalachian Spring* (1944). Martha Graham stopped dancing in 1971, but in the dancers who emerged from her group, and in the group itself, the traditions she helped to establish in modern dance continue—and nowhere more evident than in their effect on the musical comedy stage.

Doris Humphrey left the Denishawn Company in 1928. She explored the equilibrium of the dancer and emerged with a "fall and recovery" theory; that is, she observed the conflict between the dancer in motion and the forces of gravity working on him, and her choreography was based on the possibilities between the two poles. In effect, she opened up to the dancer a huge range of possible movements—the fulfillment, as it were, of the pioneering work of Isadora Duncan. Her dances included such works as *The Shakers, The American Holiday, Water Study,* and *Life of the Bee.* She was choreographer for an assortment of Broadway shows and revues as well, including such productions as *Americana* (1932) and *Lysistrata* (1930).[43] Much of her career, however, was tied up with that of Charles Weidman.

Weidman was also a member of Denishawn, though he and Humphrey left in 1928 in order to form their own school. The Humphrey-Weidman Company appeared in New York and on tours, in studio recitals, and at the Bennington Dance Festival (they taught for a while at Bennington, Vermont). His strength was in pantomime and in humor, and his best-known works include *Daddy Was a Fireman, Danse Américaine, Candide,* and *American Saga.* He worked extensively on musical comedies, and he is associated with the phrase on theatre programs "Dances by…" for such musicals and revues as *New Americana* (which featured "Brother, Can You Spare a Dime?"), *As Thousands Cheer* (Irving Berlin's score included "Heat Wave" and "Easter Parade"), *Life Begins at 8:40, I'd Rather Be Right,* and, with Humphrey, *Sing Out, Sweet Land.* Their company split up in the 1940s and Humphrey continued to teach and to choreograph for other companies (José Limón's, for example— he had been a solo dancer with them). Weidman formed his own troupe, for which he did the choreography; Ted Shawn's work had been done well, and the male dancer had an important place in the theatre.

Still another generation of modern dancers follows, creating their own works for dance performances as well as for musical comedies and revues. If José Limón, for example, is still represented in the ballet world with *The Moor's Pavane*, he is happily remembered for his dances for Jerome Kern's *Roberta*. In the late 1930s, Katherine Dunham began to make her way in the world of dance.[44] She brought ethnic dance to the stage— African and Caribbean (Cuban, Haitian, and Jamaican)—in the dances she created and in the work of the Dunham Dancers, in films and on Broadway. Her techniques and her dances were later incorporated into the repertory of the Alvin Ailey Company. She was the first to organize a troupe of black dancers to explore black folklore in dance. She and her company appeared in several Broadway shows, and she herself created several Broadway shows, mostly revues, in the 1940s. Out of Martha Graham's Company came Merce Cunningham and Paul Taylor, and each now has his own company. Most modern dancers, however, study some ballet as well, and here we segue to the second strand forming twentieth-century dance in America—ballet.

If the modern dance was able to grow here because ballet had long been sleepily pushing audiences out of the theatre, the revival of ballet itself found an audience waiting to come back. Probably one dancer had most to do with this revival— Anna Pavlova. Even as Fanny Elssler had caused a wave of ballet interest in nineteenth-century America, so Pavlova in her American tours awoke a nation to the love of ballet. After her American debut (in 1910), the way was paved for a succession of events. Diaghilev came with a company of Russian dancers. Nijinski arrived and toured the country. Gertrude Hoffman brought a troup of 200 Russian dancers to the Winter Garden in New York. The Metropolitan Opera featured Russian ballet, and Pavlova danced there with her own company. Fokine and Mordkin established ballet schools here. An explosion, indeed! And one finds each of these ballet stars helping the course of our popular theatre as well—Mordkin dancing in a Shubert revue, Pavlova dancing in a Hippodrome revue, Michel Fokine choreographing a Hippodrome revue and ballets for the 1923 *Ziegfeld Follies* and musical comedies (for example, *Aphrodite*, with costumes designed by Leon Bakst).

Ballet companies began to open all over the country; the best known were two based in New York, the American Ballet Theatre and the New York City Ballet. Before those, however, the Ballet Russe de Monte Carlo came to America in 1933 and returned again and again, until, for most Americans, it *was* the ballet. It was directed by Colonel Wassily de Basil. Though the company split and found other directors, it nevertheless managed to survive into the 1960s, only a shadow of the glorious company (Massine, Danilova, Markova, Eglevsky) which had helped to make ballet an institution in America.

In 1934 Lincoln Kirstein and Edward Warburg opened the School of American Ballet, designed to train American dancers and choreographers; George Balanchine was hired, and a company was to grow out of the school. The company failed, as did its successor, the Ballet Caravan, but the school remained in operation. Kirstein and Balanchine tried again, in 1946, drawing on the school for the Ballet Society, and this company eventually became the New York City Ballet, one of the great dance troupes of the world.

In 1940 what is now called the American Ballet Theatre was formed with a repertory of Russian, French, English, and American ballets. Its roots are also tangled in history, but its emergence from American soil proved tremendously exciting for the dance's future here. While many artists have gone back and forth between the companies (Jerome Robbins, for example, was associate artistic director under Balanchine yet soon showed up at the American Ballet Theatre), it was probably the American Ballet Theatre which did more for native dance by using American-style ballet with American choreographers—*Fancy Free* (later a full-length musical comedy, *On the Town*), by Jerome Robbins, Agnes de Mille's *Rodeo*, Eugene Loring's *Billy the Kid*, Michael Kidd's *On Stage!*, Eliot Feld's *Harbinger*.

By the mid-1960s New York had added two more major companies, the Joffrey and the Harkness Ballet, and still later the Alvin Ailey Company came into being. Important ballet companies sprang up all over the country: the Philadelphia Ballet, the Page-Stone Ballet Company in Chicago, the San Francisco Ballet, the National Ballet in Washington, D.C., for example.

And regional ballet companies (non-professional companies, largely made up of students from local ballet schools, frequently complemented with one or two professionals) proliferated at an astounding rate—by 1971, over 300 were performing all over the country.

By 1965 dance had become one of America's major art interests. Modern dance and classic ballet—"These two disciplines . . . and their interplay are absolutely unique to the United States," said Clive Barnes. He was fascinated, too, with the way resident dance companies work in collaboration with local dance companies.[45]

An example of the popularity ballet now enjoys may be seen from a quick look at some appearances in New York City. On Sunday, January 5, 1975, for example, nine professional dance companies were performing (New York City Ballet, American Ballet Theatre, Murray Louis Dance Company, Nancy Sparinger Dance Theatre, Eliot Feld Ballet, Les Ballets Trockadero de Monte Carlo (real ballet, albeit comic and in drag), Solaris, and Charles Weidman Theatre Dance Company). Most gave both matinées and evening performances that day; during the month, a total of forty-six dance troupes passed through the city. The federal government supported many dance troupes in the 1970s, and these companies traveled all over the country, performing for new audiences. In New York some theatres actually produced dance (as opposed to merely renting space). The Theatre of the Riverside Church, for example, has been producing dance events by providing New York audiences with choreographers and dancers regularly for seventeen years. The Riverside Dance Festival of 1983 presented thirty-four companies and for choreographers' showcase programs was barraged with 2,250 applicants for places. In fact, New York alone has four other theatres producing dance. And some of America's most important dance owes its existence to those producing theatres—the Riverside showed Ruth St. Denis' "Masque of Mary" in 1934, for example.[46] Add all this to dances available through colleges and universities, through dances in musicals and night clubs, and the total is indeed staggering.

The popular theatre added still a third strand to dance on American stages. The relationship between social dancing and the theatre again pressed forward. The Turkey Trot and Bunny Hug were taken up all over the country; yet they began in vaudeville. The Charleston moved from the people to the stage even as the Black Bottom (*George White's Scandals* of 1926) and the Varsity Drag (*Good News*, 1927) moved from the stage to the ballroom, or whatever room people chose to dance socially. Popular dances introduced in the ballroom by Irene and Vernon Castle quickly found their way to the popular stage. American blacks offered much to theatre dance, in steps, rhythms, and ethnic heritage. The popular musical stage displayed tap dancing, soft shoe dancing, ballroom dancing, and trick dancing in vaudeville shows, revues, and musical comedies; such dance stars as the Astairs, Ray Bolger, and the Champions provided much of the style used by choreographers in drawing the various strands of dance together.[47]

With dancing as with all other aspects of our musical stage, a peculiar sort of cross-pollination takes place. Opera, of course, is heavily dependent upon ballet, and opera houses were one of the early ways by which ballet could find a toehold in this country. Today, our larger opera houses feature their own ballet troupes. Most of our serious dancers have appeared in and choreographed popular shows. And the line between serious and popular was almost completely erased when Agnes de Mille choreographed Rodgers and Hammerstein's *Oklahoma!* in 1943. Here, for the first time, dance was not only integral to the action, but it went even further in pushing the plot forward and in developing characterizations. Gilbert Seldes was only one in a long line of critics who made much of the event. He found *Oklahoma!* to be a turning point in American Dance history; ballet had been shrouded in snobbish mystery.

Then, seeing a straight ballet in the midst of a musical, the American public discovered you could like it without having to speak French. It was a cultural revolution—and all to the good. It deprived the intellectuals of a piece of property they were running into the ground and shook the ground under the feet of the reverse-snobs who held that the intellectuals were incapable of doing anything the public really liked.[48]

All available dances were used in our musical comedies—modern, ballet, ethnic, popular—and a wide range of dancers choreographed them. We have already noted some of Charles Weidman's work; other choreographers used all sorts of dances until a mixture, in the Broadway musical, seemed to emerge. We find Blanchine arranging dances for the *Ziegfeld Follies of 1936*, for *On Your Toes* ("Slaughter on Tenth Avenue," danced by Ray Bolger), *Babes in Arms*, and *I Married an Angel*. Agnes de Mille, who did much to integrate dance into musicals, is represented by, among many others, *Brigadoon* and *Carousel*. Michael Kidd's *Finian's Rainbow*, Hanya Holm's *Kiss Me Kate* and *My Fair Lady*, Helen Tamaris's *Annie Get Your Gun* and *Up in Central Park*—all shows choreographed by dancers with long professional careers in all aspects of the dance. We have already seen some of Jerome Robbins' early work, and now we note his *Fiddler on the Roof* and *West Side Story*. The latter, with dance so much a part of the story that it becomes inseparable from all other aspects of the show, indicates how far dance has come in this country and probably points the way toward a future for musicals, where all theatrical arts are combined in a total work and where no one aspect can be isolated from the rest. A later chapter on the musical demonstrates an even closer relationship between dance and musical comedy.

The dance in America, then, can be found in separate performances, or in opera houses, night clubs, revues, and musical comedies. It has come a long way, and it, too, helps keep alive our musical stage heritage.

1. William Dunlap, eighteenth-century librettist, playwright, theatre manager, and historian; sometimes called the "Father of the
American Theatre."

Actor and Manager

2. Sol. Smith, nineteenth-century actor, manager, critic, writer, and historian. The Billy Rose Theatre Collection, The New York Public Library at Lincoln Center.

3. G. L. Fox in Burlesque *Hamlet*.

4. John Brougham, the "American Aristophanes." The Billy Rose Theatre Collection, The New York Public Library at Lincoln Center.

5. Lydia Thompson, whose British Blondes helped change the nature of Burlesque. The Billy Rose Theatre Collection, The New York Public Library at Lincoln Center.

6. Fanny Elssler, who started a dance craze in nineteenth-century America.

7. Celeste, a dancer and pantomimist in nineteenth-century melodrama.

8. Pavlova, who revived America's love of ballet. The Billy Rose
Theatre Collection, The New York Public Library at Lincoln
Center.

1. Gabriel Ravel.   2. Jerome Ravel.   3. François Ravel.   4. Antoine Ravel.   5. Mr. C. Lehmann.   6. Mr. Blondin.   7. Mr. Merzetti.   8. Mad. Merzetti.   9. Med. Amé.   10. Med. J. Ravel.   11. Mr. Amé.

THE RAVEL FAMILY IN JEANNETTE AND JEANNOT.

9. The Ravels in a typical dance-spectacle-melodrama performance. The Billy Rose Theatre Collection, The New York Public Library at Lincoln Center.

10. Blacks of the North and South as depicted by Boston minstrels.

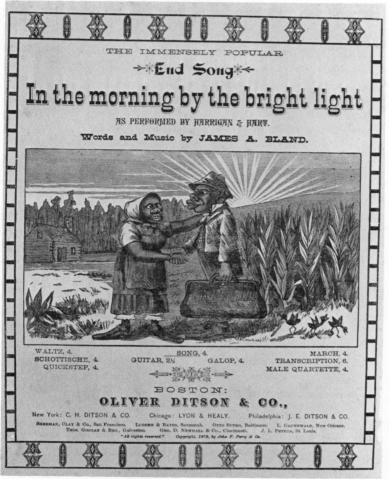

11. Harrigan and Hart's early career as minstrels, performing a song by James A. Bland, one of America's first black composers.

12. A melodeon, sometimes called a box house or in Cheyenne, Wyoming, a honky-tonk. The Billy Rose Theatre Collection, The New York Public Library at Lincoln Center.

13. Tony Pastor, who cleaned up vaudeville and made it a national entertainment.

14. Adah Isaacs Menken in the spectacular equine melodrama, *Mazeppa*. The Billy Rose Theatre Collection, The New York Public Library at Lincoln Center.

15. A scene from *The Black Crook*, a spectacle-dance of great publicity. The Billy Rose Theatre Collection, The New York Public Library at Lincoln Center.

16. Sigmund Romberg's operetta, *The Student Prince* (1924). The Billy Rose Theatre Collection, The New York Public Library at Lincoln Center.

17. Harrigan and Hart in a Mulligan Guard pose. The Billy Rose
Theatre Collection, The New York Public Library at Lincoln
Center.

18. The Four Cohans (George M., left) in vaudeville. The Billy Rose Theatre Collection, The New York Public Library at Lincoln Center.

19. The original New York production of *Show Boat*. The White Studio, The Billy Rose Theatre Collection, The New York Public Library at Lincoln Center.

20. The New York production of Rodgers and Hart's *Pal Joey*, starring Gene Kelly. The Vandamm Studio, The Billy Rose Theatre Collection, The New York Public Library at Lincoln Center.

The Black Crook

─────────────────────

In a brief intermission, it is important to inspect the myth behind a work which, more than any other, has been accepted as a landmark in American musical theatre. *The Black Crook*, furthermore serves as a nice transition between ballet and burlesque.

Dates and events are frequently useful pigeonholes into which may be neatly tucked whole periods of literature or significant literary trends. One knows them to be oversimplifications, but so long as their limitations are recognized, they remain useful tools for teaching, talking, and writing. Occasionally, however, history is hung from a date so unreliable and so unjustified that delineation of material is blurred rather than clarified, traditions are obscured rather than illuminated, and fields of research are closed rather than opened. American theatre history offers a perfect example of the misused common reference point. The year 1866, with the production of *The Black Crook*, has been accepted as the landmark for the beginning of American musical comedy.

Now, musical comedy is a lively and successful part of the American stage and an important part of our cultural history; it certainly warrants attention. But nothing about *The Black Crook* justifies its position as the precursor of our modern musical stage; all its forms and conventions derive from a long tradition, established well before 1866. Perhaps its removal as a roadblock may provide scholars with a way back to a rich stage heritage as well as a way forward to a more careful analysis of the components of our current musical theatre.

Certainly there is nothing unique about the plot of *The Black Crook*.[1] Perhaps a summary may be useful here.

The scene is laid in and around the Hartz Mountains in 1600. Rodolphe, a starving painter, loves Amina. But the count of Wolfenstein also loves her and intends to move her to a suitable place, educate her, and marry her. Rodolphe protests and is captured by the count's men. Meanwhile, the Black Crook, Hertzog, finds he is losing power with age; he decides to visit Zamiel, who offers him a year of life for each soul he damns during the coming year. Hertzog decides Rodolphe will be his first candidate.

The second act begins in a vault beneath the Castle of Wolfenstein where Rodolphe is thrown into a rat-infested cell. When Hertzog arrives, he shows Rodolphe a picture of Amina with the count, and Rodolphe seems to be won over to Hertzog. Assorted scenes pass in which little happens but much spectacular scenery is displayed; then, in scene 4, the action moves again: Stalacta, queen of the fairies, had been in danger from Zamiel; her followers resolve to take revenge, and then they perform a dance. Rodolphe approaches in a boat and the boat overturns, and Stalacta saves him and gives him a magic ring.

The third act involves a masquerade ball. Rodolphe and Wolfenstein fight, but Rodolphe kisses his magic ring and fairies come to rescue him.

In Act IV Rodolphe and Amina have somehow managed to find each other. But they are discovered and seven scenes are required—involving duels, a burning forest, Pandemonium, a flaming chasm, the underground world of stalactites, and a long procession—before the lovers are united at the final curtain.

The plot, then, is neither more nor less convoluted than most melodramas of the period. As the *New York Times* reviewer remarked in his column of September 17, 1866, "No one need go to see the play—it's a very odd mixture of 'Der Freischutz,' 'Undine,' the 'Naiad Queen,' and several little Teutonic nursery tales." The *New York Tribune* agreed: "the drama is—rubbish."

And modern critics, such as George Freedley, who calls *The Black Crook* "a completely ridiculous melodrama," all concur. But Freedley goes on to note that the production was the "most elaborate of all nineteenth century musicals in America."[2] And this is the clue to the function of the plot: it was, as Joseph Whitton of the financial department of Niblo's Gardens cheerfully chronicled in his *Inside History of "The Black Crook,"* merely a clothesline on which to hang scenery, costumes, ballet, and so forth.[3]

There is no doubt that *The Black Crook* must have been a tremendous stage spectacle. The *Times* critic (September 17, 1866) said that "everybody should, and apparently everybody does, go to see the magnificent spectacle." The *Tribune* (September 17, 1866) referred to "gorgeous scenes." The *Times* of September 3, 1866, had reported, "[s]uch a stage was never seen in this country before. Every board slides on grooves and can be taken up, pushed down or slid out at will. The entire stage may be taken away; traps can be introduced at any part at any time, and the great depth of the cellar below renders the sinking of entire scenes a matter of simple machinery."

Perhaps the best way to appreciate the spectacular element is to envision Act II, scene 4, the "Grotto of Golden Stalactites." We are in a cavern of gold. In the distance we discern an open lake and a shore beyond it. Vistas extend in all directions. Since part of the scene takes place beneath the water, we can see silver water with fish and "nondescript amphibia." Diminutive fairies are asleep in golden shells. Gold, jewels, emeralds are everywhere. Gnomes wander about. A mist gradually disperses as the moon rises slowly to the strains of the forty-third musical selection. Blood appears on the face of the moon. The moon disappears when the fairies arm themselves. The queen rises slowly from the water and steps onto the shore. Music plays and the fairies dance. They arm themselves again. A huge image cast on glass reveals the approach of strangers. Then a boat appears on the lake; it is overturned. After the queen has rescued its occupants, she listens to their tale. An elaborate dance follows which involves sprites floating on water. Meanwhile cleverly contrived shellfish catch silverfish. Jewels rise from the sea. A golden boat studded with precious stones appears. A long, elaborate tableau follows, and a slow curtain rounds off the scene.

When it is noted that the preceding scene takes place in a "Wild pass in the Hartz Mountains," and the succeeding scene is a masquerade in the illuminated gardens of Wolfenstein, the stress on spectacle is apparent. This stress was not new to the American stage. American scenic art first began to flower in the eighteenth century with the introduction of pantomimes that depended heavily upon the elaborate scenery, costumes, and machinery devised by Alexander Placide and M. Francisquy for the French companies that were then popular.[4]

The influence of beautifully staged pantomimes was reinforced by still another eighteenth-century musical stage form—the masque. Popular masques, such as the *Masque of Neptune and Amphitrite*, which was almost always performed immediately after Shakespeare's *The Tempest*, included chariot-drawn seahorses, gods and goddesses, views of the rising sun, and spirits hovering in the air.[5] By the 1790s, with the increased interest in the panorama and diorama, the masque catered so heavily to a taste for the spectacular that a libretto such as *Americania and Elutheria; or, a new Tale of the Genii*, which was performed in Charleston in 1798, reads very much like *The Black Crook*.[6] The extravaganza finally became a separate stage form, and spectacles were frequently announced as embellished with "new scenery, decorations, and flyings."[7] These were either integrated into the plays, inserted between the play and the farce, or exhibited by themselves as feature attractions.[8] In the heyday of the extravaganzas, Clifford Hamar notes, "the actor sometimes found himself crowded entirely off the stage, the manager relying chiefly on the magic of paint and canvas to pack the house."[9] And so, there were extravaganzas before *The Black Crook* (notably those of Laura Keene), and many afterward (Gerald Bordman lists them in his *The American Musical Theatre*).[10] Critics have even attempted to categorize them, and Deane L. Root lists some of these spectacles: equestrian, military-nautical, burlesque, fairy, and romantic. They were primarily spectacular in nature (indeed, they were as frequently called spectacles as extravaganzas), which means they were judged primarily by their non-musical elements. Transformation scenes, magic, crowds of actors—the bigger the better—these were the elements making up extravaganzas. Some, after *The Black Crook*, made names for themselves thanks to songs or dances (for example, Loie Fuller and *A Trip to Chinatown*), but for the most part, while music was always important in extravaganzas, it was not one of the prime elements.

Some extravaganzas worth noting include *Humpty Dumpty* in 1868 (which included pantomime and ballet), *Chow Chow, or A Tale of Pekin* (1872), an extravaganza which was also referred to as a "spectacular pantomime" or a "ballet extravaganza"; and *The Deluge*, in 1874, a "grand spectacular drama" that featured 500 ballet and auxiliaries on stage. Probably the last extravaganzas in New York—as opposed to extravagant elements (see, for example, Ziegfeld's *Follies*)—were presented at the Hippodrome. But *The Black Crook* added no new elements and no new ways of integrating spectacle, music, and drama. It did, however, offer the traditional forms on a very large scale. The same old dish was served up as before, but more lavishly than ever, for those with appetite enough and time.[11]

What of its ballet? Advertisements for *The Black Crook* specifically referred to "the beautiful ballet troupe" (*New York Times*, September 12, 1866), and reviews, too, mentioned "the English and French ballet troupes who were received with enthusiasm" (*New York Times*, September 13, 1866). The *New York World* said: "During the two hundred and odd years of its existence New York has never enjoyed the presence of so beautiful, varied, efficient, facile, graceful and thoroughly captivating a *corps de ballet* as the one herein introduced." The *Clipper* concurred: "The *ballet* may be termed an attractive adjunct to the drama, by no means necessary to its proper development, but adding a new attraction by its connection with it"; and the *Tribune* was even more enthusiastic: "In respect to the Ballet, it is the most complete troupe of the kind that has ever been seen in this country."[12] The critics of the period were perhaps carried away by their enthusiasm, but their exaggerations have unfortunately given rise to current claims that *The Black Crook* was "the first ballet production of any substance in America."[13]

The Black Crook's ballet *corps* was not the first European company in America, nor was it the first production to combine ballet and drama. In American pantomime (for example, the "dance of Two Pierrots," 1735) the familiar, standard postures of pantomime characters came to be used frequently for brief dances. Dances used as *entr'acte* entertainments had characters and told stories. And in 1792 Alexander Placide introduced the ballet form to the American people with his French ballet troupe.[14] At first, Americanizations of works performed in Paris and London were given, but eventually American ballets were written, and in the eighteenth century ballet soon drifted away from drama and dance and became a vehicle for costume, scenery, and machinery. (Note, for example, Suzannah Rowson's benefit bill which included, "a Pantomime Ballet, directed by Francis. Representing a ship on a rocky coast stranded—Her Captain preserv'd, some few mariners landed; By a gang of Blood-thirsty banditti surrounded," as well as other dances, choreographed by M. Lege with music by Raynor Taylor.)[15] The serious pantomime *La Forêt Noire*, with its similarity to early melodrama and its spectacular scenic effects, was one of the most popular stage pieces in many cities in the 1790s.[16] If *The Black Crook*'s integration of dance and drama has any claim to originality it lies not so much with the ballet as with the cry, "Bring on the girls!"

It was as a girlie show that *The Black Crook* achieved, and for many years maintained, its reputation. Jarrett, who with Palmer was responsible for bringing the dancers to this country, remarked: "Legs are staple articles and will never go out of fashion while the world lasts."[17] The names of thirty-one dancers were listed in the original bill plus "fifty Auxiliary Ladies selected from the principal theatres of London and America." Comments about this large chorus were both purple and constant. It was rumored that the chorus girls and dancers were to be nearly nude, and ladies who attended the show wore long veils to conceal their identity.[18] The *Tribune* of September 17, 1866, referred to the "large number of female legs," and reviews mentioned *The Black Crook* "not only as a 'leg show', but as a sink of abomination."[19] *The New York Times* (September 13, 1866) spoke of "the witching *Pas de Demons*, in which the Demonese, who wears no clothes to speak of, so gracefully and prettily disported as to draw forth thunders of applause." The *Times* critic went back to see the show on the seventeenth and reported "such unembarrassed disporting of human organism has never been indulged in before." *The New York World* (September 17, 1866) described "a regiment of lithe, active beauties bent on turning old heads by kicking their two regiments of young heels high in the air." Again, "[e]veryone knows how shocking a Parisian ballet must be, from hearsay, and therefore everybody is going to Niblo's post-haste to learn from actual observation." And again, "this matchless feast of natural beauty prepared for the enthusiastic student of anatomy." And still again: Niblo's is "a vast paradise of houris." The overawed critic for *The New York Clipper* (September 22, 1866) called *The Black Crook* an "undress piece," and noted: "as an irredeemably fast young man once remarked, 'we have not seen such a sight since the day we were weaned.'" The costumes are such, the *Clipper* went on, that if our ladies wore them, their "Extravagant wardrobes could be such at least/ reduced to silk tights, puff drawers and chemise...."

In fact, the *Clipper* had such difficulties recovering from "the beautiful and extravagant display of natural feminine charms" that subsequent issues continually harked back to them. The issue of September 29 referred to "symmetrical legs and alabaster bosoms so lavishly presented to our view," and the October 13 issue remembered with pleasure the "bare dance" at Niblo's. *The Black Crook* was still popular in 1869, when *The Galaxy* referred to its "sensuous beauty,"[20] and *Appleton's* spoke of the "glaringly indecent" aspects of burlesque which display "the most intoxicating forms of beauty" and present "women garbed, or semi-garbed, in the most luxurious and seductive dresses possible.... One is dazzled with light and color, with gay songs, with beautiful faces and graceful limbs."[21] The Reverend Charles B. Smythe rebuked three thousand people at Cooper Union on November 18, 1866, saying that in *The Black Crook* the attitudes are indelicate, the ladies expose their figures from head to toe, and they wear short skirts and thin, gauze-like undergarments.[22] Wheatley, manager of Niblo's Gardens, exploited the show's reputation by publishing a time-table "showing at what hour a lover of natural beauties may drop in, take a peep at a favorite scene, or dancer, or leg, or something, and, after enjoying the sight, return to the bosom of his family."[23]

The Black Crook, then, did help build the rage for burlesque in America and cater to the growing American appetite for girlie shows. It did not, however, as some later critics have erroneously claimed, either "originate burlesque in this coun-try" or stand out as "the first of the leg-displaying entertain-ments, the first to make an appeal in that way to the increasingly tired business man."[24] Again, a more careful look at American theatre history places even this element of *The Black Crook* into a continuing tradition. Leading New York theatres had featured masquerade balls in scanty costumes as far back as the 1820s, and in the decade before *The Black Crook*, New York thrilled to the beauty of Lola Montez ("her feet, legs and ankles were almost faultless") in 1851 and 1852 to the posturings of Ada Isaacs Menken. ("The smart set and the prudes alike ac-tually believed they were looking at a woman in the nude. The flesh-colored tights worn by Ada were completely unknown in 1861, and the audiences thought they were gazing on bare skin.")[25] The 1840s had featured *tablaux vivants* with naked women in each tableau, the sole restriction being that they must not move while the curtain was up. But perhaps the display of female anatomy in *The Black Crook* was so much more crass and lavish than anything seen on the stage before that the show deserves, at least on this score, the fame it has enjoyed. However, no proof exists that the road which leads to burlesque carries either scholar or tired businessman to mus-ical comedy.

Justified notoriety thanks to legs, yes; but thanks to music, no. The music for *The Black Crook*, much of which is still available, was by an assortment of composers. The score for the first production was largely by Operti, but in addition there were songs and ballet music by Thomas Baker, Jacobi, Lothian, Frederic Clay, G. Blackwell, Mons. Ronzani, and others.[26] Additional music was tacked on whenever and wherever the piece was produced. The program of the Academy of Music for October 10, 1892, lists music by A. W. Hoffman plus four popular airs (including "Ta-ra-ra-boom-de-ay"). New music by Lothian was included in performances at Whitman's Continental Theatre in Boston, and three grand ballets were tossed in by unknown composers for Hooley's Theatre in Chicago. Advertisements for the show never mentioned the composers at all, and most critics ignored the music altogether, although *The New York World* (September 17, 1866) did complain about the band and the hackneyed selections of "new" music.

There are various reasons why one is reluctant to grant *The Black Crook* the label of genuine musical comedy. The music was written by a conglomeration of composers, rather than by one. There is a complete lack of collaboration between librettists and composers, with a consequent disunity of musical conception. As might be expected, the music fails to illuminate particular kinds of action or particular characters. Undistinguished music was certainly not uncommon on the early American musical stage, but *The Black Crook*, in this department, exemplifies the most backward, rather than the most advanced, level of achievement to which the musical had risen.

By the end of the eighteenth century, music for most comic operas in America had a single composer. The development from ballad operas (such as *The Disappointment*, which used old music set to new words) through pasticcios (such as *May Day in Town*, or *New York in an Uproar*, which used music, some old, some new, by a variety of composers), to comic operas (such as *The Archers*, which used music by one composer) was accomplished in a very few years. And by 1800 it was the boast of new shows that (unlike *The Black Crook*) they had music composed especially for the show, the entire show, music by such men as Benjamin Carr, Victor Pelissier, James Hewitt, and Alexander Reinagle.[27] Musically, then, *The Black Crook* is a weak link in the chain that leads from early works such as Benjamin Carr's *The Archers* to modern musicals like Bernstein's *West Side Story* or Sondheim's *Sweeney Todd*.

Although *The Black Crook* did not lead directly to musical comedy, it perhaps has some importance in the history of vaudeville. True, something very like vaudeville performances had been seen in this country in the 1790s (see, for example, the detailed program of a show led by Mr. Powell, in the New York *American Minerva,* January 22, 1796); but it was *The Black Crook* which first displayed a gargantuan appetite for all sorts of popular theatrical arts. By September 20, 1866, new ballet divertissements, new costumes, and new scenery had been added to the show, as well as a four-year-old dancer. In October 1867 a ballroom scene, two new ballets, and a mechanical donkey had been tacked on, not to mention a troupe of 150 children! In New York alone, *The Black Crook,* after its original run was over (the 475th performance was given on January 6, 1868), was revived in 1870, 1871, 1873, 1874, 1876, 1882, 1883, 1886, 1889, 1892, 1893, 1894, 1895, and 1896. Aside from those innovations the show was sometimes swelled by an infant ballet, animals, contortionists, a ventriloquist, gymnasts, a Christmas Harlequinade, "hand-bell ringers," and roller skaters.[28] Every new entertainment sensation was somehow fitted into the show.

Finally, no account of *The Black Crook* myth would be complete without an account of the business arrangements which help to explain so large a part of the show's popularity. Jarrett and Palmer had imported dancers, costumes, and scenery from Europe in order to produce a ballet, *La Biche au Bois,* at the Academy of Music. But fire destroyed the theatre, so costumes, scenery, and contracts for the dancers were sold to William Wheatley, the manager of Niblo's Gardens. The latter owned a melodrama by Charles M. Barras which could serve as background for the new ballet corps.[29] Starting from this elaborate beginning, the producers lavished huge additional sums on the show and then proceeded to use a reputation for expense to attract crowds. *The New York Times* for September 12, 1866, contains an advertisement for *The Black Crook* which specifically mentions an outlay of $50,000 ($55,000, according to Whitton, p. 16). To the Ravels, then performing at Niblo's, went $10,000 to get them off the stage and leave it clear for rehearsals. During the run of the show, 218 people were engaged daily in one capacity or another at Niblo's, and costs were just over $6,000 per week. *The Black Crook* ran for sixteen consecutive months, and the box office sale in that period was

$1,100,000 (nightly receipts were nearly $2,500). Eventually, Wheatley made a profit of $300,000, Jarrett and Palmer an equal sum, and Barras $60,000.[30] The managers laid constant stress on their expenses, and the show was no doubt made to seem more important through the huge amount of money spent on it. The lure of elaborateness continued in other cities. Whitman's Continental Theatre in Boston, for example, mentioned in its playbill an outlay of $20,000 on the production.

The kind of publicity *The Black Crook* received no doubt also helped its reputation, and back of this publicity lies a peculiar story. Bennett, of *The New York Herald*, was forced to rent Barnum's American Museum building when the *Herald* edifice burned down; but he felt the price was exorbitant. To get even, he refused to take advertising for Barnum's new museum, located in another building. But Barnum was a member of the New York Theatre Managers Association, and he was able to persuade the other managers to withdraw their advertising from the *Herald*. This part of the dispute is on record; what is not generally known, however, is the debt Bennett felt he owed Wheatley, the manger of Niblo's, for another matter. He repaid the debt, not by reviewing *The Black Crook*, for that would have been against his express policy at that time, but by lambasting it. And so the *Herald* accused *The Black Crook* of every kind of immorality known to man—and people fought to get into Niblo's.[31] Combine Bennett's diatribes with those of a series of ministers, and the success of *The Black Crook* was assured. The atmosphere of naughtiness caught on, and, as in so many cases of public moral censure, stirred up more interest than it discouraged.

The Black Crook was able to travel all over the United States thanks to a legal altercation. Barras sold to various managers the right to all performances in a given state; but when Tom Maguire bought the California rights for a production at Maguire's Opera House, San Francisco, a rival theatre put on something very similar called *The Black Rook*. Maguire tried to obtain an injunction but was refused; the judge thought the work corrupt and said that "the piece under dispute was not even subject to copyright since it cannot be denied that this spectacle of *The Black Crook* merely panders to the pernicious curiosity of very questionable exhibitions of the female person."[32] And so, from then on, the famous *Black Crook* could be put on anywhere without the necessity of paying royalties.

Interest in the show never completely died down; it was seen in Boston, Chicago, Los Angeles, San Francisco, Newark, Indianapolis, Cleveland, and Hoboken.[33] Christy's Minstrels put on a burlesque of the work, written by G. W. H. Griffin, for ninety nights.[34] Typical is the scene where the Black Crook summons up the evil one, and chants: "I'll call to aid the Evil One,/ He's just come from Washington./ He'll aid me in my dire distress,/ Then send me on to Con-geress!" Songs from the show were published separately as *Gems from the "Black Crook,"*[35] and a novel based on the show emerged in 1873.[36] A 1929 revival in Hoboken featured lyrics by Christopher Morley and the ballets were arranged by Agnes de Mille.[37]

In her *American Humor*, Constance Rourke says, "The lighter theatre is still a deeply ingrained American form, fresh and characteristic, a place of overflow and experiment.... It has become immensely accomplished, particularly in dancing and broad impersonation; yet it has not used the long and many traditions which lie behind it."[38] It is because of comments like these that *The Black Crook* myth is so dangerously misleading. The American musical stage does use the long and many traditions of its past, so much so that today's musical has some right to be considered an indigenous form. *The Black Crook*, while good fun and tremendously popular, neither originated the features that made it popular nor culminated any significant musical trends. Its unwarranted reputation has only the effect of keeping scholars out of a relatively unexplored yet significant section of American cultural history—that vast area of musical drama that lies before 1866, before *The Black Crook* ever paraded its lovely women across the stage at Niblo's Gardens in New York.

SCENE 4

Burlesque, Revue, and Vaudeville

Until the late nineteenth century, variety (later called vaudeville) and burlesque, first cousins, led separate lives. Then, for
a brief period, they overlapped, then both died together. Still
another close relative, the revue, managed to survive. Each
was part of our musical theatre, drawing sustenance from it,
and helping to keep it alive and healthy.

Several sources flowed together to form the mainstream of
burlesque. For most of the nineteenth century, "burlesque"
referred to a travesty, a satire, a parody of something. At a
time when most Americans understood democracy to mean their
right to revolt against authority, any literary form which seemed
to have rules was fair game. Perhaps this accounts for the
surprising amount of burlesque throughout the 1800s. What is
significant here is that all burlesques were performed with
music prominently featured.

Scholars are fond of tracing this type of satire back to Aristophanes, but as far as America is concerned, *The Beggar's
Opera* will serve. Gay's musical, so popular with the first acting
companies in America, parodied pastoral drama and grand opera, with an assortment of swipes at the British government
en route. After the usual variety of English imports, Americans

soon began writing their own burlesques, and found the form especially congenial to the new nation.

Many Americans wrote these travesties, burlesques, early in the nineteenth century, satirizing history and grand opera. Men such as William Mitchell, William B. Burton, and John Brougham ("the American Aristophanes") made their names through producing or writing burlesques. From the 1840s through the 1880s, especially, one finds Americans mining the lode. Any serious work, any contemporary event might be subject to an immediate satire.[1] Mat Field, who worked with Noah Ludlow's company, wrote *New Orleans Assurance* (a send-up of Dion Boucicault's *London Assurance*), and the 1842 manuscript reveals a large number of songs, most sung to airs from popular plays. The techniques of the ballad opera were ideally suited to satire. Another of Field's better-known parodies was of *La Bayadère, or the Maid of Cashmere* which he called *Buy it, Dear! 'Tis Made of Cashmere.*[2]

Almost anything might be the subject of burlesque. Fanny Elssler's dance *La Tarantule*, the tarantula, emerged in San Francisco, performed by Lola Montez, as the Spider Dance, and Lola dramatized the plight of a woman attacked by spiders. The famous British actor William Charles Macready was especially fair game as a result of his altercation with the American actor Edwin Forest—a typical burlesque was called *Mr. Macgreedy.*

Cinderella was a popular opera, and represented one of the early attempts at grand opera in the South; Rossini's music from *Cinderella* as well as from some of his other operas was used.[3] It was ready to be burlesqued. A letter from theatre manager Sol. Smith in 1841 gives some idea of how these early burlesques were managed:

We have got up a most exquisite burlesque opera called *Schinder Eller, or the Doctor and the Little Dutch Sleeper*—words paraphrased from Cinderella by Matt Field—music adapted from the opera. . . . Elssler is the *Cinderella* and Dr. Stillman, the sarsaparilla man, the *Prince*. . . . Only think of Dr. Mesmer (in the place of the *Fairy Queen*) being projected out of an alligator's mouth, head foremost, and alighting on his feet in an attitude! *Schinderella* comes up standing in a tub of sarsaparilla! Frogs, very large ones, with glistening eyes, made of any quantity of foil leaf are seen swimming in the swamp; steam boats passing and repassing in the lake beyond; railroad cars running down and from the lake. . . . In the last scene a magical change takes place. The doctor's laboratory is transformed into a ballroom of the St. Louis Hotel, and, after the Cracovienne by *Eller*, a *pas de quatre* takes place between two bottles of sarsaparilla syrup and two boxes of sarsaparilla pills![4]

The burlesque was in one act and played an hour and a quarter.

Still another reminiscence helps to make clear our early use of burlesque. Lester Wallach remembered Mitchell's producing, about 1838, at the Olympic Theatre in New York, "travesties on everything that was played anywhere else. He had an actor named Horncastle, who had been a tenor singer in my father's company at the National, a fellow who had some talent for turning serious matter into burlesque. When, for instance, the opera of 'Zampa, the Red Corsair,' was brought out, they travestied it and called it 'Sam Parr and his Red Coarse Hair.' "[5]

One of the more curious aspects of these burlesques was the occasional practice in one theatre of burlesquing in the latter part of the evening what had been presented seriously in the first part. A variation of the practice in the 1850s found the burlesque flourishing as a form, with managers watching Broadway productions, waiting for them to become familiar hits, and then offering burlesques of them.

The best-known actor of burlesque was George L. Fox.[6] He was born in New England in 1825 and got most of his stage training in the part of the Yankee rustic so popular in plays of the day. He was manager of his own company for a while (and even called it a "comic opera company"), but his name has come down to us primarily as a burlesque star, and primarily as the star of a burlesque *Hamlet* in 1870. Burlesque of Shakespeare began to flourish in the 1840s; in the 1850s, burlesques of Shakespeare began to show up extensively in minstrel shows, where they remained popular for forty years, especially in the 1860s and 1870s.[7] With songs sung to sprightly or folksy tunes, social and political comments—anti-British, anti-aristocratic, anti-foreigner and immigrant—were important in all burlesques.

As far as Fox's *Hamlet* was concerned, newspapers commented on the extensive music throughout, and some brief moments from the show clearly indicate burlesque's relation to our musical stage. W. H. Draper notes that "an embryo musical comedy appeared to have been made of the tragedy." He goes on: "At the height of the court scene, Hamlet entered to slow music.... After Polonius had given Laertes the stern warning to 'Look out for number one,' Ophelia subsided into a song and walk around.... Songs such as a duet of 'Johnny, Fill Up the Bowl,' and as background for the ghost scene, 'I am a Native Here,'" were among the musical numbers of the travesty. And a final touch was noted by a newspaper in 1870, "The consternation of the king and the triumph of Hamlet are shown by a sudden, mad chorus of 'Shoofly.'"[8]

If Fox was the leading actor of burlesque, there is no question that our leading creator in the form was John Brougham. Some of his titles indicate the areas he punctured: he burlesqued Stone's *Metamora, or the Last of the Wampanoags* in 1847 with *Mat-a-mora, or the Last of the Pollywogs*; other of his works include *Columbus el Filibustero!* (1857), and *Much Ado About a Merchant of Venice* (1869). In 1855 he hit the "noble savage" theme with *Po-ca-hon-tas, or The Gentle Savage*. It ran for months as a main attraction, and until 1884 it was a standard afterpiece in theatres across the United States. Richard Moody points out that "Brougham's musical burlesques pointed the way for the vaudeville sketch and Broadway-revue 'blackouts'. An excerpt from *Po-ca-hon-tas* demonstrates the form:

Pooteepet: Now, let's be off, as we've no time to lose.
Dimundi: Those gentlemen can keep time, I suppose.
  [*To Orchestra*]
Pooteepet: Then, if you please, as we've good time before us,
  We'll just take time enough to sing a chorus.
  [*Addressing Leader*]

Chorus
Air—"Pop Goes the Weazle"
As we're going on a train
  We must see and load a

Hamper with the drink of Maine.
  Pop goes the soda.
Hampered thus, no Indian corn
Can we now forebode, a
Bumper fill then (in a horn),
  Pop goes the soda.

Exeunt omnes

Scene 3
Union Square in the City of Weramocomoco.
The assembled Upper Tendom of Tuscarora,
discovered.

Chorus
Air—"Hark 'tis the Indian drum"
Hark 'tis the ingine bell,
Look out for the locomotive
We off the track must go.
                                  Though
  His majesty is rather slow.
He must be how come you so,
With Smith's New England rum:
The rum, the rum, etc., etc.

Enter Pocahontas, evidently in very indifferent spirits, her over-
    burthened soul bursts forth in melody
Pocahontas
Air—Notturne, Grazioso vel Filosofoso
Oh, some are right
Who don't invite
Within their vest
So dangerous a guest
As love, that hies
To this abode,
And heavy lies—

Dyspeptic load.
It sets one frying
And sadly sighing,
You can't lodge here, no way,
So love good day,
'Twill never pay
To let you stay
So love good day, good day, good day,

I'm better off without thee
Verily.
And do not care about thee,
No, not I.[9]

Many authors wrote burlesques, generally with music stolen from any available source. And although William Mitchell helped bring about the new school, it was principally his New York theatres which helped to popularize the form and send it all over the United States. Perhaps a few titles will help to show the range of topics covered: *A Lad in a Wonderful Lamp*, *The Bohea Man's Girl*, *Fried Shots*, *Lucy Did Sham Her Moor*, *Man Fred*, *Cinder Nelly*, *Wench Spy*, *Mrs. Normer*, *Richard Number Three*, *Her Nanny*.

Plays, operas, ballets—all were fair game, and all featured song and dance. By 1868 of the seven theatres open in New York, at least six featured some form of burlesque. *Appleton's Journal* of 1869 lamented the fact:

[Burlesque] sets out with respecting nothing—neither taste, propriety, virtue, nor manners. Its design is to be uproariously funny and glaringly indecent with the most intoxicating forms of beauty.... One is dazzled with light and color, with gay songs ... and startled with the coarse songs ... and the abandoned manners of the characters. The mission of the burlesque is to throw ridicule on gods and men—to satirize everybody and everything.[10]

The mention of indecency leads us to a second thread in burlesque's tapestry—nudity. *Tableaux vivants* were introduced in America in 1831–1832.[11] These were living pictures, that is, nudes arranged on stage so as to form a picture; the performers, if that is the word, were not permitted to move, and an orchestra played while the curtain was up. These *tableaux* might serve as afterpiece to a play, or an opera, or a ballet, or even as entertainment in a variety performance. Breeches roles, where actresses took men's parts in a given play, were also popular, since women's legs could be viewed here in a semi-legitimate fashion. An additional dimension was added by Adah Isaacs Menken in the melodramatic production of *Mazeppa*. *Mazeppa* was first seen on stage in England in 1839, adapted by Henry Milner. In 1861, at the Green Street Theatre in Albany, Menken appeared in the title role, "completely nude except for the flesh-colored tights that covered her exquisite figure from her neck to her ankles." She was strapped to the back of a horse, and nearly every story of melodrama or burlesque shows a picture of *Mazeppa* with an undressed Adah Isaacs Menken, singer, dancer, and actress strapped to the horse's back. Her success, as Allen Lesser affirms, particularly in offering "the female figure unadorned... led eventually to the development of a new type of musical comedy entertainment which reached its peak in the soubrettes of the Eighties and Nineties." And so the second thread of burlesque established its connection with our musical stage.

New York audiences of the 1860s demanded both melodrama and some realistic touches, especially in staging; Menken provided both. She continued for most of the decade to perform in *Mazeppa* all across the United States, and her performance was the subject of burlesques by minstrel companies, such as the San Francisco Minstrel's *Mazeppa à la Menken.*[12]

The Black Crook, if it did nothing else, helped provide sustenance for those with a taste for nudity. In fact, many critics feel that *The Black Crook* was "the musical show that originated burlesque in this country." The dancers startled everyone with the amount of flesh displayed (through tights, of course), and it was called "the most magnificent girl-and-music show" that this country had ever seen.[13]   The next step was to cash in on the newly revived interest in girlie shows. Lydia Thompson and her troupe of British Blondes fit the bill precisely, with their stress on leg shows and female exposure—yet continuing in the burlesque tradition. Thompson's company arrived in 1868 with a traditional burlesque, *Ixion, ex-King of Thessaly*, but the costuming, or lack of it, helped bring burlesque into modern times. The comic operas of Offenbach had helped prepare audiences for the music and the dancing, even as Adah Isaacs Menken had helped prepare for the semi-clad women.[14]

By May 1869 fourteen of New York's sixteen theatres featured the new type of show. Where *Mazeppa* had featured but one woman in flesh-colored tights, and where the chorus line of *The Black Crook* had worn them, now the entire production was in tights. Olive Logan, writing in 1870, railed against burlesque companies, but she inadvertently helps us to visualize these musical-stage entertainments. She speaks of "the shameless can-can dancing, and their perversion of simple nursery rhymes into indecent songs." She goes on to say that even ballet had been turned into "a pander to vice and sensuality." The New York stage, she says, "presented one disgraceful spectacle of padded legs jigging and wriggling in the insensate follies and indecencies of the hour." She goes on to mention the race as to who could sing the vilest songs, dress with the greatest immodesty, dance the most indecent dances.[15]

Meanwhile, still another burlesque strand was being woven, this one in the West. Honky-tonks, a term applied to dance halls, saloons, and dime museums, were growing in popularity. In these, women were expected to sing and to dance, and to sell beer and themselves. The shows were coarse, vulgar, and immensely popular. While it is possible to trace a line from honky-tonks through rathskellers and, later, cabarets and night clubs, the immediate effect of the honky-tonk entertainment spread from the West through the South and then East, where the next stage lay in the hands of A. J. Levitt.

In 1870 Levitt formed the first burlesque shows as we have come to understand the term. He joined the atmosphere of the honky-tonk with the three-part structure of the minstrel show: comic sequences separated by musical interludes and ending with a walk-around; the olio with specialty acts; and an afterpiece, a musical, and sometimes a burlesque of a popular drama. Minstrel shows themselves, in attempts at novelty, had begun to substitute women for men, and soon all-female minstrel companies arose. Then, put some of the female minstrels into tights, and the transition into burlesque was nearly complete—witness such companies as Blanche Selwyn's Red Riding Hood Minstrels. Some attempts were made to clean up burlesque, or at least to return to the world of travesty, such as E. E. Rice's productions (his *Evangeline*, 1874, is a case in point); Rice's burlesques were traditional, including mandatory singing voices in his performers, but smut was now essential to burlesque, and Rice soon gave up. Levitt, however, had the formula down pat. His Rentz-Santley Novelty and Burlesque Company used

Mme. Rentz's Female Minstrels, and by merging the lady minstrel show with vaudeville and with travesties, and calling the whole burlesque, he was able to popularize the form. He brought out a new edition every season, something the revue would make popular again years later. His shows' reputations were hurt by "turkey" shows and "behind-the-tent"companies, in which dirt was all-important to the exclusion of almost everything else.

The Rentz-Santley series of burlesque shows continued for about ten years, though the form of the burlesque show remained relatively stable until about 1890.[16] Sam T. Jack was putting on burlesque shows in New York and Chicago, and a dancer with him, known as Little Egypt, was responsible for the next breakthrough. Her fame came with the Chicago World's Fair in 1893, and her dance, the Hootchee-Kootchee, attracted nationwide attention. No burlesque company could in future be without the belly dance, the exotic dance—the Hootchee-Kootchee, and the solo performer, the cooch dancer, who performed it. Little Egypt's influence extended later to modern dance, where the exotic made an early appeal, especially as performed by Ruth St. Denis. Dance, always a part of the burlesque show, now became a dominant element as movements as sexually suggestive as possible were combined with as much exposure as possible and were more and more demanded by audiences.

In the early 1890s, burlesque houses were active in St. Louis, Boston, Grand Rapids (Michigan), Buffalo, Washington, Philadelphia, Providence, Minneapolis, Detroit, Albany, Newark, Troy, Baltimore, Louisville, Pittsburgh, and, of course, New York. Their popularity led to attempts to organize the shows, and so in 1900 one found the Variety Managers' Association (Samuel A. Scribner, president) competing with the Eastern Circuit of House Managers (George Krauss, president). In the West, the Empire Association was formed, and by 1905 it included Spokane, San Francisco, Butte (Montana), Portland (Oregon), Carson City and Reno (Nevada), and Ogden and Salt Lake City (Utah). Occasionally, burlesque shows featured a one-act musical comedy and followed this with an olio (that is, an assortment of entertainments, including cooch dances) and an afterpiece (and this, too, might be an abbreviated musical comedy; *Wine, Women and Song* was an example of this type of show, as was the *Dreamland Burlesquers* of 1908).

Gradually, these circuits came to be called wheels, that is, a collection of shows which theatre owners circulated on a rotating basis. The years from the turn of the century through 1930 were prosperous for burlesque shows. Some wheels collapsed even as new ones were formed, and their shows were seen throughout the country. The Columbia, or Eastern, Wheel competed successfully with musical comedies and revues; the American Wheel competed successfully with stock burlesque (companies gathered to perform in only one theatre with changing programs; these resident stock companies did not travel). In 1923 alone the Columbia Wheel was rotating thirty-eight shows for a season of forty weeks; and each show featured thirty-five to forty performers. In 1928 the Mutual Wheel had forty-nine theatres from Minneapolis to New York. Prosperity indeed! The fact is that while stock burlesque companies tended to stress smut for their audiences, the burlesque wheels, with their songs, dances, and "bits" (individual comic sequences, unrelated to each other or to the rest of the show) sat somewhere between musical comedies and vaudeville.[17]

And this is precisely why burlesque was forced to keep changing. From the beginning its identity was never clear, since it tended to overlap other musical stage forms, to draw from them and to give to them.[18] If, for several years, managers went abroad to find musical farces suitable for conversion to their burlesque shows, so their finest entertainers frequently left for vaudeville or musical comedy. A good early example of the latter tendency is the Weber and Fields Music Hall which featured travesty (such as *Hoity-Toity*) before those fine comedians settled into vaudeville. Jazz became popular in the honky-tonks, and many black musicians found their first recognition in burlesque. In fact, burlesque tended to become an adjunct of the music industry precisely because the guaranteed long runs of the various shows on a wheel meant a huge amount of exposure for a new song. Publishers actually began to help with staging numbers, then to dress a company or a number.

As burlesque moved toward musical comedy, it tended to lose

audiences. Only the dirty shows were able to survive, though musical acts continued to be central even to these. Still, many of burlesque's unique features were preempted—by the revue, for example, which picked up nudity and bits (these were called blackout sketches in revues). Burlesque's last gasp came with the introduction of the strip tease in the 1930s. And here is the last irony of burlesque. Insofar as it tried to be vaudeville, or revue, or musical comedy, its audiences left; the only direction that guaranteed an audience was toward more and more smut, thus risking being closed down altogether. Still, for a time the striptease, always more or less a part of burlesque, revived the burlesque show and made it again one of the most popular forms of entertainment on the American stage. Bare breasts had been seen before; in fact, nudity with and without tights had long been one of burlesque's distinguishing characteristics. The new strippers danced as they teased and as they removed their clothes; the comedians alternated with the strippers and with the chorus girls, singing and dancing, even as the leader of the orchestra joked aloud with the performers. And *Variety* reported that as late as 1936 burlesque had the lowest rate of unemployment of any branch of show business. When the wheels disappeared, the resident stock companies took over, as the Minsky Brothers did, for example, in New York.[19]

Ann Corio, a leading stripper, wrote of her days in burlesque and mentioned going on the road with a company larger than those touring Broadway musicals, a company which included strippers, a boy-and-girl dance team, a singing juvenile, twelve to fourteen chorus girls, the music conductor, among other performers.[20] The elaborate revue helped to kill burlesque, though a lot of other factors did, too, especially the rise of television as an entertainment medium.

But before the 1930s, burlesque shows in the Broadway area were pushed as miniature musical comedies. In fact, it was as musical comedies that serious writers on the theatre criticized them. Burns Mantle asked, for example, whether burlesque was better than the more common musical comedies. He claimed that he had hoped to find burlesque different and was disappointed. Another critic warned burlesque that it would hurt itself by offering the public weak musical comedy.[21] Still, for quite a while burlesque was happy to advertise itself as "The Working Man's Musical Comedy." And there is no question that it took from and gave to musical comedy as it did to other aspects of the American musical theatre from vaudeville to serious dance. If comedians were the diamonds of burlesque, their foil was our musical stage.

The revue achieved a semblance of form in mid-nineteenth-century France. But the elements of revue had been enjoyed in America before that. If one were forced to name a beginning in America, he might start with Raynor Taylor. Taylor traveled in the South and then in the mid-Atlantic states giving one-man or two-character performances of shows for which he wrote both text and music. Before he died in 1825 he had composed the music for melodramas and serious pantomimes (as well as many non-theatrical works), but his own shows, "burlesque olios" or "extravaganzas" they were called, were closest to modern intimate revues. He mixed comic songs with recitations and with burlesques of Italian operas; he sang and played the piano and acted. John Tasker Howard cites part of one of his programs: "The Poor female ballad singer, a pathetic song; Hunting Song; Algerian captive; Sailor's song; Ding Dong Bell, or the Honeymoon expired, being the courtship and wedding of Ralph and Fan; Character of smart Dolly, a laughing song; Rustic courtship or the unsuccessful love of poor Thomas, a crying song with duet, trio, etc." When the English actor Charles Mathews appeared here with a similar program, Americans, thanks to Taylor, had been adequately prepared.[22]

The French, however, gave initial shape and name to the genre. They devised an annual performance consisting of a series of scenes, each scene reviewing events of the past year and commenting satirically on them. This format moved to America, and our acknowledgment was in keeping the French spelling, "revue." In England, James Robinson Planché claimed to have brought the revue to that nation with his *Success; or a Hit If You Like It*, in 1825.[23] John Brougham attempted this sort of revue, that is, a satire on the year's events, in New York in 1869, but the form did not gain popularity at this time in

America. In Europe, however, satirical scenes on current events were adapted as cabaret entertainment.

The minstrel show paved the way for the revue as it had done for the burlesque show and would for vaudeville, too. Revue, in fact, became a somewhat more refined vaudeville show. Early revues in America were filled with the elaborate decor of extravaganzas. George W. Lederer produced in 1894 *The Passing Show*, which differed from vaudeville primarily in that the text, lyrics, and music were written expressly for the show, but the content, with sketches, songs, acrobatics, and girls, was old hat. Other revues followed: *Merry Whirl* in 1895, *In Gay New York* in 1896, *All of the Town* in 1897, and *In Gay Paree* in 1899. By the turn of the century, revue had become a permanent fixture on the New York stage.[24]

The revue gradually became one part of an evening's entertainment, frequently satirical in nature. Paris was again responsible for the revue's next development. The *Folies-Bergère*, which had been functioning as a sort of music hall or vaudeville house since 1869, added the spectacular presentation and exploitation of girls. The first attempt at imitating the French *folies* occurred in England in 1904 with the *Follies* of Henry Gabriel Pélissier, but the major breakthrough to follies in their twentieth-century guise, to modern revue, came with the innovations of Florenz Ziegfeld in America.

Ziegfeld presented a series of turns, some satirical, some spectacular, with the majority containing a little of each. Revue's relationship to burlesque came with the use of bits (called "blackouts" in revue) and undraped women; it took various turns and used them as well. Ziegfeld's first *Follies* in 1907 used unrelated songs, sketches, dances, and tableaux with one cast throughout. Before Ziegfeld, the revue had stressed satire, as the original French revues had done. Since many writers and composers contributed material to a revue, it was the producer who set the style and tone. And Ziegfeld was unsurpassed as a producer.[25]

His yearly productions of the *Ziegfeld Follies* ran for twenty-one editions and set the standards by which all other revues were judged. Yet many of the Ziegfeld revue's characteristics first saw the light of day in the Hippodrome shows. The Hippodrome was massive from any point of view, including a stage 110 feet deep and 200 feet wide, a stage which could be dropped in part to allow an aquatic spectacle, a stage designed for circus acts yet one which strongly influenced our musical theatre in the years following the turn of the century. The pattern of a typical Hippodrome bill was set when the monster theatre opened in 1905: three parts—a musical, a ballet, and a melodrama, each dependent upon much elaborate music. In each part, a story line was used, but only to provide some sort of motivation for the big scenes. In a musical as many as 280 chorus girls might be used; the ballet, *Dance of the Hours*, brought 150 dancers upon the stage. And the quality seems to have been high despite the emphasis on spectacle, since, for example, *The New York Times* found the "grace of execution overshadows anything yet seen in New York." An assortment of producers reigned over the Hippodrome, including the Shuberts and later Charles B. Dillingham, who managed in a revue of 1916, *The Big Show*, to feature Anna Pavlova.[26]

The Hippodrome's spectacle, loosely tied together by either a story or a motif, was the immediate predecessor of the revues of Ziegfeld. His first *Follies* had other influences as well. Ziegfeld had been in Paris in 1906, and the idea of a Follies probably came to him then. The title, however, was borrowed by Harry B. Smith, who wrote the book for this first production, from a popular newspaper column, "Follies of the Day."[27] Ziegfeld's first wife, Anna Held, suggested to him that he adapt the *Folies-Bergère*'s use of contemporary skits, dances, songs, and vaudeville turns. And Ziegfeld's first *Follies*, in thirteen acts, was little more than a series of vaudeville turns held together, not by assorted acts which happened by, but by one cast, "vaudeville in fancy dress," said David Ewen—at least in its early days. He might have failed at the outset, since this show was not well received in New York, but it was popular on the road, and this encouraged him to try other editions. He was particularly good at pulling talent from everywhere; witness featuring Fanny Brice (from burlesque) and Bert Williams in 1910. His 1927 *Follies* found Irving Berlin writing the entire score. And here is the key difference between the revue and vaudeville: text, lyrics, and music, however unrelated to each other, and written and composed by however many artists, were all written expressly for one show.

Altogether, Ziegfeld produced twenty-one editions of his *Follies*, from 1907 to 1931, and almost all major composers and singers and dancers were used in one or another of his *Follies*. So popular did he make the revue that many other series followed—eight *Greenwich Village Follies*, four *Music Box Revues*, thirteen *George White's Scandals*, nine *Earl Carroll Vanities*, six *Artists and Models*, five *Blackbirds*, several *Passing Show* and *Hitchy Koo* editions, plus at least one hundred single revues in the 1920s alone.[28] Some idea of the lavishness of these revues may be indicated by the fact that several revues required twenty different sets.[29]

Many of the single revues made names for themselves because of the talent they brought to the theatre, such as *Cocoanuts* in 1925, featuring the Marx Brothers (and music by Irving Berlin). For composers, the revue was an ideal testing ground, since only rarely did one composer write an entire score and, further, there was little need for continuity. True, in the best revues, such as those of Ziegfeld, the music grew out of the situation; yet the situations were unrelated to each other. In fact, given an assortment of scenes, one of the prime obligations of the producer was the ability to sort out scenes so as to make the maximum impact. Noël Coward, a master of the revue form in England, wrote of the importance of the running order of the sequences, though first in importance, he said, were the songs, the sketches, and the dances.[30]

In America the stress in the 1920s was first on what one critic called "the allure of female flesh," though here, too, it was crucial that this allure be "embellished with music and dancing and presented in lavish and exotic settings." Some revues stressed women more than others—*Earl Carroll Vanities*, for example, made their reputation almost entirely as elaborate girlie shows—but all were dependent upon music and dance. The decades of the 1920s and 1930s were golden years for revues; they were probably the most popular form of American stage entertainment.[31]

American composers chose the revue as a means of introducing their music without the risks or demands of inventing an entire score. Even those composers who wrote all the music for a revue were able to write for one section unconnected to any other, sometimes just a series of unconnected songs. George M. Cohan wrote all the music for several revues as did Irving Berlin. Most revues used from one to half a dozen or more composers; the 1907 *Follies*, for example, featured the music of eight composers. Victor Herbert, Rudolf Friml, and Sigmund Romberg, whose reputations were primarily in operetta, wrote for a wide assortment of revues. Men whose names would be synonymous with musical comedy received their early acceptance here: Richard Rodgers (whose first real success came with the *Garrick Gaieties*; this series later featured an opera-farce, *Triple Sec*, by Marc Blitzstein), Jerome Kern, B. G. De Sylva, Vernon Duke, George Gershwin, Ray Henderson, Harold Arlen, Burton Lane, Cole Porter (especially in the *Greenwich Village Follies*), and many others. Some, Sissle and Blake for example, allowed their reputations to grow with contributions to English revues.[32]

An important aspect of music for revues is that while composers were hired to do parts of the score, the entertainers themselves frequently brought in songs they liked, and these interpolated songs, in many cases, were the hits of the show. In fact, new songs were often tested in performance; thus a given revue is difficult to describe with any accuracy, since the score was often changed during the run.[33]

The world of dance found ready acceptance in the revue, both classical ballet and modern dance, and the sort of mixture of both that theatrical dancing came to represent, as well as the newest ballroom craze. Interestingly enough, revue programs frequently mentioned dances with their choreographer in addition to ballets with *their* choreographer; the same revue (the *Ziegfeld Follies of 1927* is an example) needed both. Dancers and choreographers whose names shone later in other theatre genres (and some who had already established international reputations) came to the world of popular musical theatre through the revue. Anna Pavlova performed in *The Big Show* in 1916. Dances by Robert Alton and Jack Cole are mentioned frequently in playbills of the time. Martha Graham appeared in the *Greenwich Village Follies*. The Albertina Rasch Ballet danced as a part of several revues. Busby Berkeley dances were featured in revues, notably the *Earl Carroll Vanities* of 1928. One finds José Limón in a 1933 revue, *As Thousands Cheer*, and the Charles Weidman Dancers on the bill. Weidman's Dancers were complemented by the totally different technique of Ray Bolger the following year in *Life Begins at 8:40*. The Astaires joined a flood of entertainers moving over from vaudeville, and dancers Ann Miller and the Castles began to be seen on the revue stage. Ruth St. Denis and Ted Shawn, Alicia Markova and Anton Dolin, Michel Fokine, Helen Tamaris, George Balanchine in America, and Massine and Frederick Ashton in England—names responsible for the best in twentieth-century dance—all found the atmosphere and the popularity of the revue congenial to their creative efforts.[34]

Many revues featured a name band or orchestra rather than an anonymous aggregation of musicians, and the result was an extraordinarily high quality of performance to accompany the singers and dancers and to present the new music. John Philip Sousa and his band, Paul Whiteman's Orchestra, Vincent Lopez, Mantovani—all were at one time associated with a revue, as were such choral groups as Fred Waring's and Robert Shaw's.

Even revue sketches found a surprising assortment of writers: Guy Bolton and P. G. Wodehouse (*Miss 1917*), Ring Lardner (*Ziegfeld Follies of 1917*), Moss Hart, George S. Kaufman, Heywood Broun, Maury Riskind, Howard Dietz, Marc Connelly, Dorothy Parker, Robert Benchley, F. P. A., Robert A. Sherwood, E. B. White, Ben Hecht, Jean Kerr. Some distinguished names from the literary world appear here, all finding this aspect of the American stage, the American musical stage, a place to experiment and to reach a broad section of the populace.

The list of singers in revues ranged from famous opera stars to such popular voices as Al Jolson, Eddie Cantor, Ruth Etting, Marilyn Miller, Elsie Janis, and Helen Morgan.

While girls continued to be the main attraction of most revues, the method of presenting them varied from the elaborate, revealing costumes of Ziegfeld to no costumes at all as occasionally featured by Earl Carroll. If the *Follies* of 1907 presented fifty girls, Ziegfeld had learned their worth by 1927 when ninety appeared. Each of the major series had its own emphasis or distinctive feature. For example, the *Greenwich Village Follies* put its faith in much dancing, especially an innovation called the "Ballet Ballad." But whatever the unusual feature of the revue, music was essential. It is no accident that over 500 songs were published from the *Ziegfeld Follies* alone, or that George Gershwin should have attempted a one-act opera (still occasionally performed) for one of *George White's Scandals*.[35]

The opulence of the 1920s revues was forced, in the 1930s, to give way to fewer revues (the annual editions, for example, were too expensive) and to smaller ones (the depression was no help here).[36] Still, a decade which boasted *The New Yorkers* in 1930, with Durante, Clayton, and Jackson, with Cole Porter music, Ann Pennington dancing, and with the Fred Waring singers; *Simple Simon* (1930) with Ed Wynn, Ruth Etting, ballet, and the music of Rodgers and Hart; *The Band Wagon* (1931), with Fred and Adele Astaire and Tilly Losch, book by George S. Kaufman and Howard Dietz, dances by Albertina Rasch, and songs by Dietz and Schwartz; *Face the Music* (1932) with songs by Irving Berlin and book by Berlin and Moss Hart; *As Thousands Cheer* (1933) with Marilyn Miller, Ethel Waters, José Limón, and the Charles Weidman Dancers, with book by Moss Hart and Irving Berlin, and songs by Berlin; *Life Begins at 8:40*, with Bert Lahr, Ray Bolger, the Charles Weidman Dancers and songs by Ira Gershwin, E. Y. Harburg, and Harold Arlen, and dances by Robert Alton—a decade in which these formed only a small part, such a decade cannot be said to find the revue in decline.[37]

Irving Berlin's *This Is the Army* and only a few other large revues appeared in the 1940s: *Seven Lively Arts*, for example, and *Call Me Mister*. The form was starting to disappear, though the titles indicate the one means by which the revue managed to stay alive: its contemporaneity. The *Americana* of 1932, for example, with its satiric farewells to Jimmy Walker and its hit song, "Brother Can You Spare a Dime?" *Pins and Needles* in 1937, albeit using an amateur cast, had songs by Harold J. Rome and in a light-hearted manner discussed the assorted dilemmas of members of the International Ladies Garment

Workers' Union. Timeliness was at the heart of *This Is the Army* at the beginning of World War II, even as current issues were central to *Call Me Mister* at its end. Russell Nye suggests that "Americans used the popular drama . . . as a way to explore the aims, ideals and problems of their society—as well as for entertainment."[38]

And here is the clue to the revue's next phase: the intimate revue. The stress here is neither on girls nor on spectacle, but instead on wit, sophistication, making the best of a small cast with good music and an assortment of situations, each designed to comment on some aspect of contemporary society, the whole held together by the theme of the show. These intimate revues depend upon one writer for cohesiveness, usually, rather than a potpourri of talents. This sort of revue is easily created in a cabaret (thus carrying the revue back to its very roots in Paris) or in an Off-Broadway house; Ben Bagley's *Shoestring Revues*, the *Scrambled Feet* of 1979, or *Tuscaloosa's Calling Me* are examples of the intimate revue as it continues its happy way across a variety of stages. Occasionally, an intimate revue lands on Broadway and proves the viability of the form, as when *Beyond the Fringe*, for example, arrived on Broadway from England to the enthusiastic cries of delighted critics and audiences alike.

Elements of the revue may still be seen in such shows as *Chorus Line*, though only an occasional intimate revue still makes a name for itself. The usual reasons given for the decline of the revue—cost, movies, television—all have some validity. But it is also possible that many of the artists connected with the revue sensed the potential of the musical. Certainly one begins to see the revue decline even as musicals begin to make their way into the consciousness of the American theatre audience.

The revue and burlesque cannot be seen whole without some understanding of their relationship to vaudeville. All three were an essential part of America's musical stage. "Variety" was the term used to describe what later became vaudeville, and variety shows were popular on America's stages almost from the beginning. It is true that the first theatre to feature

variety acts exclusively was built in the late 1840s or early
1850s, and it may be true that the first theatre to use the name
"vaudeville" to describe these variety acts was John W. Ran-
some's in the 1880s (though the term "vaudeville" had been
used here as early as 1840)[39]—but it is undoubtedly true that
these acts were an important part of America's theatrical entertainment long before any of these dates. All through the
eighteenth and throughout most of the nineteenth centuries
even legitimate theatres featured, during the production, between the acts, and between the various productions on an
evening's bill, such delights as songs, dances, rope dancing,
and almost any other sort of act an enterprising manager might
locate. So, from the beginning of drama in this country, there
was a little touch of vaudeville in the night.[40]

Variety acts could be featured easily and could travel easily.
They were a part of every minstrel show. No circus was complete without them. They are as much a part of the story of
show boats and river boats as any other form of entertainment
produced on these aquatic, peripatetic theatres. Summer gardens, such as New York's Vauxhall and Ranelagh in the eighteenth century, and Niblo's in the nineteenth, found it easier
to hold an audience on a hot summer's evening with a variety
of acts (mostly musical) than with one or two productions. Niblo's Gardens had been famous since 1830 for summer seasons
which included variety entertainment and Mitchell's Olympic,
in the same decade, specialized in variety acts and burlesques,
from bursts of song to double shuffles. Later, variety acts were
at the heart of museums, honky-tonks, and free-and-easies as
well, and helped serve to train performers for the big time.

"Concert halls" or "concert saloons" were still another nineteenth-century means of aiding the growth of vaudeville; low
or no admission prices (the sale of food, drink, and tobacco gave
the proprietors their profit) brought audiences to such variety
acts as music, dancing, burlesque skits, and character
monologues.[41]

The movement of variety acts all over the United States
helped sustain America's love for musical theatre. In Salem,
Massachusetts, for example, in 1815, variety entertainment
was listed on the bill. J. S. Potter converted the Idaho Saloon

in Boise to the Idaho Theatre and provided plays along with songs and dances. Throughout the early years of settlement in Seattle, variety entertainment was provided—both in its reputable strain and in its licentious (the former in respectable halls and theatres, the latter in box houses).[42]

By the 1850s dozens of concert saloons appeared in lower Manhattan, and by the mid-1860s, variety resorts could be found in principal cities from coast to coast and in smaller communities, too. As vaudeville traveled, it began to assume a format of its own, largely derived from that of the minstrel show. The interrelationship of America's musical stage forms was becoming still more pronounced. In this case, the minstrel show provided, in its olio, a model for a diverse assortment of individual acts; the circus, too, provided the basis for a mélange of entertainment. For an additional fee, one might stay after a circus performance and see variety acts; in some circuses these acts might be the sort of living statuary so important to the development of burlesque. Interestingly enough, vaudeville began its phenomenal growth after the Civil War, in the same period as the beginning of the English music hall. In the music hall a soloist or group performed a turn, and a series of these turns made up a bill; the turn was primarily a song, with occasional dancing. An American "Variety Concert Troupe," similar to the music hall, could find plenty of employment as it meandered all over the country with farces, songs, dances, and the like. Many cities around the country were privileged to see an evening's entertainment comprised of an olio of variety acts followed by an afterpiece, that is, a short musical comedy or burlesque, even as the minstrel shows had been doing since the middle of the century.

The two strains of variety, clear by the 1850s, found their own showplaces even as we saw in Seattle; "box houses" (where the balcony was partitioned so the audience could see and not be seen), saloons, free-and-easies, honky-tonks, and music halls were the habitats of lewd acts; the cleaner shows might be found in museums, town halls, amusement parks, and showboats. Probably the first places to display respectable variety acts prominently were the museums. Whatever other exhibits a museum might feature, theatre was sure to be an element, and here P. T. Barnum and other showmen could offer variety acts. As far back as the 1830s, the museums were anticipating the variety halls of the 1860s and 1870s. Tony Pastor, later called the "Father of Vaudeville," was a variety performer at Barnum's Museum (acrobatics, clowning, dancing, singing) at the beginning of his career. Dime museums (derived from Barnum's) flourished in the 1880s and 1890s; later, they served as training grounds for vaudeville performers. B. F. Keith started one of these museums in Boston, and Kohl and Castle opened one in Chicago. The usual museum entertainment had a hall of freaks and curiosities on one floor and thirty- to fifty-minute variety shows hourly.[43]

By the 1860s variety had established a thoroughly disreputable name for itself; it was developing in tandem with burlesque, and each tended to feature assorted specialty acts. Variety borrowed freely, said Bernard Sobel, "from the varied forms of native American variety entertainment, as exemplified in minstrel or medicine show, circus concert, dime museum, town hall entertainments, beer hall or honky tonk, even, in later years, from the legitimate stage, concert hall, grand opera, ballet, musical comedy and pantomime."[44] Yet its reputation, even where undeserved, was of a form of entertainment fit for men only. It was at this point that Tony Pastor came along, with his determination to make variety family entertainment. His own background included circuses, museums, minstrel shows, and variety. He opened his first variety theatre in 1865 and stayed there from 1865–1875; he put on shows at this theatre, formerly the Bowery Minstrel Hall and now renamed Tony Pastor's Opera House, with the determination to present cleaned-up shows, family entertainment. Dozens of saloons presenting variety were situated in lower Manhattan by the late 1850s, and these "concert saloons" had spread across the rest of the nation, both in larger cities and in smaller communities. Gradually, variety took over theatres and moved out of saloons, and even the name "vaudeville" was an attempt to replace the disreputable "variety." Pastor was not the first to try to clean up variety, but he was aggressive in his efforts, and soon the entire clean vaudeville movement marched under his banner.

Pastor's first company, accompanied by an orchestra of five to eight pieces, included a singing comic, a songstress, a duo singing Irish songs and performing double clog dances, a dancer, still another songstress, a blackface comic, and Pastor himself, specializing in topical songs. In fact, Pastor's contributions to our musical stage, beyond those acts he brought before the public, included his own two new songs each week. Known as the "man of a million songs," he presented about 2,000 new songs during his long career, many of which he composed himself. The topicality of these songs helped prepare the way for the intimate revue, even as many of his performers (Harrigan and Hart are an excellent example) helped make long strides toward the development of the American musical.

The format used by Pastor was typical of variety: a mix of songs, dances, comedy, circus acts, and drama. He had his own stock company plus a *corps de ballet*; his shows featured an afterpiece, which the entire company performed, and these were mostly pantomimes or burlesques or melodramas—all heavily dependent upon music. In 1875, Pastor moved to the Metropolitan Theatre on Broadway, where he stayed for six years; he opened his last showplace, Tony Pastor's Fourteenth Street Theatre, in 1881. By the mid-1890s he gave up the afterpiece (as did other variety houses). His virtual monopoly on Fourteenth Street was largely broken by Keith and Albee's Union Square Theatre with "continuous vaudeville," meaning two or three shows daily, a format all vaudeville houses including Pastor would soon be forced to adopt. Keith and Albee had featured a cut-down light opera as part of their Boston shows, though light opera was dropped in New York for a while.[45]

When Tony Pastor left the Fourteenth Street Theatre in 1909, it was turned into a burlesque house, but by then big-time vaudeville had virtually taken over and forced an entirely new approach to the world of burlesque. Aside from the discovery of such stars as Lillian Russell and the Four Cohans, Pastor's reputation rests with giving vaudeville a clean image, thereby launching it as national entertainment. He stressed ladies' nights, he gave away free gifts, and he demanded clean acts; he condemned smoking and drinking in the theatre. His stress on musical acts, clean musical acts as most of his biographers have noted, "has culminated in the musical comedies of the legitimate theatre." Pastor's influence was great, but music was always a part of vaudeville, making vaudeville truly a musical stage form. Charles Hamm notes, "Songs were always an essential element in vaudeville. There were ballad singers, offering the sentimental popular songs of the day. There were blackface singers doing minstrel songs; dialect songs of all sorts—German, Jewish, Irish, Scandanavian—by singers skilled in the portrayal of racial and ethnic groups; juvenile singers; character singers."[46] And there was a rich exchange between opera and vaudeville. Add dances to all of this, plus an assortment of acts dependent upon music, and the form emerges still more clearly.

Traveling vaudeville shows, companies especially created to perform variety shows, were also a part of Pastor's triumphs— Nate Salsbury's Troubadours, for example, or Barnabee's "Patchwork of Song and Story." The popularity of Pastor's shows caused immediate imitations in other cities. Soon B. F. Keith, joined by E. Albee in Boston opened a vaudeville house, opened others in an assortment of cities, and was soon running the greatest vaudeville circuit in the world.

After 1860 vaudeville added to the country huge amusement enterprises and chains of theatres. Before 1860, independent shows (menageries, circuses, minstrel shows, show boats, and the like) traveled the country; after 1860 the monopolistic practices of big business began to affect the amusement field. Railroads helped, as large troupes were able to move from city to city with relative ease, enlarging their field of operation and appealing to a large, diversified mass audience. And it was vaudeville, with its basically musical stage, which appealed to this audience and sent its acts everywhere.[47]

A quick look at the rise of vaudeville circuits demonstrates its range; its effects on mass entertainment are being felt even today. The greatest period of vaudeville's expansion were the years 1890–1910. During much of this time, not only was vaudeville fantastically popular, but small-time and big-time vaudeville circuits were being established everywhere. Percy Williams, for example, built the Brooklyn Orpheum in 1902 specifically for vaudeville and eventually owned eleven more variety theatres. There was the Sullivan and Considine circuit in the first decade of the twentieth century with vaudeville theatres all over the West and as far east as Louisville. In the 1890s Martin Beck had the Orpheum Theatre in San Francisco and later dominated the West Coast with big-time vaudeville. Kohl and Castle, who owned vaudeville theatres in the Chicago area, joined with Beck to form the Western Vaudeville Managers Association and thus to control all big-time vaudeville west of Chicago. Meanwhile, B. F. Keith and E. Albee, eventually in control of the entire country's big-time and much of its small-time vaudeville, had been expanding from their original Boston theatre into Providence and Philadelphia. F. F. Proctor, with continuous performances, had beaten them to many cities with dozens of theatres featuring 10–20–30 vaudeville and with as many as twenty acts on a bill.

In 1900 Albee organized the Vaudeville Managers Protective Association and in 1906 the United Booking Office, both organizations guaranteeing the managers and later Albee himself a near monopoly of vaudeville talent. By 1896 there were ten variety theatres in New York alone and six in Chicago; by 1910, New York supported thirty-one vaudeville theatres and Chicago twenty-two. By 1913 the United States saw 2,973 vaudeville theatres (Brooklyn alone had fifty-three, Cincinnati thirteen, Philadelphia fifty-one, and Boston thirty). Decline, when it came, came swiftly: by 1926, there were only a dozen theatres in America offering nothing but big-time vaudeville. Still, the mix of vaudeville with movies was quite popular for a long time, so that even though its demise was imminent, the Albee-Keith chain, for example, was still in command of 350 theatres as late as 1925.[48]

And all of this excludes shows that bordered on vaudeville but are not a part of the overall count. The Shuberts, for example, put on "unit" shows which were condensed revues and musicals. For a long time, one of the most important purveyors of vaudeville, and of musical theatre generally outside regular theatres, was the tent show. In tent repertoire, a traveling company of performers came to town, put up a tent, and offered a free concert outside the theatre, followed by a concert inside the tent, then a play, with vaudeville between the acts. Frequently after the performance came a separate vaudeville or tabloid (usually abbreviated to tab) show. The tab show might be a revue, or more frequently a cut-down musical comedy. Tent repertoire began in the late nineteenth century, and by 1920 there were about 400 tent theatre organizations, nearly all playing a forty-week season with from six to twelve bills. Each company stopped for about one week in a given community, with about 16,000 communities seeing these shows annually. One estimate is that tent rep gave 96,000 performances each year before 76,800,000 people. Occasionally, they used "circle stock" in the Midwest; in this arrangement the company was based in one small town and then worked a circle around it, playing six different towns during the week, returning to each town on the same night, week after week.

In tents, audiences saw minstrel shows (black and white), tab shows, medicine shows, movies, *Uncle Tom's Cabin*, and *Ten Nights in a Barroom*. Tent shows could avoid the monopolistic practices of the theatrical syndicate. With an entire company prepared to sing and dance, with even members of the tent show orchestras doubling as actors, singing and dancing, with tent shows appearing before towns with populations of from 5,000 to 10,000, tent shows unquestionably helped to disseminate musical theatre all over America. Again, what is nearly incredible is the number of people exposed to the popular theatre, a theatre heavily musical in nature.

Even the notorious medicine shows, traveling by wagon, offered free entertainment in order to hawk medicines. By the 1890s about 150 medicine shows were wandering across the country, and their main feature was usually the musical program, with singers, dancers, minstrels, and musicians.[49]

As it gradually developed, vaudeville drew materials from all other forms of show business—from musical comedy, burlesque, drama, the minstrel show, the circus, opera, ballet, sports, the concert hall, and the legitimate stage. But vaudeville was not merely an amalgam of miscellaneous elements; its format and performance techniques were unique and uniquely American. The vaudevillian, appearing but once in each show, no matter how big his name, had but a limited time (from ten to thirty minutes, depending upon his star status) in which to win over the audience.[50]

The songs that an entire nation sang for over fifty years were introduced on vaudeville stages and made popular by repetition from coast to coast. Syncopation, ragtime, and jazz found wide audiences through vaudeville; dances, too, were introduced in much the same fashion (note the Cakewalk, for example, with its roots in the minstrel show). And all this had a form almost as rigid as the sonnet—eight or nine acts, each with a fairly clear place on the bill, each reflecting on the other, each needing its particular place on the program to achieve its maximum effectiveness.

Probably the best way to see vaudeville's far-reaching effect is to follow the itinerary of one performer over one season. Bert Lahr, comedian, singer of comic songs, later musical comedy star, helped as did all vaudeville to pull an entire nation together (and parts of Canada, too). His route in the 1926–1927 season, from August to July, was followed, with variations, by all in vaudeville. He performed in St. Louis, Chicago, Minneapolis, Winnepeg, Vancouver, Seattle, Portland, San Francisco, Los Angeles, San Jose, Oakland, San Francisco (different theatre from first visit), Los Angeles (different theatre), Denver, Kansas City, St. Louis (different theatre), Chicago (different theatre), Des Moines, Davenport, Chicago (same house as second visit there), Cleveland, Toledo, Detroit, Indianapolis, Cincinnati, Dayton, Louisville, Columbus, Canton, Akron, Youngstown, Erie, Syracuse, Rochester, Ottawa, Montreal, Providence, Boston, New York, Philadelphia, Baltimore, Washington, New York (different theatre), Brooklyn, Newark, Mt. Vernon (New York), Paterson (New Jersey), New York (third theatre).[51]

When, in 1932, the Palace in New York switched to movies only, the final nail was hammered into vaudeville's coffin. Movies had been encroaching on vaudeville for some time, but at the beginning had served as the "chaser," designed to get the audience out of the theatre, albeit in a pleasant frame of mind. Movies, radio, a major depression—all these helped to kill vaudeville, but for about fifty years, variety shows in a huge number of theatres, drawn together by chains of circuits throughout the country, for big-time vaudeville as well as for small-time (Marcus Loew was king here), variety shows had tremendous significance. Not only were they important sociologically—in the homogenization of a culture—but in addition they provided standards for entertainment, and they helped, through songs and dances, to tie the entire country together. Not only did vaudeville bring urban entertainment to small-town America, it created a taste for song and dance, and vaudeville tended to retain its popularity because, unlike the legitimate theatre, it drew audiences from all walks of life.

Comedians were important, though probably not as important as they were to burlesque; critic after critic, however, begins with song and dance in describing vaudeville. Joe Laurie, Jr., for example: "Singing, like dancing, was the foundation of honky-tonks, variety, and vaudeville."[52] C. and L. Samuels refer to "The great glowing wonder of the big time was its women singers."[53] The great names here, women associated with particular songs, included Eva Tanguay, Elsie Janis, Irene Franklin, and Nora Bayes, and the list of women superstars could easily include Sophie Tucker, Louise Dresser, and Fritzi Scheff. The fact is, there were literally thousands of singing acts in vaudeville, from solo voices to various combinations, from opera stars who sang in vaudeville to vaudeville stars who were discovered for opera.

Vaudeville picked up every dance craze from the cootch dance through "Salome dances"—the latter followed the dance of the seven veils in Richard Strauss's opera *Salome*. Gertrude Hoffman danced it at Hammerstein's Victoria on Broadway, and soon—the dance known now as the Salome dance and the dancers as Salome dancers—it showed up in vaudeville and burlesque. Ballroom dances, too, were made popular by their appearances in vaudeville shows.

Vaudeville maintained a close relationship with all forms of musical theatre. Many vaudeville stars went to and from burlesque and the revue. Tabloid musicals (or tabs) started about 1911 and flourished through the 1920s. The Palace called condensed versions of operettas "flash acts," although sometimes they were short revues or even mini musicals, and they were normally the penultimate act before intermission. In its declining years the Palace found itself in competition with movie houses which added to the film live tabloid versions of popular musicals—the Paramount, for example, drew crowds with a tab version of *The Band Wagon* (with Fred Astaire) and at Loew's State a film was offered along with some vaudeville acts and a tabloid *Girl Crazy.*[54]

Vaudeville became the place where minority groups found an opportunity to enter the society. Talent was the only requirement, and members of minority groups found their chances here. Jews could appear and laugh at themselves; so could the Irish and the Germans (in "Dutch" comedy acts). Blacks could find an outlet for creativity permitted them in no other branch of American culture: performers such as Bert Williams and George Walker; and composers such as Gussie Davis, Jim Thornton, Bob Cole, Bill Johnson, J. Rosamond Johnson, Irving Jones, and James Bland.

Whatever the reasons for vaudeville's flowering—the stress on "clean" family entertainment, the desire for popular amusements, the availability of theatres and talent, the lack of competition from other media—it grew at an astounding rate all over the country. The story of the business side of vaudeville is not a pretty one, but the story of vaudeville's relationship to the American musical theatre follows the pattern of cross-pollination we have seen in effect since the eighteenth century.

In its range of acts, in its willingness to experiment, in its reliance on the musical stage of the past and its contribution to the musical stage of the future—in all these, vaudeville helped contribute to the musical stage of the future—in all these, vaudeville helped contribute to the pattern which is America's musical stage.

SCENE 5

Musical Comedy

All forms of musical theatre we have noted are encompassed in the twentieth-century musical. But the musical in simpler, somewhat different structure, derives ultimately from those cousins of *The Beggar's Opera* which played on American stages in the eighteenth century. The rise of the minstrel show or melodrama, for example, did not preclude development of the musical, though elements from each became assimilated into the musical, America's most indigenous musical stage form.

The comic opera of the eighteenth century hardly changed as Americans began to write them and to include native themes. What was significant was their appearance in theatres all over the young country. And where the comic opera could not go, the circus and later the minstrel show could and did. The musical interacted with many forms in its journey from the eighteenth century, each form producing some change. The number of songs varied, as did the relationship between song and character or song and situation. Still, the musical was one of the first dramatic forms to open the frontier, and it did so with all the elements familiar to us today: songs (solos, duets, trios), dances, ensemble work, comic subplot, music growing out of the action, some attempt at characterization through music, reasonably strong book, plots and characters drawn from American life, and themes drawn from American experience. Even the practice of having one person write both book and lyrics and for another to write the music was usual in the eighteenth century.

The infusion of spectacle into the repertory thanks to elaborate productions (*Cherry and Fair Star*, for example) and the acrobatics and transformations of such troupes as the Ravels and the gratuitous excitement of melodrama, resulted in a loosening of the structure of comic opera in order to provide that spectacle.

But it is a mistake to think that comic opera died in, say, 1808 with James Nelson Barker's *Indian Princess* or 1824 with Micah Hawkins' *The Saw-Mill* or 1825 with Samuel Woodworth's *The Forest Rose*. Musicals may have added all the popular elements of the day and may have become virtually indistinguishable from melodrama or even variety shows, but the form continued. It was deeply rooted in the repertory, so much a part of the American experience that it could absorb from everywhere without total loss of identity; it could experiment before a willing audience. It overlapped with comic plays, since these always included incidental music and an interpolated song or two.

Many practices of the musical theatre remained unchanged from their introduction here through the twentieth-century— the practice of performing music before the play and between the acts, for example, or of using the conductor as resident composer, or of interpolating songs and dances into the action in order to permit the performers to display some specialty act. The introduction of opera contributed to the changes in the musical; operas frequently arrived here from Europe not in their original form but in adaptations, in English, with spoken dialogue and with complex music simplified. Charles Hamm says that these adaptations of Italian opera "became the most popular musical fare on the American stage in the 1820s, 1830s, and into the 1840s."[1]

The 1840s found three musicals opening in New York and taking the city captive—the three "Mose" plays.[2] Frank Chanfrau played Mose, a Bowery fireman, soon to become one of the mythic figures of American lore, along with the riverboat man, the lumberjack, and the Yankee. Music and songs from a variety of sources, especially minstrel shows, were added to the works and helped keep them tuneful as well as fascinating to a wide swathe of audience who could identify with someone very like themselves.

Musicals which took their audiences on a tour, such as *A Glance at New York in 1848*, were modeled on some English importations by Pierce Egan, beginning with *Tom and Jerry; or, Life in London*. Tom and Jerry made their principal impact on American musicals in the 1840s and 1850s. Virtually plotless, each production provided scenes with music tied loosely together by some theme indicating the places to be musically and scenically visited. These mid-century productions were primarily extravaganzas and, aside from the unifying character of Mose, contributed little form to the musical. These musicals (or comic operas) continued to play all over the country, but, as Bordman notes, "early works such as *The Archers* [1796] are probably closer in form to later comic operas."[3]

The 1860s brought a stirring of new life to the musical, if not in form, then at least in notoriety. *The Black Crook* followed the extravaganzas of Laura Keene in the 1850s and 1860s, such as *The Seven Sisters* in 1860 with music by Thomas Baker, and led to a taste for elaborate staging, wild transformations, magnificent if abbreviated costumes, melodramatic situations, and a mixture of ballet, song (by assorted composers), and spectacle, all suspended from a plot ludicrously convoluted when not outright absurd. Just as any available music might be thrown into an extravaganza, so might any available act be used. Many extravaganzas crossed American stages in the years to come, and the mixture of musical elements continued to be popular for many years. In fact, the popularity of *The Black Crook* caused many later theatre historians to decide that American musical comedy began in 1866 with the first performance of this extravaganza. A sort of game followed, where each writer on America's musical stage names a candidate for the first American musical and begins the history at that point. The result is as many candidates for "first" as there are suggested authors for the plays of Shakespeare. Such works as *The Archers*, *The Brook*, Harrigan and Hart's "Mulligan Guard" plays, George M. Cohan's *Little Johnny Jones*, the Princess

Theatre musicals, *Show Boat*, and *Pal Joey* have all had their proponents.

In any case, concurrent with *The Black Crook* were all the other forms discussed in the previous chapters. Furthermore, a form of musical, the "farce-comedy," was popular in the 1860s and for a decade or two after: here we had songs, dances, and other specialty acts tied together with some simple scheme, such as a day in the country—in effect, a variety show, except that in variety each performer did his specialty and disappeared, while in the farce-comedy the performers maintained their roles all through the performance and got several chances to sing and dance. The first, the best known, and the most influential was *The Brook*.

Nathan Salsbury formed Salsbury's Troubadours in 1875, and the organization lasted for thirteen years.[4] They used variety acts, already-popular music (as ballad opera had done and for the most part the minstrel show did, too), and burlesque to shape the musical farce-comedy. The second work they produced, *The Brook*, in 1876, helped to establish and to popularize the form. A small cast (five) took an assortment of parts. The plot was made quite clear in its full title and subtitle: "THE BROOK 'For man may come and man may go but I flow on forever' Depicting the Pleasures of a Jolly Pic-Nic." It involved no more than all five deciding to take a trip down river in Act I. Act II showed the picnic with such delightful sequences as mixing the fish bait with the coffee, opening a food basket only to find it filled not with food but with their theatre costumes, thereby providing the means for the various acts. In Act III they returned home. The costumes and props which they removed from the basket permitted what were essentially a series of vaudeville turns, including some burlesques of opera and many songs, dances, and recitations. The attempt to attract a family audience with naturalness and energy and sheer fun helped provide a standard which other companies soon followed and which added these elements also to the musical in its journeys throughout the United States. As far west as California in the 1860s, says E. M. Gagey, historian of the region, "only musical comedy in its protean forms could share honors successfully with King Melodrama."[5]

Still, other trends in the "protean" musical manifested themselves at nearly the same time. Ethnic humor had always been present on the musical stage, most obviously in the minstrel show, but it now began to be stressed more heavily with powerful results for the history of the musical. Possibly the result of floods of immigration, possibly as a means of entry into the society, ethnic groups courted laughter, and ethnic humor continued to grow on the musical stage. One of the first characters to emerge from this new interest was the tremendously popular Fritz, as portrayed by Joseph Kline Emmet.[6] Emmet's background had been in musical theatre (that is, minstrel and variety), but after *Fritz, Our Cousin German* (1870), his identity in a "Dutch" (that is, German) act, complete with comic accent, became confirmed. The play was written by Charles Gayler, though not as a musical. However, not uncommon at the time were plays with one or two songs, and in the case of *Fritz, Our Cousin German* spots were provided in the action for popular songs. Evidently, *Fritz* was a hit as was Emmet, and the latter began to compose many of his own songs. A place in the script, generally near the end of the second act, was provided for Emmet to perform an assortment of musical numbers, and they were the highlights of the show. Fritz was revived again and again and no doubt provided the comic basis for Dutch acts, one of the standbys of vaudeville in years to come. A whole series of sequels kept their popularity: *The New Fritz, Our Cousin German* (1878), *Fritz in Ireland* (1879), *Fritz Among the Gypsies* (1883), *Fritz, the Bohemian* (1884), and *Fritz in a Madhouse* (1889). In addition, the original *Fritz* continued to be much in demand and was performed in England as well. There were other attempts to cash in on these ethnic beginnings. Probably the most popular as well as the most influential were the Harrigan and Hart musicals.

Edward ("Ned") Harrigan was born in New York City in 1844. He gained his theatrical experience in melodeons (he sang and played the banjo) and in minstrel troupes. In 1871 in Chicago he met Anthony J. Cannon ("Tony Hart"), and the two joined together in variety acts, written by Harrigan, that sounded suspiciously like typical minstrel routines. Hart's background had included singing and dancing in circuses, saloons, and minstrel shows. When Harrigan and Hart began putting on shows in New York, all the music was written by David Braham. Braham had been born in England, but he came to America at an early age; his first job in America was with a New York orchestra that accompanied Pony Moore's minstrels.[7]

It is important to note that the plays of Harrigan and Braham, starring Harrigan and Hart, represented a change in the direction of the American musical, or, if not a change, an important addition. Yet the background of the three men responsible for the shows included, in each case, the minstrel show. The type of humor, of songs, of characters; the pacing; the level of humor; the very themes—all these were contributions the minstrel show made directly to vaudeville and indirectly to the musical itself.

Between 1875 and 1895, Harrigan ran four different theatres in New York; and in a day when long runs were almost unheard of, twenty-three of his plays had runs of more than a hundred performances. Altogether, he wrote eighty to ninety sketches for the theatre and about thirty-five plays. As social historian, in his lifetime he was compared to Goldoni, Hogarth, Balzac, Zola, and Dickens. No other American dramatist had explored New York's lower class with such understanding, love, accuracy, and fun—particularly Germans, Italians, blacks, and Irish. He wrote of conflicts among these groups, with an incredibly sharp eye for the details of their lives, and these conflicts made up the center of his works, though much of the popularity of each play was derived from the approximately six songs included in each one.[8]

Harrigan and Braham's first major hit was a song called "The Mulligan Guard," composed in 1872. It was later incorporated into a long sketch, and the sketch's popularity led to the full-length (about forty minutes) *Mulligan Guard Picnic*. The songs had no particular relevance to the action, nor did they arise from it in any structural fashion; in fact, "The Mulligan Guard" came in like this:

Dan Mulligan: Now come over to Mc Quade's, and I'll play you a game of hand ball for a five.

McSweeney: I'm with you, Dan.

Dan: Come on. Do ye remember the old tune?

And they sing "The Mulligan Guard," some of whose lyrics go:

> We crave your condescension,
>   And we'll tell you what we know
> Of marching in the Mulligan Guards,
>   From the South Ward below;
> And our Captain's name was Hussy—
>   A Tipperary man—
> He carried his sword like the Russian Duke,
>   Whenever he took command.

CHORUS

> We shouldered guns,
>   And marched, and marched away,
> From Jackson [in some versions Baxter] Street
>   Way up to Avenue A;
> Drums and fifes did sweetly, sweetly play,
>   As we marched, marched, marched in the
>   Mulligan Guards.

The Skidmore Guards (a black troupe) fought the Mulligan Guards, and their chief song is introduced in similar fashion in three stanzas and a chorus:

Puter: I'm agin de shedding of blood, but when it comes to dem people [that is, the Irish], why, you all know me.

Company: Um—Um—

Captain Sim: [Sings] "Skidmore's Fancy Ball"

Still another song from *The Mulligan Guard* eventually proved to be one of their most popular.

Tommy: I say Pop give de boys a song as send off.

Omnes: A song Mr. Mulligan.

And he proceeds to sing "The Babies on Our Block."

So popular was the original Mulligan Guard song that it began to show up in unlikely places—in Kipling's *Kim*, where it is sung on the plains of India; in England, where the Coldstream Guards marched to it; and even in Paris:

> Armes en bras nous marchons gaiement
> De la rue Baxter jusq' à l'Avenue A.
> Les fifres, tambours, on les écoute doucement,
> Quand les Mulligans marchent là, là![9]

Harrigan and Hart split up as a team in 1884, but Harrigan continued to write and to perform; his popularity remained at a peak for another ten years. He wrote his last play in 1903, though he continued to act until 1909, two years before his death. During his career, he and Braham wrote more than 200 songs. His company toured all over the United States, and he sent a road company (The Hanley Combination) on tour with the various Harrigan pieces.

The original Mulligan Guard sketch, as Richard Moody points out, "celebrated and satirized the ridiculous pseudomilitary target companies that were manned by the immigrants who were excluded from the regular militia."[10] By 1889 at least 300 organizations like the Mulligan Guard existed in New York City, and so a built-in audience was ready to see itself portrayed on the stage. Add to this the fact that in 1850, one-fourth of New York City's population were Irish-born, and something of the basis for the Mulligan Guard series, including such works as *The Mulligan Guard Ball, The Mulligan Guard Chowder,* and *The Mulligan Guard Nominee* becomes evident. While Harrigan wrote many other pieces, the seasons 1879–1880, 1880–1881 saw six Mulligan Guard works on stage, with two more in 1883 and 1884.

Braham's theatre orchestra (three violins, viola, cello, bass, flute, clarinet, two cornets, trombone, timpani) was used to entertain outside the theatre as well. But Braham made his name primarily in composing for Ned Harrigan's stage works. His basic rules—never have two songs in the same show in the same time, and all tunes must fit the voices of the actors (in

what was basically a stock company)—worked over a long period of time, and his tunes were sung everywhere, especially
in New York's Lower East Side.

At first, variety acts preceded the Harrigan and Hart sketches.
Gradually, the sketches lengthened into plays, and the variety
acts disappeared, though some were incorporated into the plays
themselves. Harrigan and Hart, and especially the Mulligan
Guard series, were in large part responsible for obscuring the
line between variety and the musical. The roots of all their
work were solidly American, from the minstrel shows' dialogue
to portraits of real people, from the type of humor to the nature
of the songs themselves. Thanks to the work of Harrigan and
Braham, the American musical gained still other resources to
draw upon.

The ethnic appeal of the musical did not come to an end with
the Mulligan Guard or with the later works of Ned Harrigan.
Nor did farce-comedy (variety entertainment encapsulated
within a thin plot, lots of spectacular scenic effects, and a few
songs to break up the rhythm of the piece). Later farce-comedies
tended to use specially composed music rather than music gathered from anywhere and everywhere. The end of farce-comedies
came, to a great extent, with the productions of Charles Hoyt.

The structure of Hoyt's productions was similar to that of
Harrigan's plays—farce-comedies, or comedies with music.
While he used no blackface, he nonetheless derived much of
his material from the minstrel show, as had Harrigan, Hart,
and Braham. Cecil Smith found that Hoyt "translated minstrel-
show music and dancing into fresh terms."[11] He did not bother
with even a pretext for introducing songs and dances, and in
one of his works referred to these as "musical interruptions."
He developed a following with such pieces as *A Tin Solider, A
Rag Baby* (directed by Julian Mitchell who would later direct
for George M. Cohan and later still for Florenz Ziegfeld), *A
Hole in the Ground*, and others, for a total of seventeen farce-
comedies plus one comic operetta. Hoyt's biggest hit, one which
set a record in the American theatre with more than 650 performances in its first production, was *A Trip to Chinatown* (first
performed in 1890, though it did not open on Broadway until
1891), the culmination of the farce-comedy form.[12]

Yet all during *A Trip to Chinatown*'s run, performers and specialty acts shuttled in and out of the production. For example, on February 19, 1891, Loie Fuller began an engagement in the show with her spectacular skirt dancing, making butterfly wings and other shapes from yards and yards of skirts which she manipulated with sticks under an elaborate lighting system.[13] She left the company on June 25, whereupon the management announced new dancers and new dances on June 27. The music of the show, or at least most of the music, was composed by Percy Gaunt. Immediate hits included "The Bowery!," then, later in the run, "Reuben, Reuben, I've Been Thinking," and, on the road, "After the Ball." A typical minstrel song, in dialect, "Push Dem Clouds Away," was also featured. Yet when Douglas L. Hunt printed the farce-comedy in *America's Lost Plays*, he found several versions of the play to work from, and a rather startling handling of the songs. He discovered that the various versions "differed so vastly as presented that it is not at all certain that even Hoyt's own songs were always sung in the same spots or that the same songs were sung all through the long run and by the many road companies presenting the piece."[14] Worse still, although as editor he was told by a performer who had been in one of the road companies which songs were in the play, he frequently, lacking cues, had to place them "where they seemed most logically to belong."[15]

Still, *A Trip to Chinatown*'s mixture of farcical situations, its delightful songs (however irrelevant), and its variety turns, provided enjoyment for audiences in every part of the country, including a rather unusual time when a road company played in New York City while the original company was still on Broadway. Something of the nature of the characters may be gathered from their names alone: Welland Strong ("a man with one foot in the grave"), Ben Gay and his nephew Rashleigh Gay, Wilder Daly, Willie Grow, Cora Fay, and so forth.

Hoyt tended to use Harrigan's method of turning out farce-comedies but with a broader appeal, that is, his characters were fresher and more native American, thereby attracting a wider audience. His themes, too, tended to be broader than life in the tenements. In short, a middle-class audience was what Hoyt strove for and got. Furthermore, where Harrigan and Hart tended to emphasize types (the Irishman, the German, the Negro), Hoyt did attempt some individuality, some breath of life. In his lack of vulgarity and use of national themes and depiction of the everyday experiences of ordinary people, Hoyt not only helped keep the musical alive and well but prepared the way for its next proponent—George M. Cohan.

A sort of sidelight shines about now. In 1896 *The Geisha* was the first American production ever to be labeled a "musical comedy."[16] The term was useful for a while, as was "farce-comedy" or "comic opera." However, from the 1920s on, when our musical stage took the whole world as its oyster, the term "musical" seems best able to express what America's musical stage is up to.

Before looking at Cohan's contributions to musical comedy, another powerful influence on the history of the American musical must be considered. The Negro musical theatre developed into a strong influence on the musical; it grew and flourished in Manhattan in the late 1890s and early 1900s.

After the Civil War, blacks began to form their own minstrel troupes, but their groups employed basically the same structures made popular by whites since the 1840s. One of the terrible ironies of the history of theatre in America was the necessity for black men to put on blackface in order to be accepted as proper minstrels. When blacks began to create their own shows, the influence of minstrelsy remained strong, largely because almost all black entertainers had been minstrels. And so, a gradual process began in which blacks continued on one level to retain the mannerisms of the minstrel show and on another to begin to depict on stage their own mores, their own behavior, their own past.[17]

Black theatre's first real departure from the minstrel show appeared in 1890 with *The Creole Show*, though the early 1870s had seen *Out of Bondage*, a farce-comedy. Still, *The Creole Show* was probably the first meaningful separation from the minstrel show. Sixteen young women were used in a sort of high-voltage chorus line. This provided one of the first opportunities for black women to appear on the stage, since all women's roles—the "wenches" parts—in minstrel shows were played by men. *The Creole Show* was produced by Sam T. Jack and was an attempt to glorify the black woman. It started the line of descent which led to the musicals of Cole and Johnson, and Williams and Walker. It opened in Boston and played in Chicago before arriving in New York.

In 1897 Bob Cole organized and headed the first black stock company in New York City, and here blacks could receive formal training. The following year, Cole created the blacks' first complete break with the minstrel show, *A Trip to Coontown*. It has been called "the first Negro musical comedy," and it featured an all-black cast and a continuous plot. It ran for three seasons and was the first show to be written, produced, managed, and staged by blacks. Soon afterward, Cole joined with J. Rosamond Johnson in vaudeville, in writing songs, and in collaborating on the writing of white musical plays.[18]

Meanwhile, a team of vaudeville comedians turned producers and brought out one of the most important black musicals of the period. Bert Williams and George Walker had formed a partnership in California and traveled the country together, singing, playing the banjo, and telling jokes in vaudeville and medicine shows. In New York they attempted to bring out a different sort of black production, one which was closer to the mainstream of the musical and farther from the minstrel show. Their works have been called farce-comedies, revues, and musical comedies, though there was little difference between them and the sort of show which Harrigan and Hart and Charles Hoyt had turned out. Their contributions were twofold: as producers of black shows which moved away from minstrelsy (though a strong minstrel element remained in the dialogue) and toward genuine Negro comedy; and as performers in the shows they produced. Their musicals included *Sons of Ham* (1900), *In Dahomey* (1902), *In Abyssinia* (1906), and *Bandana Land* (1907).[19]

In Dahomey was particularly important, since it was the first black show to reach Broadway.[20] Willams and Walker appeared as Shylock Homestead and Rateback Punkerton; Bert Williams had already achieved the persona of the put-upon man whose life was unhappy and who was both the cause and the effect of bad luck. From "I'm A Jonah Man" ("When I was young my mamma's frens to find a name they tried./ They named me after Papa and the same day Papa died./ For I'm a Jonah, I'm a Jonah man"), with music and lyrics by Alexander Rogers of *In Dahomey*, it was not a long step for Williams to becoming to the brilliant headliner singing "Nobody" ("When life seems full of clouds and rain,/ And I am full of nothin' but pain,/ Who soothes my thumpin', bumpin' brain?/ Nobody!"), with words by Rogers and music by Bert Williams, in the *Ziegfeld Follies*. *In Dahomey* is in three acts; the book is by Jesse Shipp, the music mostly by Will Marion Cook, and the lyrics by Cook and the famed black poet, Laurence Dunbar. Many of the songs were by others and were interpolated as star turns or musical interruptions. Certainly, there was no organic relationship between the songs and the story. In 1903 *In Dahomey* ran for seven months in London. Amongst other things, Williams and Walker are credited with popularizing the Cake Walk and establishing the precedent of beginning a dance craze on the stage of the musical.

All through the United States black theatres were erected; they served as training ground for black performers and provided continuity during the period from 1911 to 1920 when black shows were rarely seen on Broadway. Still, black companies toured in extensive black circuits, and several cities had their own black stock companies.[21]

The next great breakthrough in the black musical came with *Shuffle Along* in 1921; it began the return of black shows on a regular basis. It was written, directed, produced, and staged by Eubie Blake, Noble Sissle, Flournay E. Miller, and Aubrey Lyles. A chorus line of "partially garbed girls," H. T. Sampson says, danced with precision and abandon and "gave birth to the speed show which was to characterize black shows during the next twenty years," and which was one of the major contributions blacks made to the American musical.[22] More even than this, *Shuffle Along* "restored authentic black artistry to the mainstream of the American theatre," said Robert Kimball. "A daring synthesis of ragtime and operetta, it had an enormous impact on the development of the Broadway musical. . . . It featured jazz dancing, [and] was the first black musical to play white theatres across the United States."[23] Ragtime had been present in black musicals for decades, but in *Shuffle Along* this blend of dance forms and African rhythms became so important that it influenced all musicals of the 1920s. Jazz dancing, too, affected white shows, so much so that Ziegfeld and George White hired girls from *Shuffle Along* to teach the girls in their shows.

Other black composers and lyricists quickly followed, and their path had clearly been opened by *Shuffle Along*. The *Blackbirds* revues (five, from 1928 through 1939) and the musical *The Wiz* (1975) demonstrate something of the vitality and the long life of the black musical. The use blacks made of syncopation in ragtime, in the blues, and in jazz was a strongly influential element of the black musical. Add to all this a large assortment of hit songs which have become standards, plus such dances as the Lindy Hop, the Blackbottom, and the Charleston, and the influence of black theatre on the American musical becomes even clearer.

Still, the type of play-with-songs that Harrigan wrote so well was beginning to wear thin, though his influence continued for some time in the farce-comedies of Hoyt and even in the musical mélange which was *Shuffle Along*. In fact, it is only with George M. Cohan that the musical begins to assume a somewhat different guise.

Of course, American musicals reflect the times in which they are written—this provides their great flexibility and is ultimately their triumph. So, an era of jazz will find jazz on the musical stage even as a later time will find a proliferation of rock musicals (*Hair, Two Gentlemen of Verona,* and *Grease,* are good examples), or country Western (*The Best Little Whorehouse in Texas* or *Pump Boys and Dinettes*). It is irrelevant to say (as most critics do) that jazz changed the shape of the musical. What is relevant is the way the form changes, the ways in which book, music, lyrics, and dance work together. From this point of view, the American musical saw some great changes in the twentieth century and a good many important creative artists working within the form.

The first name to be reckoned with is George M. Cohan. If he did little more than had been done by Nate Salsbury's troupe or by Harrigan and Hart, he did it with flare, with excitement, with a deep underlying patriotism, and with a sense of the idiom, both linguistic and musical, of his day. The great period of American operettas coincided with Cohan's career but where operettas took place in a never-never land with romantic plots and music close to operatic, Cohan insisted that his materials be drawn from America—characters, experiences, settings, and music. Especially in the pacing was Cohan's style different from that of operetta, perhaps indicating the bustling, energetic tempo of the audience Cohan wrote for. In his autobiography, he recalls a speech he made to the cast of his musical *The Governor's Son* (1901) before the opening curtain: " 'Ladies and gentlemen,' I began ... 'don't wait for laughs. Side-step encores. Crash right through this show tonight. Speed! Speed! and lots of it; that's my idea of the thing. Perpetual motion.... And don't forget the secret of it all,' I added. 'Speed! A whole lot of speed!' "[24]

The Four Cohans (George, his sister, and his parents) began as a vaudeville team. At first, Jerry, George's father, wrote the sketches they used in their vaudeville turn. Soon, George began to write vaudeville sketches, and he quickly expanded them into full-length musical comedies. The farce-comedy, the play with music, was the shape his work took, and he himself announced his indebtedness to Harrigan, a debt he paid with the hit song "Harrigan" in *Fifty Miles from Boston* (1908). After *The Governor's Son* George wrote *Running for Office* (1903) and then his first big hit, *Little Johnny Jones* ("The Yankee Doodle Boy," "Give My Regards to Broadway") in 1904. One year later he brought out *Forty-five Minutes from Broadway*, with the title song, "Mary's a Grand Old Name," and "So Long, Mary" as the memorable songs the audience hummed on the way out of the theatre. Working at an incredible pace, staging his shows, co-producing them with Sam Harris, writing book, lyrics, and music—and performing in them as well—Cohan turned out *George Washington, Jr.* ("You're a Grand Old Flag") in 1906, *Fifty Miles from Boston* in 1908, material for the Cohan and Harris Minstrels in 1909, *The Man Who Owns Broadway* in 1909, *The Little Millionaire* in 1911, three revues in 1914, 1916, and 1918 (this last revue contained some songs by Irving Berlin), and a burlesque of operetta, *The Royal Vagabond* in 1919. All together, he wrote twenty-one musical plays out of a total of nearly eighty works for the theatre. He himself claimed to have written 500 songs and musical numbers in addition to all his various stage works.[25]

Obviously, Cohan was concerned with the musical stage during much of his career. His attempt at creating a minstrel show was a mistake, since the form was almost dead; yet he seemed to realize how much the minstrel show had contributed to the kind of theatre with which he was most comfortable. His creation of the "personality revue" was still another means of attempting to work with dance and music. His musicals were also a means to reconcile forms he was comfortable with rather than a conscious striking out for something new. His dependence on the farce-comedy structure came from the past. The half-dozen songs of a Harrigan plot were the same number used, for example, in *Forty-Five Minutes from Broadway* (as compared, for example, to *Of Thee I Sing*, 1931, with nineteen songs, or *One Touch of Venus*, 1943, with sixteen songs). The very dialogue came from variety, with straight man's lines constantly offered for the sake of the answer. The choice of American themes and characters was also a part of the theatre of his youth.

The new elements, however, did make a difference. He refused to be influenced by the flood of operettas inundating American stages through the 1930s, except for the one satire on operetta he wrote later in his career. Instead, he updated Harrigan with an appeal to a middle-class audience. He speeded the pace of the musical, while operetta took its own sweet time. He changed the typical farce-comedy plot from comic to melodramatic, quite conscious in this case of doing something different. He insisted on colloquial speech larded with slang, and thus his vernacular language helped to ward off the convoluted, unrealistic speech of the operetta. And, of course, his constant flag-waving helped give him a clear identity. If his plots were overly simple, still there was some attempt to fit the songs into them rather than dropping them like pebbles into a clear pond. And if the brashness of a Broadway character (usually someone very like Cohan himself) was repeated again and again, still that character could be added to some of the other archetypes the musical stage had helped to foster.

A few exciting songs keep Cohan remembered today, but in

his own time he kept alive, modified, and passed on the American musical to a new generation of artists and audiences. And it was in the 1920s that the American musical, with so much tradition behind it, and so many and varied forms, began to burgeon again.

It is difficult to say what specifically produced excitement and innovation after a dry period. Certainly the musicals did not die after Cohan stopped writing them in profusion. In fact, one finds more than forty new musicals in the 1911–1912 season and thirty-eight in 1917–1918. But a sort of mediocrity, despite the numbers of musicals, causes the musical of the late 1910s to serve as little more than transition to the 1920s.

It is possible that a mass audience began to move away from the romantic picture of the world inhabited by operetta's denizens after World War I; the horror of that conflict may have helped to seal operetta's fate, early in the 1930s. The growing interest in films may have also begun to draw a mass audience and to leave a different sort of person sitting in the live theatre. All that would be needed to push the process along would be a depression, where almost any sort of entertainment would cost too much for many. No doubt, too, the effect of sound in film and the development of radio would draw audiences from the theatre.[26] For a large chunk of that audience which had been drawn to vaudeville and to burlesque, movies, radio, and later television would supply the entertainment needs. The musical, too, might have disappeared, but as always a strong tradition, a heritage, enabled the form to bend, to change, to find a way to appeal; and an audience, nurtured in the oldest theatrical tradition in America, found in the musical, even as musicals experimented and changed, something to enjoy.

And something else happened. An amazing number of brilliant artists, composers, and lyricists, found their way to the musical. Most had broken in on another form of musical theatre—vaudeville or the revue, for example. Any one of them might have made a name, thanks to inborn genius combined with appropriate background and a confluence of physical events—plus the deeply ingrained American musical stage heritage. But add to all these a large assortment of talents, and a burst of musicals followed.

Still, the second decade of the twentieth century saw a series of shows that added some different aspects to the musical and led the way to others. Many critics find the Princess Theatre shows tremendously significant in the development of the musical, though it is hard to say why.[27] In their autobiographical *Bring on the Girls*, P. G. Wodehouse and Guy Bolton wrote that Elizabeth Marbury, a dramatic agent who was running the small Princess Theatre with Ray Comstock, first thought of the different approach to musicals. No more than two sets were to be used with eight to twelve girls, and an orchestra of eleven. The Princess Theatre held only 299 seats.[28]

The Princess shows lasted from 1915 to 1919 and featured such outstanding hits as *Very Good Eddie* (Kern music, Bolton book, and Greene lyrics), *Oh, Boy!*, and *Oh, Lady, Lady* (both created by the team of Kern, Bolton, and Wodehouse). Probably what excited the critics, then and now, was the insistence on a fairly tight book; what is interesting is that the authors of that book evidently saw it as little different from what had gone before, though they, too, became caught up with "firsts." They wrote: "It [*Very Good Eddie*] was a farce-comedy which would have been strong enough to stand on its own feet without the help of music, the first of its kind to rely on situation and character laughs instead of the clowning and Weberfieldian cross talk with which the large-scale musicals filled in between the romantic scenes."[29] There had, of course, been attempts before to fit the songs to the action and the characters. But the Princess stories were well written and the dialogue brisk and funny. Probably what really was responsible for the Princess Shows' popularity was the intimacy of the theatre. The result was a lower-key musical where large production numbers would have been impossible—out of place—and where the small gesture and the subtlety of delivery and of wit became possible.

Aside from the Princess shows, the revue and operetta were going their happy ways, showing no signs of decline till the late 1920s and early 1930s. An interesting point is the number of shows that used two composers, one with a reputation for operettas and one coming along in the musical. It was as if producers were aware of the transition and were providing a bridge from operetta to musical. In 1916, for example, both

Victor Herbert and Irving Berlin composed the score for *The Century Girl*; in 1917 Herbert and Jerome Kern wrote *Miss 1917*, and in 1920, *Sally*. Also in 1920 Sigmund Romberg and Richard Rodgers composed *Poor Little Ritz Girl*; and in 1928 Romberg and George Gershwin wrote the music for *Rosalie*.

The second decade of the twentieth century also saw the emergence of those brilliant talents who would help to give the musical another of its periodic lifts to glory. By 1920 Irving Berlin, for example, had been actively involved in the musical stage for nine years with many musicals and revues behind him. Jerome Kern, in this decade, wrote some of the music for at least ten musicals plus ten more by himself (including music for revues), and still had the best part of his career before him in 1920. Cole Porter had written two musicals before 1920, and George Gershwin's *La!La! Lucille* made its debut in 1919.[30]

All of these men were concerned with the musical as it had developed separately from the operetta, as it had been handed on by Cohan, and as it had followed the oldest traditions of the American theatre. Each of them had some brief association with operetta (as Cohan had, too), but each soon turned to a different style, one uniquely his own yet peculiarly American in origin and conventions.

From this point of view, Jerome Kern was probably most important. Aside from his Princess shows, he was in large part responsible for establishing the form of the musical's songs for years to come. He was associated with operetta for several years, in the sense that a freshly imported European operetta was Americanized by the addition of one or two songs by Kern. When he struck out on his own, writing the entire score himself, the experience of working for the stage, noting reactions, and composing for a particular range of voice and style all helped him considerably. He is probably most responsible for a basic change involving song. Where operettas had primarily depended upon *arioso* (an operatic vocal solo midway between recitative, or declamation, and the formal aria), Kern used popular dance rhythms, a musical line which accompanied the words so naturally that it might have been spoken, and, usually the AABA sequence of melody. The thirty-two bar sequence, with a melody repeated twice, a second melody, and the first repeated again, had the additional advantage later of fitting comfortably onto the 78–rpm phonograph record. The one song usually given credit for the displacement of European operetta *arioso* style with American song is Kern's "They Didn't Believe Me," from *The Girl from Utah* in 1924.

Soon Berlin, Kern, Porter, and Gershwin were joined by two others, Vincent Youmans and Richard Rodgers, and the 1920s saw a burst of creative energy. It seems hard to believe that Jerome Kern alone wrote thirteen musicals in the 1920s, musicals which not only added a huge number of songs to the popular repertory, but which also helped to turn Americans away from operetta and back toward a form which had been seen, in one guise or another, on America's stages for more than 200 years.

The 1920s display an incredible number of hit shows. An idea of the entire decade may be gleaned from just a shortened list from one calendar year, say, 1927. It started with *The Nightingale* (Bolton, Wodehouse, and Armand Vecsey) and *Bye, Bye, Bonnie* (score by Albert Van Tilzer) and began to pick up steam with *Rio Rita*. Arthur Schwartz wrote part of the score for *The New Yorkers*, a revue; Kern's *Lucky* opened in March as did one flop and one operetta, *Cherry Blossoms*, with a score by Sigmund Romberg. April saw, in part, an imported operetta by Emmerich Kalman and the native Vincent Youman's *Hit the Deck*. In May nine works for the musical stage opened, including revues, an operetta, and an opera. An assortment of revues (many featuring blacks) opened in the summer, and one (the *Ziegfeld Follies of 1927*) featured several songs by Irving Berlin. De Sylva, Brown, and Henderson brought in the first hit of autumn with *Good News*, and a Rombereg operetta, *My Maryland*, followed fast on its heels. Still another De Sylva, Brown, and Henderson show opened amazingly soon after their last, this one called *Manhattan Mary*. Even a George M. Cohan show, *The Merry Malones*, appeared in this brilliant year. Sigmund Romberg opened two more operettas, both in October: *My Princess* and *The Love Call*. Music by Bert Kalmar and Harry Ruby and a book by Guy Bolton and Fred Thompson were used in *The 5 O'Clock Girl*. Rodgers and Hart made their 1927 contribution with *A Connecticut Yankee*, and George and

Ira Gershwin offered *Funny Face*. Rudolf Friml composed the music to book and lyrics by Brian Hooker (famed translator of *Cyrano*) and W. H. Post for *The White Eagle*. One of the most significant shows of the decade opened in December: *Show Boat*; the music was by Jerome Kern and the book and lyrics by Oscar Hammerstein II.

It is significant that one can double the number of musical stage pieces from 1927 by including all the near-misses and flops, the shows that sustained the level of the musical without adding any particular changes, that offered large dollops of what had been successful before. But one cannot ignore a year with music by Kern, Rodgers, Gershwin, Berlin, Youmans, Schwartz, Van Tilzer, Romberg, Henderson, Friml, and Cohan; one cannot simply pass off the season as one providing continuity. What was apparent was that the best in American musical talent had found a home, a place to experiment, to express new ideas. And audiences were willing to accept, not merely because of elaborate sets and beautiful girls, but because the tradition of the musical was so much a part of the public's sense of theatre.

Many shows of the 1920s made a deep impress on the form. *Lady, Be Good!*, for example, had a score with the feel and rhythms of jazz throughout and provided still further the separation from operetta, thanks to simpler harmonies and a plainer melodic line. The one show, however, universally acclaimed both for itself and for pulling the musical in a new direction was *Show Boat*.

When *Show Boat* opened in 1927, with book and lyrics by Oscar Hammerstein II and score by Jerome Kern, it was a hit, though not of the blockbuster variety.[31] Appreciation for the show grew with each of its revivals, and it has not stopped growing. Every writer on America's musical theatre has termed it at least a turning point, and some have insisted, with a remarkably nearsighted view of history, that the musical began with *Show Boat*. Certainly, much of the praise is deserved. The various plots comprising the overall story are serious, such subjects as miscegenation, adultery, and murder all being touched upon, however briefly. Here was an attempt to move away from the terrible problems encountered in making the football team (in both senses) or bringing in bootleg liquor.

Show Boat's story covers a period of about thirty years, and Kern's music makes an attempt at accuracy of sound for the whole period, from the early sound of ragtime through that of jazz. There are also attempts at songs which are appropriate to the action and to the characters who sing them—even songs which grow out of the action. Most of the songs are in the AABA form which Kern had done so much to popularize. The exception is "Ol' Man River," which served both as a soliloquy describing the Negro's life on the Mississippi and also as a leitmotiv tying the entire musical together. Musical interpolations had been a part of musicals (and of revues) for many years; several musical interpolations were used in *Show Boat*, too, but these were not merely to show off the star's repertory or to tout some music publisher's sheet music; these interpolations served to set time and place and tone—relevant interpolations, in short.

The characters were a bit more true to life than those in earlier musicals, especially Magnolia, whom we watch grow from an infatuated young girl to a mature, self-possessed woman.

Show Boat was soon being performed by stock companies throughout America; it has been revived constantly, and several films have been made of it. It moved away from the Broadway model and seemed, outside New York, to be about concerns and people and locales different from what had gone before, that is, New York concerns and people. There was, and is, a feeling that *Show Boat* is an American as opposed to a New York show, and perhaps that has accounted for its popularity. Probably what makes *Show Boat* a significant show is not its characters or its themes, though these have contributed to its popularity. Many of the stock devices of musical comedy remained, but the tremendous number of hit songs—"Make Believe," "Ol' Man River," "Can't Help Lovin' Dat Man," "Life on the Wicked Stage," "You Are Love," and "Bill" (lyric by P. G. Wodehouse)—made audiences, then and today, more than willing to put up with dramatic clichés. It was, however, the attempt to take a musical seriously, to write a libretto with serious themes, to write music specifically for one show rather than for any show on hand, that provided a change in direction, and the best of subsequent musicals could lean on the new emphases to be found in *Show Boat.*

If it did nothing else, then, *Show Boat* demonstrated that a musical could tell a reasonably serious story. And a decade followed where a heavy stress was laid upon telling a story, frequently a satirical one. A good bit of experimentation was carried on, experimentation made possible in large part because of an audience willing to attend musicals in whatever guise. Stanley Green, in his delightful *Ring Bells! Sing Songs! Broadway Musicals of the 1930's,*[32] reports a total of 175 musical stage pieces, which he breaks down as sixty-eight musical comedies, thirty-two operettas, fifty-six revues, seventeen all-Negro musical comedies or revues (a strange category), and two operas (that is, commercial ones rather than parts of the repertory of an opera company). The point here is that musicals came into their own in this decade as they had nearly 200 years before—in the 1790s, for example, in Philadelphia and Charleston and New York. Operettas began to fade as did revues, though some of the best of the latter were seen in the ten years from 1930 to 1939.

The Depression did not eliminate the run-of-the-mill musical, which seems always to have a place on American stages as it provides a background against which new trends stand out most clearly. When lyricists of the 1930s began to criticize everything around them, audiences stayed and listened (though whether reform came about—from musicals or, indeed, any art form—is open to question). The theatre professionals realized, too, that plots and lyrics were not the only way to convey a message, and so more elaborate staging and, especially, dance began to be more relevant to the political point being made. So pervasive was this social consciousness that it began to emerge in other musical forms, from bits in vaudeville to entire sequences in revues.

Probably the outstanding musical shows of the decade which specialized in criticism, whether seriously or satirically presented, were *Strike Up the Band* (written in the 1920s but arriving on Broadway in 1930, with music and lyrics by George and Ira Gershwin and book by George S. Kaufman and Morrie

Ryskind), *Of Thee I Sing* (1931, again the Gershwins, Kaufman, and Ryskind), *Face the Music* (1932, Irving Berlin words and music, book by Moss Hart), *As Thousands Cheer* (1933, a revue with music by Berlin and sketches, again, by Hart), *Let Em Eat Cake* (1933, a sequel to *Of Thee I Sing*), *I'd Rather Be Right* (1937, music and lyrics by Richard Rodgers and Lorenz Hart, book by Kaufman and Moss Hart), *The Cradle Will Rock* (1938, music and words by Marc Blitzstein), and *Johnny Johnson* (1936, music by Kurt Weill and words by Paul Green). But Kaufman's definition of satire ("what closes on Saturday night") did not seem to affect either his or anyone else's output; the result was additional satire, on Hollywood, for example (in Rodgers and Hart's 1931 *America's Sweetheart*), or on armaments (Harold Arlen and E. Y. Harburg's *Hooray for What!*), or on current mores (Cole Porter's 1930 *The New Yorkers*).

With operetta on the way out, librettists were leery of its conventions. Not only new, but realistic plots were needed, and these came as the musical looked about at the world and found it was not especially good. But other conventions needed to be inspected as well. Elaborate dialogue gave way to realistic, the operatic song to the popular, tight form with clean melodic line; even the characters began a metamorphosis. The hero would soon give way to Pal Joey, and the 1930s saw the heroine, delicate, high born, virginal, give way to the brassy, good-hearted woman portrayed so ably by Ethel Merman. And what luck to have a Merman just when she was needed—in shows like *Girl Crazy, Anything Goes,* and *Dubarry Was a Lady.*

And so the major addition the 1930s made to the musical was not a specific point of view, or even the idea of having a point of view (the 1790s were especially good at promoting a specific idea), but rather the consistency of an idea carried throughout a show, a coherent book, and some attempt at characterization rather than whatever set character or vaudeville routine the star brought with him.

Probably the single most important change wrought by the 1930s musical is epitomized by *Of Thee I Sing* (1931). This show, with music and lyrics by George and Ira Gershwin and book by George S. Kaufman and Morrie Ryskind, won the Pulitzer Prize (as best play!). More and more, people had begun to notice the musical, to become aware of its past and its potential. A certain pride in what seems to be a peculiarly American form was developing. From now on, musicals would be more self-conscious. Just as the novel could never be the same after novelists became aware of the criticism which analyzed all of its structure (here Henry James comes to mind; point of view now becomes a tool, but it cannot be ignored)—so the self-consciousness of dealing with a distinctly American form with roots in America's past, forced on the writers of musical comedy an awareness outside of the work they were creating. After self-consciousness, nothing could remain the same. This newly acquired way of looking at things found critics taking seriously what had been a delightful target against which they could toss their best *mots*. As the book musical came into its own, and as critics and audiences came to expect something more than the straight song-and-dance-with-fluff-plot musical, so librettists and composers began to experiment. In fact, experiment, the attempt at something new and different, became almost more important than the result. Still serving as backbone for all this was the traditional musical (Cole Porter's *Anything Goes* is a superb example). But experimenting the most was, as usual, Jerome Kern.[33] Kern's 1930s shows, *The Cat and the Fiddle, Music in the Air, Roberta,* and *Very Warm for May*, with music under the action, music which worked at depth of characterization, were *sui generis*, in that they led nowhere, yet were his attempt at taking the formerly popular operetta and fitting it into the conventions of the musical.

The successful adaptation of Shakespeare's *A Comedy of Errors* by Rodgers and Hart resulted in 1938's *The Boys from Syracuse*. The revue with a single point of view showed up in the 1931 *The Band Wagon* (Arthur Schwartz and Howard Dietz, with script by George S. Kaufman). The blurred line between the musical and opera was evident in *Porgy and Bess* (1935). And a writer-poet, Maxwell Anderson, was used in *Knickerbocker Holiday* (1938, music by Kurt Weill).

Experiments led to more experiments, and the amazing thing about the 1940s and 1950s is not the number of experiments but the number of masterpieces which resulted. As Arthur Jackson has noted, the 1930s was a period of great songs, but the 1940s and 1950s a period of great shows. Not that great songs weren't written, but they were sublimated to the plot, something that really hadn't happened before. The Rodgers and Hammerstein years were at hand.

In fact, the total number of musical pieces for the stage was somewhat less than in the previous decade, just over 150 in the 1940s, about 120 in the 1950s, whereas the 1930s had viewed 175. Still, the number of musicals proper rose from the sixty-eight listed by Stanley Green in the 1930s to eighty in the 1940s and to seventy-eight in the 1950s.

The years from 1940 to 1959 included many revivals (not included in the total count), a small number of English imports, a few Broadway operas (Menotti and Blitzstein were the genre's chief representatives), eleven operettas in the 1940s and none in the 1950s, and a large supply of revues. Several series revues show up now and then, though with the passing of Ziegfeld the days of this form were numbered. The only series one could count on regularly for a while were ice revues; since they were accompanied by live, newly composed music, they must be included, though surely they are the most boring form of entertainment ever devised by the human mind, fit only for unsuspecting children and those whose ideal in art is the Venus de Milo with a clock in her belly. The 1950s revues, including a large assortment of one-person shows, were of considerably higher quality.

The revue continued to hold its own in part because of the talent of the men who created them—Irving Berlin, for example, in *This Is the Army* (1942) or Cole Porter in *Seven Lively Arts* (1944). In part, the wit shown by Dietz and Schwartz in the 1930s, with *Band Wagon* (1931), for example, and the determination to make the revue all of a piece, carried over. True, there were many weak revues, some of which achieved a measure of popularity, but these served, as did weak musical comedies, to keep the form alive and before the public.

The increasingly large number of revivals probably displayed some of the increasing self-consciousness of the musical: it's our form, it's good, and we mustn't lose it.

Despite all this other activity, it was new musicals on stage that caused most excitement. One could sense the fascination

with the musical not only with experiments, constantly renewed interest, and popularity, but with the variety of men
who composed for it: Irving Berlin, for example, and Marc Blitzstein, Cole Porter, Richard Rodgers, Frederick Loewe, Harold
Arlen, Elie Siegmeister, Kurt Weill, Morton Gould, Duke Ellington, Frank Loesser, Heitor Villa-Lobos, Vernon Duke, Jerry
Bock, Leonard Bernstein, Jule Style, Arthur Schwartz, Harold
Rome, Meredith Willson—these are only a few of the 1940s
and 1950s names which come to mind. The American musical
theatre took up composers of popular songs as well as "serious"
composers and seemed to offer them an opportunity to be heard.

Probably, however, the two decades belong most to Rodgers
and Hammerstein. Beginning with *Oklahoma!* (1943), for
twenty years they set the pattern against which other shows
would be judged, and all the experiments of the period would
be seen as departures from the musicals they wrought. *Oklahoma!* was the beginning.[34]

The story was far removed from New York, as were the characters. The glitter of an opening chorus was replaced by the
simplicity of one character sitting alone on stage. The songs
(and the choruses when used) grew out of the plot and were
appropriate to it. Agnes de Mille's dream-sequence dances moved
the story forward, so much so that no musical with serious
pretensions could do without a dream ballet for years to come.
Where Balanchine's dances had been brilliant albeit cut off
from the plot (even "Slaughter on Tenth Avenue" in *On Your
Toes* was only peripherally related to the main events of the
story), now dance had to be integrated structurally into the
story—and the 1950s would find Jack Cole, Bob Fosse, Jerome
Robbins, Gower Champion, and Michael Kidd discovering musicals as a congenial form in which to work.

More than anything, however, the sentimentality and the
simplicity of the lyrics and emotions and stories of Hammerstein combined with the absolutely appropriate music of Rodgers to form not merely the "seamless web" so many critics
were fond of noting, but also the sort of story which could travel
all over America and find an audience.

Rodgers and Hammerstein's stress on the book musical, the
musical in which the libretto might be judged on its tautness

and without which the structure collapsed, was sustained in
their other work as well. After *Oklahoma!* came *Carousel* in
1945, *Allegro* in 1947, *South Pacific* in 1949, *The King and I*
in 1951, *Me and Juliet* in 1953, *Pipe Dreams* in 1955, *Flower
Drum Song* in 1958, and their last together, *The Sound of Music*
in 1959.

The initial impact of Rodgers and Hammerstein on others
was to portray as much Americana as possible—*A Tree Grows
in Brooklyn*, for example, or *Paint Your Wagon* (both 1951).
The use of dance was another. But the longer-range effect was
the book show, where a story was told and where all elements
supported the plot. As always, a continuum of old-fashioned
musical comedies sustained the high level of expertise which
Broadway audiences were accustomed to, shows like Irving
Berlin's *Call Me Madam* (1950). Still, within the tight book
show that Rodgers and Hammerstein had perfected, there was
room for experiment, even as the tight form of the sonnet gives
the greatest scope for the poet's imagination and ability once
he agrees to stay within the basic meter and structure.

In fact, experimentation had been strong even before *Oklahoma!*. The very first year of the decade, 1940, pointed the
route. A serious story with real characters in a musical!—that
was the introduction, and the work was Rodgers and Hart's
Pal Joey. John O'Hara worked his own stories into the libretto,
with the result that a grittiness of style pervaded the show.
Too, he was aware of what an American audience would find
shocking yet stand for. A womanizer content to live on the
largesse of and be kept by a society matron of matching dubious
morality was shocking on a musical stage which had learned
to handle political problems but had not yet begun to handle
human ones. Making Joey a night club entertainer enabled
dance to be an integral part of the show, though the shortage
of potential plots dealing with dancers made this but a tem-
porary solution to the problem of what to do with dance in a
musical.

Oklahoma! (1943) and *On the Town* (1944) attempted other
means of using dance. *Oklahoma!*, using the dream-ballet, made
clear a part of the plot and furthered our knowledge of character. The device is an attempt at realism, since anyone may

dream, and at the same time allows dance to be a part of the plot. The dance itself was Agnes de Mille's demonstration of what was going on in the mind and heart of the heroine; she writes that she linked the dances closely to the drama and they were designed to augment the characters and complement the text and lyrics. The style was that peculiar amalgam of ballet and popular dance and modern dance which had formed as part of a new structure, Broadway dance—except that for *Oklahoma!* de Mille used country dance as well, and had her dancers specifically trained in it. Her insistence on using the best dancers she could find for each role also helped in the presentation of powerful dance as an integral part of the Broadway show. But dance still had to be in a dream if it were to be accepted as part of the tightly knit story.[35]

But the following year, 1944, another approach was tried, in *On the Town.* The fact that its source was Jerome Robbins' ballet *Fancy Free* may have helped. In any case, the ballet was developed into a musical comedy, with music by Leonard Bernstein, with Jerome Robbins' choreography, and with book and lyrics by Berry Comden and Adolph Green. There was no attempt to make the reasons for the dance realistic. The characters danced as naturally as they sang, and the audiences accepted the convention of dance to thrust the story forward as easily as opera aficionados accept arias instead of speech.

Oklahoma! and *On the Town* led the way to another innovation shortly to be accepted as a part of America's musical stage. The choreographer would soon be the director not merely of dance but of the entire show, and the effect on the musical was to move away from the dependence upon book and into another conception of the nature of the musical.

The 1940s and 1950s tried many approaches. Blacks made their way back into the musical in, for example, *St. Louis Woman* (1946) and *Cabin in the Sky* (1949). Early dream sequences and some exploration of psychoanalysis appear in *Lady in the Dark* (1941). Hammerstein's *Carmen Jones* (1943) attempted to make an opera contemporary in interest by changing locale and bringing lyrics up to date. There was room for the occasional try at an operetta, and *Song of Norway* (1944), with the music of Edvard Grieg, found an audience, as did *Kismet* (1953) with

Borodin's music; Romberg's *Up in Central Park* (1944) was a sort of halfway house between operetta and musical, as was his posthumously produced *The Girl in Pink Tights* (1954). American history found a fairly regular place—witness *Bloomer Girl* (1944)—and even American ballads were the stuff of musicals as in *Sing Out Sweet Land* (1944). The serious exploration of social problems in the tradition of *Of Thee I Sing* was continued with, for example, *Finian's Rainbow* (1947) and *Fiorello!* (1959). Fantasy held, when presented by men of talent, so *Brigadoon* (1947) and *Allegro* (1947) made their mark. If *The Boys from Syracuse* had shown that Shakespeare could be successfully adapted to the musical stage, then Porter would have a go, and *Kiss Me Kate* (1948), and Bernstein's *West Side Story* followed in 1957.

The Broadway opera, that is, opera designed to open on Broadway, was represented by Blitzstein's *Regina* in 1949, Menotti's *The Consul* (1950) and *The Saint of Bleecker Street* (1954), and Bernstein's *Trouble in Tahiti* (1955), though the line between opera and the musical was obscured by such through-composed musicals as Loesser's *The Most Happy Fella* (1956) and George Kleinsinger's *Shinbone Alley*. Musicals like *Candide, Lost in the Stars,* and *Sweeney Todd* now show up in the opera house. Musical experiments show up in unlikely places such as a jazz fugue in *Guys and Dolls* (1950).

A steady motif all through the Rodgers and Hammerstein decades was the picture of some aspect of American life, like Harold Rome's *Wish You Were Here* (1952) or Bernstein's *Wonderful Town* (1953) or Richard Adler and Jerry Ross's *Pajama Game* (1954) or Albert Hague's *Plain and Fancy* (1955—about the Amish, for heaven's sake). Serious works of literature became the stuff of the musical, among them *Candide* (1956) and *First Impressions* (1959, from Jane Austen's *Pride and Prejudice*) and *My Fair Lady* (1956, from Shaw's *Pygmalion*), but even the comic strip might serve, witness *Li'l Abner* in 1966, and still later *Annie,* 1977).

In those decades some powerful works stayed Off-Broadway as Blitzstein's version of Weill's *The Threepenny Opera* did in 1954 and Harvey Schmidt's *The Fantasticks* in 1960. Some moved uptown and became Broadway hits like John Latouche and Jerome Moross's *The Golden Apple* and Earl Robinson and Waldo Salt's *Sandhog*.

Occasionally a hit came along that combined all the elements in a new way, brought composers, authors, and stars together in a new combination which was magic on the stage, using all of the past and giving more than a hint of the future—such a work as, for example, *Gypsy* (1959).[36] Ethel Merman got a chance, as Gypsy's mother, to handle a more demanding role than her usual brass, and she was able to handle it; the musical itself showed through her that the old stereotypes were giving way to a more realistic handling of character. Arthur Laurents had made a name for himself as a playwright (*Home of the Brave, The Time of the Cuckoo*, and others) before attempting the libretto form with *West Side Story*, and then *Gypsy*. Jule Stein, too, had had extensive Broadway experience, with such shows as *Gentlemen Prefer Blondes, Hazel Flagg, Say Darling*, and others. And the lyricist was Stephen Sondheim, whose lyrics for *West Side Story* had proclaimed him an important presence. Jerome Robbins, who directed and choreographed the show, had also more than served his apprenticeship. The plot was in small part the story of Gypsy Rose Lee; in a larger sense it was her mother's story, and Rose/Merman's soliloquy at the end of *Gypsy*—"Well, someone tell me, when is it my turn? Don't I get a dream for myself?"—showed once again the movement of the musical from a show with songs to a music-drama.

The 1960s followed the success of *West Side Story* and *Gypsy* with a greater attention to integration (always remembering that the background for the great successes of the decade was provided by the standard song-and-dance, tired-businessman musical, though frequently of very high quality). Over 100 musicals opened on Broadway, with only a smattering of revues. Lots of imports appeared, mostly from England (*Oliver*, for example), and though some were fine, they were in the style made popular in America and offered little to modify the form.

An important influence on the musical was the emergence of Off-Broadway productions. These were easier to experiment with, since their production costs were less than those uptown. One finds, for example, four in 1967, including the excellent *Man of La Mancha*—no love story, no chorus, nothing but the idealism of a cracked brain and the adventures leading to a fatal confrontation with reality—and some glorious songs. Still another Off-Broadway hit was the 1964 *Hair*.

Though *Hair* was not the first to present rock music on the stage (*Bye Bye Birdie* in 1960 made a bow in that direction), it was the first to show something of the young's attitudes frightening so many adults: flower children, long hair, drugs, dirt, and a determination to be thoroughly anti-establishment. But they were basically good kids, so the middle-aged, middle-class audience found the work acceptable and congratulated themselves on their modern ways. The music allowed the words to be heard and was flexible enough to suggest some variations in mood. In fact, however, the musical stage had always been able to adopt new musical trends as it had always picked up dance trends. A small flood of rock musicals inundated the musical stage for a while, but the category was essentially retrogressive, since it is difficult with rock to define character, to advance the plot, or to arrange for the subtle use of music which had been the mark of the musical for so long. The kind of song hit from musicals which had always moved to records and radio and night clubs, the kind of song one left the show humming was a casualty of rock, and the rock musical was powerless to stop the trend.

The English team of Andrew Lloyd Weber and Tim Rice seemed able to use rock, but the use was deceptive. In such shows as *Jesus Christ Superstar* (1971), *Evita* (1978), and, to some extent (though rock was only a small part of the show) *Joseph and the Amazing Technicolor Dreamcoat* (to Broadway in 1982), they used a narrator as a substitute for action to set up the songs. Even this was a tradition here, going back at least as far, according to Charles Willard, as Kurt Weill and Alan Jay Lerner's *Love Life* in 1948. The "comment song" was featured—that is, musical sequences, vocal or choreographic, which do not advance the action or express character directly but instead comment through tone and point rather than emotion and character.[37] In any case, if one can imagine an opera with nothing but recitative and aria, then the essence of the rock musical comes clear.

Still, the decade of the 1960s produced some great musicals

among the more than 100 which opened, and many displayed the stirrings of ideas leading to the 1980s. As with the previous decade, Off-Broadway made major contributions to the musical, and some of these stayed Off-Broadway (*The Fantasticks* in 1960, for example), and some moved uptown to Broadway (as both *Hair* and *Man of La Mancha* did). Even the standard musical was forced away from the type of show with silly plot which served as little more than excuse for songs. *The Unsinkable Molly Brown* (1960), *Camelot* (1960), *Mr. President* (1962), and *Promises, Promises* (1968) represent the sort of upgrading standard musicals were forced to undergo in order to please an audience which they perceived as having new expectations, making new demands.

Some outstanding shows of the decade seemed to owe no allegiance to recent trends yet created the kind of magic that influenced others. Surely the team working on *Fiddler on the Roof* (1964) must have known they were doomed to failure in dealing with a Jewish community in Russia. They discovered, however, as they worked on the show, that it was about something else. In a seminar before the Dramatists' Guild Sheldon Harnick (who wrote the lyrics) spoke of the period after Jerome Robbins was signed on. Robbins kept asking what the show was about, until someone said "It's about the dissolution of a way of life." Where was the plot? Harnick again: "Robbins is the kind of director who takes total charge, because he has a total vision, a vision which encompasses every element of the show."[38] The "total vision," the show about an idea, was soon to lead away from the book musical.

It is possible that the new style of musical was so startling to Broadway audiences that they began to long for an earlier, simpler time. This yearning may have resulted in what Lehman Engel referred to as "folio" shows, where the evening looks like a musical but is in reality an assortment of songs from the total body of work of one or more composers, a close relation to a rock concert.[39] The spoken word is omitted, thereby removing a major part of our musical theatre—*Ain't Misbehavin'* (1978, songs of Fats Waller), for example, or *Eubie!* (1978, songs of Eubie Blake), or *Sophisticated Ladies* (1981, music of Duke Ellington). It is also possible that with the new self-consciousness of the musical, the beginning of an awareness of a heritage began to grow. Whatever the reason, the 1970s found a surprising number of revivals—about thirty from the past found their way to Broadway. Musicals from early in the century such as *Whoopee!* (1928), *Going Up!* (1917), *Irene* (1919), and *No! No! Nanette!* (1925) to more recent hits such as *Oklahoma!* (1943) and *Guys and Dolls* (1950) found their way back to appreciative audiences, audiences not sure what was happening with new musical works. After all, in three quarters of a century, nearly 1,700 major musicals had been produced on Broadway, and not even the most profligate society could afford to consign all of them to the dust bins of history.

This nostalgia or awareness resulted in such a company as the Light Opera of Manhattan, which did (and still does) devote itself in part to revivals of Gilbert and Sullivan and in part to revivals of the musicals of America's past. The Bandwagon, whose purpose is the revival of vintage musicals, and the Goodspeed Opera which, for the most part, does the same thing are manifestations of the same trend. Lee Theodore's American Dance Machine recreates dances from American musicals of the past. If the awareness of a heritage is only of a recent heritage, at least the movement is finally making obeisance to a past which is gradually extending down to the American theatre's roots.

The change in the musical was the result of many factors, though certainly in large part because of the change in function of the directors. Again, it was a Rodgers and Hammerstein work that led the way: *Allegro* (1947), which Agnes de Mille choreographed and directed. The director who is dancer and choreographer became a fact of life, so that one finds him or her first as dancer, then as choreographer, then as choreographer-director, and finally the show is listed "as conceived by" him or her. Before de Mille, Jack Cole had helped to establish a balletic style on Broadway. Indeed, Jerome Robbins says his contributions are "so far reaching that without him present-day theatrical dancing would not be the same. Everyone teaching jazz dance today teaches much of what Jack Cole founded and codified."[40] This was reinforced by George Balanchine with such shows as *I Married an Angel* and *On Your Toes*. After de

Mille broke ground, not only with her work for *Oklahoma!* but especially with both directing the book and arranging the choreography for *Allegro*, many others followed. Jerome Robbins made a Broadway name with *On the Town!*, followed by a series of other shows, but his work as director and choreographer for *West Side Story* expanded the director's role and enabled him to weld the dance and the drama as had earlier been done in few shows. His insistence on values outside of plot may have been responsible for the power of *Gypsy* and *Fiddler on the Roof*; certainly the movement away from complete dependence on plot may be seen in these shows. Other dancers or choreographers turned director-choreographer included Michael Kidd with, for example, *Li'l Abner* (1956) and *The Rothschilds* (1970), Gower Champion with such shows as *Hello, Dolly!* (1964), *The Happy Time* (1968), and *42nd Street* (1980); Robert Fosse, with about a half a dozen, including *Redhead* (1959), *Sweet Charity* (1966), *Pippin* (1972), and *Chicago* (1975); Joe Layton with *No Strings* (1962), and *George M!* (1968); Tommy Tune, with *The Best Little Whorehouse in Texas* (1978) and *My One and Only* (1983); and Michael Bennett, with *A Chorus Line* (1975), *Ballroom* (1978), and *Dreamgirls* (1981). Both Bennett and Fosse added the third element to their work: "Conceived, Choreographed, and Directed by" in such shows as *A Chorus Line* and *Dancin'* respectively. Popular songs might emerge from these shows ("What I Did for Love" from *A Chorus Line* is an example), but if they did, it was not because they were introduced in an overture or reprised again and again. In fact, songs were so closely tied to character and to situation that it was difficult to remove them and enjoy them out of context.

Even as the musical's audience continued to demand songs (indeed, with *My One and Only* in 1983, George Gershwin's music was brought back in a new plot), the musical continued to experiment and to use new subject matter, topics of concern to the society of its day—homosexuality, for example, treated sympathetically in *La Cage aux Folles* (1983). It was, nonetheless, one genius whose work had the effect of solidifying all this, if not actually beginning it. Stephen Sondheim's first Broadway hit was as the lyricist for *West Side Story* in 1957. He next set Jule Styne's music to words in *Gypsy* (1959). He wrote both music and lyrics for *A Funny Thing Happened on the Way to the Forum* in 1962 and for *Anyone Can Whistle* in 1964 and went back to lyrics only for Richard Rodgers' *Do I Hear a Waltz* (1965). His major breakthrough in the direction of the musical was with the music and lyrics for *Company* (1970), followed by *Follies* (1971), *A Little Night Music* in 1973, *Pacific Overtures* in 1976, *Sweeney Todd* in 1979, *Merrily We Roll Along* in 1981, and *Sunday in the Park with George* in 1984.

Sondheim himself makes clear part of the reason for *Company*'s effect. "A lot of the controversy about *Company* was that up until *Company* most musicals, if not all musicals, had plots." He is clear that the book to a show is crucial and at one point claims that "it's the book that the musical is all about."[41] His musicals were to be, if not plotless, at least with a thin plot which serves little more than to move the show from curtain to curtain. Instead, the book would deal with some concept, some theme or idea, and the musical would explore various aspects of that idea. No songs were permitted that did not have a sound dramatic situation, and all were to illuminate character. No wonder his hit songs were few, since the better they were for the show, the worse they might be out of context.

Sunday in the Park with George caused something of a sensation. Frank Rich of *The New York Times*, for example, in an article long after the show opened, called it Sondheim's "most daring musical," noted its lack of dance, and suggested that the piece is "the first truly modernist work of musical theater Broadway has produced. . . . The show forms a bridge," he wrote, "between the musical and the more daring playwriting" of Sondheim's time.[42] The American musical's freedom to experiment and still find a audience was shown again in the same 1983–1984 season, in which such traditional (from the point of view of form) musicals were produced as *La Cage aux Folles*, *Doonesbury*, and *The Tap Dance Kid*.

But if traditional musicals continued to be turned out, the effect of the Sondheim show had been quickly seen on such musicals as *Chicago, A Chorus Line, Dancin', Ballroom, Dreamgirls, Pump Boys and Dinettes*—and, presumably many more in the years ahead.

Most critics of the 1940s felt that the book musical was as far as the form could go. Yet the collapse of the book musical did not take all musicals down with it. Instead, a different way of creating the form emerged. Paul Wittke wrote that "In today's real theatre world . . . the serious and the popular are enjoying a marriage of convenience. It has been happening for years. . . . Does *Sweeney Todd* inhabit a different world from *Lulu*? Would Strauss's Marschallin spurn the Countess of *A Little Night Music?*"[43] And when the "concept" musical disappears, it, too, will be followed by something different. The only thing we can be sure of is that an artistic form with roots deep in American history will not die.

Epilogue

Without the perspective of history, commentators on the American musical theatre tend to lose their way. If the book musical seemed to be the be-all and end-all of musical theatre, then of course the musical died with the book musical. But it did not die. And if *Pal Joey* upset many critics with a hero who was a heel—arrogant, vulgar, self-seeking, pretentious, and a touch vicious—the musical did not die then, either. Nor did it expire with an attempt at telling a serious story in *Show Boat* or with the addition of a plot and the loss of a large chorus with the Princess Theatre shows. The musical did not die with the racy, colloquial language of George M. Cohan, nor was it murdered by vaudeville or burlesque or melodrama or opera, though these forms influenced its shape.

One error in concentrating upon the book musical, or any other aspect of our musical theatre, is the feeling that only it is all-important, that only it must stand alone. But it is precisely the balance of many elements which made all effects on our musical stage successful. Even as the libretto of an opera tends to seem ridiculous when read yet becomes magic when illustrated, surrounded by music, so the musical needs no stronger book than can be made to come alive by music. The health of the American musical lies precisely in its ability to change, to discard what is no longer necessary or desirable.

And the changes in the American musical incorporate all elements of our musical theatre from the circus to ballet, from melodrama to grand opera; changes which occur when a man or woman of great talent creates something different; changes which happen when the society, the audience, has different needs and is itself changed.

There is a point in the history of any art form when it is not merely attempting to emulate its successful predecessors. It is the point when a gifted artist (or artists working together), knowing the form, knowing the audience, secure in the tradition in which he works, is free to handle each work as a separate problem. The artist attempts to solve the problem. The American musical has evolved over 200 years to a point where the artist is, finally, faced with a problem and has the tools at hand to solve it. In fact, the musical is (in case anyone questions it) a serious art form as well as a popular one. The conjunction of serious and popular has happened before in history—Shakespeare is a fine example— and works to thrill the human spirit have resulted.

The coming seasons list as many musicals about to open on Broadway as straight plays. Many will no doubt be good, solid ones, and many will experiment. No one can tell where the musical is going, but it has an audience, performers, writers, and composers, and, perhaps most of all, 200 years of tradition on which to lean. A unique combination of circumstances has resulted in the excitement of the American musical; it will be instructive, and fun, to see where it goes from here.

Notes

OVERTURE. SOME HISTORY, AN ANALYSIS, AND A POLEMIC

1. Stanley Richards, *Great Musicals of the American Theatre*, 2 vols. (Radnor, PA: Chilton Book Co., 1976), 2:x.

2. Earl F. Bargainnier, "Introduction: In-Depth, The American Musical," *Journal of Popular Culture*, 12, no. 3 (Winter 1978): 404.

3. Wallace Brockway and Herbert Weinstock, *The Opera* (New York: Simon and Schuster, 1941), 2.

ACT I. SCENE 1. COMPANIES

1. The history of eighteenth-century American companies was taken from Julian Mates, *The American Musical Stage Before 1800* (New Brunswick, N.J.: Rutgers University Press, 1962), 96–135.

2. Touring patterns may be discerned from the following works: Iline Fife, *The Theatre During the Confederacy* (Ph.D. dissertation, Louisiana State University, 1949), 2; Joseph Miller Free, *The Theatre of Southwestern Mississippi to 1840*, 2 vols. (Ph.D. dissertation, State University of Iowa, 1941), 1:138; Sol. Smith, *The Theatrical Apprenticeship and Anecdotal Recollections of Sol. Smith* (Philadelphia: Carey and Hart, 1847), 102.

3. Elbert R. Bowen, *Theatrical Entertainments in Rural Missouri Before the Civil War.* University of Missouri Studies, vol. 32 (Columbia, Mo.: University of Missouri Press, 1959).

4. Ronald L. Davis, *Opera in Chicago* (New York: Appleton-Century, 1966), 8, 12.

5. Douglas McDermott, "Touring Patterns in California's Theatrical Frontier," *Theatre Survey*, 15, no. 1 (May 1974): 19.

6. Wendell Cole, "Early Theatre in America West of the Rockies: A Bibliographical Essay," *Theatre Research*, 4, no. 1 (1962): 36–45; Ronald L. Davis, *A History of Opera in the American West* (Englewood Cliffs, N.J.: Prentice-Hall, 1965), 85–86; Eugene Clinton Elliott, *A History of Variety—Vaudeville in Seattle* (Seattle: University of Washington Press, 1944), 3; Larry Robert Wolz, "A Survey of Concert Life in Texas During the Nineteenth Century." M. M. thesis, Texas Christian University, 1976; Joseph Gallegly, *Footlights on the Border* (The Hague: Mouton & Co., 1962), 19, 59.

7. Isaac J. Greenwood, *The Circus* (Washington, D.C.: Hobby House Press, 1898), 87–88, 113; Thomas Ford, *A Peep Behind the Curtain* (Boston: Redding & Co., 1850), 14; Lucille Gafford, *A History of the St. Charles Theatre in New Orleans 1835–43* (Ph.D. dissertation, University of Chicago, 1930), 54; Edmond M. Gagey, *The San Francisco Stage* (New York: Columbia University Press, 1950), 41; Glen Hughes, *A History of the American Theatre 1750–1950*, (New York: Samuel French, 1951), 173; William G. B. Carsen, *Managers in Distress* (St. Louis, MO: St. Louis Historical Documents Foundation, 1949); Edward Gladstone Baynham, *The Early Development of Music in Pittsburgh* (Ph.D. dissertation, University of Pittsburgh, 1944); Noah M. Ludlow, *Dramatic Life As I Found It* (St. Louis, MO, 1880; New York: Benjamin Blom, 1966), 330; W. Stanley Hoole, *The Ante-Bellum Charleston Theatre* (University, AL: University of Alabama Press, 1946), 44; George O. Willard, *History of the Providence Stage, 1762–1891* (Providence, R.I.: The Rhode Island News Co., 1891); Richard Moody, *The Astor Place Riot* (Bloomington: Indiana University Press, 1958).

8. Frank Costello Davidson, *The Rise, Development, Decline and Influence of the American Minstrel Show* (Ph.D. dissertation, New York University, 1952); Robert Franklin Eggers, *A History of Theatre in Boise, Idaho, from 1863 to 1963* (M.A. thesis, University of Oregon, 1963); Harold Calvin Tedford, *A Study of Theatrical Entertainments in Northwest Arkansas from their Beginning through 1889* (Ph.D. dissertation, Louisiana State University, 1965), 19–20; Firman Brown, Jr., *A History of Theatre in Montana* (Ph.D. dissertation, University of Wisconsin, 1963); Margaret G. Watson, *Silver Theatre* (Glendale, CA: The Arthur H. Clark Co., 1964); George C. D. Odell, *Annals of the New York Stage*, 15 vols. (New York: Columbia University Press, 1928), 4:255.

9. Henry Clay Barnabee, *Reminiscences of Henry Clay Barnabee*, ed. George Varney (Boston: Chapple, 1913), 171ff.

10. James Harvey Young, *The Toadstool Millionaires* (Princeton, N.J.: Princeton University Press, 1961), 191.

11. Caroline Schaffner, "Trouping with the Schaffners." In *American Popular Entertainment*, ed. Myron Matlaw (Westport, CT: Greenwood Press, 1979), 166.

12. Henry B. Williams, ed. *The American Theatre: A Sum of Its Parts* (New York: Samuel French, Inc., 1971), 8–9.

13. Michael Bandler, "Resident Theatre: Coming of Age," *EXXON USA* (First Quarter 1984): 29.

ACT I. SCENE 2. REPERTORY

1. Oscar George Theodore Sonneck, *A Bibliography of Early Secular American Music*. Revised and enlarged by William Treat Upton. (Washington, D.C.: The Library of Congress, 1945), 491.

2. Ibid., 533ff.

3. George H. Nettleton and Arthur E. Case, *British Dramatists from Dryden to Sheridan*. Revised by George Winchester Stone. (Boston: Houghton Mifflin, 1969), 526.

4. "Oh London is a Fine Town" was also called "Peggy Ramsay." The lines from John Gay's *The Beggar's Opera* are extracted from the Peter Lewis edition (New York: Barnes & Noble, 1973), 59.

5. Julian Mates, *The American Musical Stage Before 1800* (New Brunswick, N.J.: Rutgers University Press, 1962), 141.

6. Milton Gerald Hehr, *Musical Activities in Salem, Massachusetts: 1783–1823* (Ph.D. dissertation, Boston University, 1963), 351.

7. Noah M. Ludlow, *Dramatic Life As I Found It* (St. Louis, Mo., 1880; New York: Benjamin Blom, 1966), 330.

8. Joseph Miller Free, *The Theatre of Southwestern Mississippi to 1840*, 2 vols. (Ph.D. dissertation, State University of Iowa, 1941), 1:138.

9. Lucille Gafford, *A History of the St. Charles Theatre in New Orleans, 1835–43* (Ph.D. dissertation, University of Chicago, 1930), 24.

10. W. Stanley Hoole, *The Ante-Bellum Charleston Theatre* (University, AL: University of Alabama Press, 1946), 44.

11. John Durang, *The Memoir of John Durang*, ed. Alan S. Downer (York, PA: Historical Society of York County and University of Pittsburgh Press, 1966), 122–126.

12. Henry W. Adams, *The Montgomery Theatre, 1822–1835* (University, AL: University of Alabama Press, 1955), 14, 16.

13. Ronald L. Davis, *Opera in Chicago* (New York: Appleton-Century, 1966), 6; Joseph Gallegly, *Footlights on the Border: The Gal-*

veston and Houston Stage Before 1900 (The Hague: Mouton & Co., 1962), 19–21.

14. David Grimsted, *Melodrama Unveiled: American Theatre and Culture, 1800–1850* (Chicago: University of Chicago Press, 1968), 108, 259.

15. Selma Jean Cohen, "The Fourth of July, or the Independence of American Dance," *Dance Magazine*, 50, July 1976, 49–53.

16. Sol. Smith, *Theatrical Management in the West and South for Thirty Years* (New York: Harper & Bros., 1868), 238.

17. William Dunlap, *History of the American Theatre*, 2 vols. (1833; New York: Burt Franklin, 1963), 1: 129–130.

18. Joe Cowell, *Thirty Years Passed Among the Players in England and America* (New York: Harper & Bros., 1844), 75.

19. Alexis de Tocqueville, *Democracy in America*, 2 vols., Henry Reeve text, rev. Francis Bower and further corrected by Phillips Bradley (Paris, 1835, 1840; reprinted New York: Vintage Books, 1954), 2: 85, 86.

20. Glen Hughes, *A History of the American Theatre 1700–1950* (New York: Samuel French, 1951), 216–217.

21. *Papers on Literature and Art* (London: Wiley & Putnam, 1846), Part 2, 134.

22. Arthur Hobson Quinn, *A History of the American Drama from the Civil War to the Present Day* (New York: Appleton-Century-Crofts, 1936), 2, 6.

23. Lloyd Morris, *Curtain Time* (New York: Random House, 1953), 185.

24. Deane L. Root, *American Popular Stage Music 1860–1880* (Ann Arbor, Mich.: UMI Research Press, 1981), 62.

25. Garff B. Wilson, *Three Hundred Years of American Drama and Theatre* (Englewood Cliffs, N.J.: Prentice-Hall, 1973), 147, 242.

26. Louis B. Wright, *Culture on the Moving Frontier* (New York: Harper and Row, 1961), 158–159.

27. Allen Churchill, *The Great White Way* (New York: E. P. Dutton, 1962), 12.

28. Brooks Atkinson, *Broadway* (New York: Macmillan, 1971), 7, 11, 97–98.

29. Burns Mantle, ed., *The Best Plays and Year Book of the Drama in America* series (New York: Dodd, Mead, 1947 ff.).

30. Cecil Smith and Glenn Litton, *Musical Comedy in America* (New York: Theatre Arts Books, 1981), 347.

31. Jack Beeson, "American Opera: Curtains and Overtures," *Columbia University Forum*, Fall, 1960, vol. iii, no. 4, pp. 21, 24, 25; Gael M. O'Brien, "Opera Enjoying a Boom on U.S. Campuses," *The Chronicle of Higher Education*, Sept. 27, 1976, xiii, 4, p. 8.

32. Charles Hamm, *Music in the New World* (New York: W. W. Norton, 1983), 447–452; Edward Ellsworth Hipsher, *American Opera and its Composers* (Phila.: 1927; reprinted New York: Da Capo Press, 1978), 442; Ronald L. Davis, *A History of Opera in the American West* (Englewood Cliffs, New Jersey: Prentice Hall, Inc., 1965), 15, 27, 86, 114, 135, ff.

ACT I. SCENE 3. PERFORMERS

1. Cited in Julian Mates, *The American Musical Stage Before 1800* (New Brunswick, N.J.: Rutgers University Press, 1962), 83; original sources for this and other eighteenth-century references are in fn. 35, 54, 61–64, 143, 161, 163, 185 of Chapter IV.

2. John Durang, *The Memoir of John Durang*, ed. Alan S. Downer (Pittsburgh: Historical Society of York County and University of Pittsburgh Press, 1966), xii–xiii.

3. Ibid., 83.

4. Alan S. Downer, "Players and Painted Stage, Nineteenth Century Acting," *PMLA*, Vol. 61 No. 2, June 1946, 522.

5. Anna Cora Mowatt, *Autobiography of an Actress* (Boston: Ticknor, Reed, & Fields, 1854), 320.

6. Ibid., p. 219.

7. Noah M. Ludlow, *Dramatic Life As I Found It* (St. Louis, MO: 1880, reprinted New York: Benjamin Blom, 1966), 612.

8. Warren's roles are cited in Henry Clay Barnabee, *Reminiscences of Henry Clay Barnabee*, ed. George Leon Varney (Boston: Chapple, 1913), 178; William B. Wood, *Personal Recollections of the Stage* (Philadelphia: Henry Carey Baird, 1855), 473.

9. Julian Mates, "American Musical Theatre: Beginnings to 1900," in *The American Theatre: A Sum of Its Parts*, ed. Henry B. Williams (New York: Samuel French, 1971), 230.

10. Joseph Leach, *Bright Particular Star, The Life and Times of Charlotte Cushman* (New Haven, Conn.: Yale University Press, 1970), 28ff.

11. David Dempsey with Raymond P. Baldwin, *The Triumphs and Trials of Lotta Crabtree* (New York: William Morrow, 1968), 130.

12. Downer, "Players and Painted Stage," 547, 573.

13. Anne Hartley Gilbert, *The Stage Reminiscences of Mrs. Gilbert*, ed. Charlotte M. Martin (New York: Charles Scribner's Sons, 1901), 24, 29–31.

14. Mowatt, *Autobiography of an Actress*, 313.

15. William Davidge, *Footlight Flashes* (New York: The American News Co., 1866), 88–89.

16. Sol. Smith, *The Theatrical Apprenticeship and Anecdotal Recollections of Sol. Smith* (Philadelphia: Carey and Hart, 1847), 132.

17. George C. D. Odell, *Annals of the New York Stage*, 15 vols. (New York: Columbia University Press, 1928), 2: 146, 149, 249, 303, 380.

18. Theodore Thomas, *A Musical Autobiography*, ed. George P. Upton (Chicago: 1905; reprinted New York: Da Capo Press, 1964), 21ff; George O. Willard, *History of the Providence Stage, 1762–1891* (Providence, R.I.: The Rhode Island News Co., 1891), 116–117, 131; William G. B. Carson, *The Theatre on the Frontier*, 2d ed. (New York: Benjamin Blom, 1965), 215, 236.

19. Sol. Smith, *Theatrical Management in the West and South for Thirty Years* (New York: Harper and Bros., 1868), 23.

20. William Green, "Broadway Book Musicals: 1900–1969," in Williams, *The American Musical Theatre: A Sum of Its Parts*, 266.

21. Richard Moody, "American Actors and Acting Before 1900: The Making of a Tradition," in Williams, *The American Musical Theatre: A Sum of Its Parts*, p. 46.

ACT II. SCENE 1. AMERICAN OPERA: COMIC, GRAND, AND OPERETTA

1. J. Aiken, *Letters from a Father to his Son, 1792 and 1793* (Philadelphia: 1796), 59.

2. Donald J. Grout, *A Short History of Opera*, 2d ed. (New York: Columbia University Press, 1965), 491, 492.

3. Cited in Oscar G. Sonneck, *Early Opera in America* (New York: London, Boston, 1915), 140.

4. Wallace Brockway and Herbert Weinstock, *The Opera* (New York: Simon and Schuster, 1941), 142.

5. Charles Hamm, *Music in the New World* (New York: W. W. Norton and Co., 1983), 195.

6. Alexis de Tocqueville, *Democracy in America*, 2 vols. Henry Reeve text, rev. Francis Bowen, corrected and ed. Phillips Bradley (1835, 1840; reprinted New York: Vintage Books, 1954), II:85.

7. Iline Fife, *The Theatre During the Confederacy* (Ph.D. dissertation, Louisiana State University, 1949), 23.

8. In Montrose Moses, ed., *Representative Plays by American Dramatists*, 2 vols. (1918; reprinted New York: Benjamin Blom, 1964), 1:569ff.

9. Sol. Smith, *Theatrical Management in the West and South for Thirty Years* (New York: Harper and Bros., 1868), 87.

10. Philip Hone, *The Diary of Philip Hone 1828–1851*, ed. Allan Nevins (New York: Dodd, Mead & Co., 1936), 837.

11. Cited in Blanche Muldrow, *The American Theatre as Seen by British Travelers 1790–1860* (Ph.D. dissertation, University of Wisconsin, 1953), 373–374.

12. Francis Trollope, *Domestic Manners of the Americans*, ed. Donald Smalley (New York: Vintage Books, 1960), 133–134.

13. William G. B. Carson, *Managers in Distress: the St. Louis Stage, 1840–1844* (St. Louis, Mo.: St. Louis Historical Documents Foundation, 1949), 170.

14. Hone, *The Diary of Philip Hone*, 24.

15. William George Burbick, *Columbus, Ohio, Theatre from the Beginning of the Civil War to 1875* (Ph.D. dissertation, Ohio State University, 1963), 22; Ronald L. Davis, *A History of Opera in the American West* (Englewood Cliffs, N.J.: Prentice-Hall, 1965), 15, 38, 41, 83, 88.

16. Noah M. Ludlow, *Dramatic Life As I Found It* (St. Louis, Mo., 1880; reprinted New York: Benjamin Blom, 1966), 614–615.

17. Sol. Smith letter to H. Chippendale, April 2, 1845, Harvard University Theatre Collection.

18. John Tasker Howard and George Kent Bellows, *A Short History of Music in America* (New York: Thomas Y. Crowell, 1959), 136.

19. Ibid., 127–128, 130–131; Andrew H. Drummond, *American Opera Librettos* (Metuchen, N.J.: Scarecrow Press, 1973), 1.

20. Donald Jay Grout, *A Short History of Opera*, 2d ed. (New York: Columbia University Press, 1965), 490.

21. Drummond, *American Opera Librettos*, 63.

22. H. Earle Johnson, *Operas on American Subjects* (New York: Coleman-Ross Co., 1964), 64–65.

23. Ibid.

24. Jack Beeson, "American Opera: Curtains and Overtures," *Columbia University Forum*, Vol. 3, No. 4, Fall 1960, 24–26; additional statistics on numbers of American operas cited in the *Sonneck Society Newsletter*, Vol. 8, Summer 1982, 37.

25. Oscar G. Sonneck, "Ciampi's 'Bertoldo, Bertolino e Cacasenno' and Favert's 'Ninette A La Cour'—A Contribution to the History of Pasticcio," *Miscellaneous Studies in the History of Music* (NY: 1921. Reprint. New York: Da Capo Press; 1968), 112.

26. Julian Mates, *The American Musical Stage Before 1800* (New Brunswick, N.J.: Rutgers University Press, 1962), 144–145.

27. Edward Ellsworth Hipsher, *American Opera and Its Composers* (Philadelphia, 1927; reprinted New York: Da Capo Press 1978), 48–49.

28. Gerald Bordman, *American Operetta* (New York: Oxford University Press, 1981), 70.

29. Anecdote by Deems Taylor, Forward to Stanley Green, *The World of Musical Comedy* (New York: Grosset and Dunlap, 1962).

30. William Dunlap, *Musical Works of William Dunlap*, ed. Julian Mates (Delmar, N.Y.: Scholars' Facsimiles & Reprints, 1980).

31. Micah Hawkins, *The Saw-Mill: or A Yankee Trick* (New York: J. and J. Harper, 1824; reprinted in *The Magazine of History with Notes and Queries*, Vol. 32, No. 3, Extra No., No. 127, 1927; Vera Brodsky Lawrence, "Micah Hawkins, the Pied Piper of Catherine Slip," *The New-York Historical Society Quarterly*, Vol. 62, No. 2, April 1978, 156.

32. David Ewen, *Panorama of American Popular Music* (Englewood Cliffs, N.J.: Prentice-Hall, 1957), 106.

33. David Ewen, *The Story of America's Musical Theatre* (Philadelphia: Chilton Book Co., 1961), 7–8, 10.

34. Bordman, *American Operetta*, 27.

35. Jacques Offenbach, *Orpheus in America*, trans. Lander MacClintock (Bloomington: Indiana University Press, 1957), 21.

36. Bordman, *American Operetta*, 41–50.

37. Ewen, *Panorama*, 109–115.

38. Ibid., 116–129; Ewen, *The Story of America's Musical Theatre*, 13–27, 30–45; Bordman, *American Operetta*, 94, 98, 107ff.

ACT II. SCENE 2. MINSTREL SHOW AND CIRCUS

1. Glen Hughes, *A History of the American Theatre 1700–1950* (New York: Samuel French, 1951), 137; Lawrence Hutton, *Curiosities of the American Stage* (New York: Harper and Brothers, 1891), 115–117; Molly N. Ramshaw, "Jump, Jim Crow! A Biographical Sketch of Thomas D. Rice (1808–1860)," *The Theatre of Southwestern Mississippi to 1840* (Ph.D. dissertation, State University of Iowa, 1941), 252; W. Stanley Hoole, *The Ante-Bellum Charleston Theatre* (University, Ala: University of Alabama Press, 1946), 35, 63; Gilbert Chase, *America's Music* (New York: McGraw-Hill, 1955), 264.

2. Rice's lyrics, consisting of fifty stanzas, are in the Harvard University Theatre Collection.

3. Noah M. Ludlow, *Dramatic Life As I Found It* (St. Louis, Mo.: 1880; reprinted New York: Benjamin Blom, 1966), 332.

4. George C. D. Odell, *Annals of the New York Stage*; 15 vol.: Columbia University Press, 1927), 3: 472, 641, 686; Frank Costellow

Davidson, *The Rise, Development, Decline and Influence of the American Minstrel Show* (Ph.D. dissertation, New York University, 1952), 66, 44, 68; Hans Nathan, *Dan Emmett and the Rise of Early Negro Minstrelsy* (Norman: University of Oklahoma Press, 1962), 67–69; Gary D. Engle, *This Grotesque Essence, Plays from the American Minstrel Stage* (Baton Rouge: Louisiana State University Press, 1978).

5. The visitor is cited in Blanche Muldrow, *The American Theatre as Seen by British Travellers 1790–1860* (Ph.D. dissertation, University of Wisconsin, 1963), 325.

6. Rice's *Othello* manuscript is in the Theatre Collection of the New York Public Library at Lincoln Center.

7. Arthur Hobson Quinn, *A History of the American Drama: From the Beginning to the Civil War*, 2d ed. (New York: Appleton-Century-Crofts, 1943), 334; Sigmund Spaeth, *A History of Popular Music in America* (New York: Random House, 1948), 70; Odell, *Annals of the New York Stage*, 4: 216; Chase, *America's Music*, 248; Davidson, *The Rise*, 132, 173; Nathan, *Dan Emmett*, 81, 155, 208.

8. John Bernard, *Retrospections of America, 1797–1811*, ed. from manuscripts by Mrs. Bayle Bernard (New York: Harper's, 1887), 207.

9. William C. Macready, *Macready's Reminiscences, and Selections from His Diaries and Letters*, ed. Sir Frederick Pollock (New York: Harper's, 1875), 587.

10. Carl Wittke, *Tambo and Bones* (Durham, N.C.: Duke University Press, 1930), 6, 9.

11. Frances Trollope, *Domestic Manners of the Americans*, ed. Donald Smalley (1832; reprinted New York: Vintage Books, 1960), 7.

12. Davidson, *The Rise*, 211; Richardson Wright, *Hawkers and Walkers in Early America* (Philadelphia: J. B. Lippincott, 1927), 187; Randolph Edmonds, "The Blacks in the American Theatre 1700–1969," *Pan-African Journal*, Vol. 7, No. 4 (Winter 1974), 312, 313.

13. Visitors commenting on blacks are cited in Muldrow, *The American Theatre*, 444, 445, and 446 respectively; English newspaper in an undated, unspecified clipping in Harvard University Theatre Collection.

14. Emmett and Christie are cited in Davidson, *The Rise*, 74 and 81 respectively; *Democratic Review and the United States Magazine*, November 1847, cited in Davidson, 82; account of early years of minstrel show in Nathan, *Dan Emmett*, 113ff, except where otherwise noted, and from accounts in playbills.

15. Nathan, *Dan Emmett*, 114–117.

16. Richard Moody, *America Takes the Stage* (Bloomington: Indiana University Press, 1955. Reprint. Millwood; N.Y.: Kraus Reprint Corp., 1969), 29.

17. Mark Twain, *Mark Twain in Eruption*, ed. Bernard De Voto (New York: Harper's, 1940), 111.

18. Walter Thornbury, 1873, writing of his American experience prior to the Civil War, cited in Muldrow, *The American Theatre*, 446, 379.

19. Ibid., 378.

20. Nathan, *Dan Emmett*, 175.

21. Nathan, *Dan Emmett*, 175; Chase, *America's Music*, 248; Davidson, *The Rise*, 138; John Tasker Howard and George Kent Bellows, *A Short History of Music in America* (New York: Thomas Y. Crowell, 1959), 105.

22. Davidson, *The Rise*, 85.

23. Howard and Bellows, *A Short History*, 103; Davidson, *The Rise*, 74, 108, 173.

24. Sources on the geographical range of the minstrel show include: Wendell Cole, "Early Theatre in America West of the Rockies: A Bibliographical Essay," *Theatre Research*, Vol. 4, No. 1, 1962, 36, 39, 41; Edmond M. Gagey, *The San Francisco Stage: A History* (New York: Columbia University Press, 1950), 4, 64, 31; Edward Gladstone Baynham, *The Early Development of Music in Pittsburgh* (Ph.D. dissertation, University of Pittsburgh, 1944), 230; Elbert R. Bowen, *Theatrical Entertainments in Rural Missouri Before the Civil War* (Columbia: University of Missouri Press, 1959), 44, 45; William G. B. Carson, *Managers in Distress: The St. Louis Stage, 1840–1844* (St. Louis, Mo.: St. Louis Historical Documents Foundation, 1949), 262–263; George O. Willard, *History of the Providence Stage, 1762–1891* (Providence: The Rhode Island News Co., 1891), 172; Richard Moody, *The Astor Place Riot* (Bloomington: Indiana University Press, 1958), 118; Ronald L. Davis, *Opera in Chicago* (New York: Appleton-Century, 1966), 6; Robert Franklin Eggers, *A History of Theatre in Boise, Idaho, from 1863 to 1963* (M.A. thesis, University of Oregon, 1963), 16; Firman Brown, Jr., *A History of Theatre in Montana* (Ph.D. dissertation, University of Wisconsin, 1963), 59; Joseph Gallegly, *Footlights on the Border: The Galveston and Houston Stage Before 1900* (The Hague: Mouton & Co., 1962), 59, 73; Margaret G. Watson, *Silver Theatre: Amusements of the Mining Frontier in Early Nevada 1850–1864* (Glendale, Calif.: Arthur H. Clark, 1964), 59; Eugene Clinton Elliott, *History of Variety-Vaudeville in Seattle, from the Beginning to 1914* (Seattle: University of Washington Press, 1944), 5–7; Iline Fife, *The Theatre During the Confederacy* (Ph.D. dissertation, Louisiana State University, 1949), 46ff.

25. Lester S. Levy, *Grace Notes in American History: Popular Sheet Music from 1800 to 1900* (Norman: University of Oklahoma Press,

1967), 99, 102; Richard A. Dwyer and Richard E. Lingenfelter, eds., *The Songs of the Gold Rush* (Berkeley and Los Angeles: University of California Press, 1964), 9.

26. Henry Clay Barnabee, *Reminiscences of Henry Clay Barnabee*, ed. George Leon Varney (Boston: Chapple, 1913), 92.

27. Cited in Muldrow, *The American Theatre*, 446.

28. Cited in John Tasker Howard, *Stephen Foster, America's Troubadour* (New York: Tudor Publishing Co., 1945), 196.

29. Wilfrid Mellers, *Music in a New Found Land* (New York: Alfred A. Knopf, 1967), 246.

30. For circus background in eighteenth-century America, see Julian Mates, *The American Musical Stage Before 1800* (New Brunswick, N.J.: Rutgers University Press, 1962), 20–28; and Isaac J. Greenwood, *The Circus: Its Origin and Growth Prior to 1835* (Washington, D.C.: Hobby Horse Press, 1898), 101–102, 114, 90, 109, 113; and Bowen, *Theatrical Entertainments*, 31, 32, 39, 40; and Gagey, *San Francisco Stage*, 71.

31. John Durang, *The Memoir of John Durang*, ed. Alan S. Downer (Pittsburgh: Historical Society of York County and University of Pittsburgh Press, 1966), 43.

32. James S. Moy, "Entertainments at John B. Ricketts' Circus, 1793–1800," *Educational Theatre Journal* (Vol. 30, No. 2, May 1978), 192.

33. William Dunlap, *Diary, 1766–1839*, 3 vols., ed. Dorothy C. Barck (New York: New–York Historical Society, 1930), 1:144, entry for September 12, 1797.

34. Thomas P. Parkinson, "Circus Music," *The Sonneck Society Newsletter*, Vol. 9, Spring 1983, 13–14.

35. George L. Chindahl, *A History of the Circus in America* (Caldwell, ID: Caxton Printers, 1939), 19, 45, 240–272.

36. Norman Clarke, *The Mighty Hippodrome* (South Brunswick, N.J., and New York: A. S. Barnes, 1968), 138.

37. Parkinson, "Circus Music," 13–14.

38. Myron Matlaw, "Tony the Trouper: Pastor's Early Years," *The Theatre Annual* Vol. 24, 1968, 76, 85.

ACT II. SCENE 3. MELODRAMA AND DANCE

1. *La Forêt Noire; or, Maternal Affection* (Boston: John and Joseph Russel, 1797), Act I, scene v.

2. M. Willson Disher, *Melodrama: Plots that Thrilled* (New York: Macmillan, 1954), xiii.

3. Elbridge Colby, *Early American Comedy* (New York: New York Public Library, 1919), 7–8.

4. Noah M. Ludlow, *Dramatic Life As I Found It* (St. Louis, Mo., 1880; reprinted New York: Benjamin Blom, 1966), 216.

5. David Mayer, "The Music of Melodrama," in *Performance and Politics in Popular Drama*, ed. David Bradby; Louis James, and Bernard Sharratt (Cambridge: Cambridge University Press, 1980), 51, 62.

6. Larry Robert Wolz, *Opera in Cincinnati: The Years Before the Zoo 1801–1920* (Ph.D. dissertation, University of Cincinnati, 1983), 26.

7. Colby, *Early American Comedy*, 8.

8. Thomas Holcroft, *A Tale of Mystery* (1802), in *British Plays of the Nineteenth Century*, ed. J. O. Bailey (New York: Odyssey Press, 1966), 229.

9. James Nelson Barker, *Indian Princess; or, La Belle Sauvage* (1808), in *Representative Plays by American Dramatists*, ed. M. J. Moses (Reprint. New York: Benjamin Blom, 1964).

10. N. H. Bannister, *Putnam, the Iron Son of '76* (Boston: 1859).

11. David Grimsted, *Melodrama Unveiled: American Theatre and Culture 1800–1850* (Chicago: University of Chicago Press, 1968), 259, 260, 261; James Russell Grandstaff, *A History of the Professional Theatre in Cincinnati, Ohio, 1861–1886* (Ph.D. dissertation, University of Michigan, 1963), 13.

12. Julian Mates, *The American Musical Stage Before 1800* (New Brunswick, N.J.: Rutgers University Press, 1962), 36–37.

13. Charles Durang, *History of the Philadelphia Stage: 1749–1855*, newspaper articles arranged and illustrated by Thompson Westcott, 1868, in the library of the University of Pennsylvania.

14. John Durang, *The Memoirs of John Durang*, ed. Alan S. Downer (Pittsburgh: Historical Society of York County and University of Pittsburgh Press, 1966), 118ff.

15. Lillian Moore, "John Durang the First American Dancer," *Chronicles of the American Dance*, ed. Paul Magriel (New York: Henry Holt and Co., 1948), 22, 59, 103.

16. Playbills in the Museum of the City of New York.

17. See note 1 of this scene.

18. Henry Clay Barnabee, *Reminiscences of Henry Clay Barnabee,* ed. George Leon Varney (Boston: Chapple, 1913), 58.

19. Henry W. Adams, *The Montgomery Theatre 1822–1835* (University, AL: University of Alabama, 1955), 14, 16; Joseph Gallegly, *Footlights on the Border: The Galveston and Houston Stage Before 1900* (The Hague: Mouton and Co., 1962), 20.

20. Olive Logan, *Before the Footlights and Behind the Scenes* (Philadelphia: Parmeles and Co., 1870), 563.

21. Joseph E. Marks, *America Learns to Dance* (New York, 1957; reprinted New York: Dance Horizons, n.d.), 50, 84, 25, 39, 98.

22. Joe Cowell, *Thirty Years Passed Among the Players in England and America* (New York: Harper and Bros., 1844), 75.

23. Frances Trollope, *Domestic Manners of the Americans,* ed. Donald Smalley (New York: Vintage Books, 1960), 134–135.

24. William B. Wood, *Personal Recollections of the Stage* (Philadelphia: Henry Carey Baird, 1855), 204–205.

25. William Dunlap, *History of the American Theatre,* 2 vols. (London 1833; reprinted New York: Burt Franklin, 1963), 2:326.

26. *A Peep Behind the Curtain, by a Supernumerary* (Boston: Redding and Co., 1850), 28–29, 57.

27. George Ellington [pseud.], *The Women of New York* (New York: New York Book Co., 1869; reprinted in *Dance Magazine,* January 1964, 33.

28. Philip Hone, *The Diary of Philip Hone, 1828–1851,* ed. Allen Nevins (New York: Dodd, Mead & Co., 1936), 272–273.

29. Cited in George C. D. Odell, *Annals of the New York Stage,* 15 vols. (New York: Columbia University Press, 1928), 4:432.

30. Ludlow, *Dramatic Life As I Found It,* 496, 346–347, 385, 374, 378.

31. *Cherry and Fair Star* (n.p., n.d.), is in the William Vaughn Moody Collection of the University of Chicago Library.

32. Cited in *Dramatic Life As I Found It,* Ludlow, 513–514.

33. Ibid., 361–362.

34. Ivor Guest, *Fanny Elssler* (Middletown, Conn.: Wesleyan University Press, 1970), 130ff, 132, 185.

35. Ludlow. *Dramatic Life As I Found It,* 536–538.

36. Hone, *Diary,* 479–481.

37. Barnabee, *Reminiscences,* 189.

38. Lillian Moore, "John Durang: the First American Dancer," *Chronicles of the American Dancer,* ed. Paul Magriel (New York: Henry Holt & Co., 1948), 37.

39. Walter Terry, *The Dance in America,* rev. ed. (New York: Harper & Row, 1971), 30–31.

40. Winthrop Palmer, *Theatrical Dancing in America,* 2d ed., rev. (Cranbury, N.J.: A. S. Barnes, 1978), 20, 34–35.

41. Cited in Walter Sorell, *The Dance Through the Ages* (New York: Grosset and Dunlap, 1967), 190.

42. Terry, *Dance in America,* 45ff.

43. Gerald Bordman, *American Musical Theatre, A Chronicle* (New York: Oxford University Press, 1978), 479.

44. Matteo, "Ethnic Dance," *The Dance Catalogue*, ed. Nancy Reynolds (New York: Harmony Books, 1979), 152.

45. Clive Barnes, "An Explosion of Dance," *American Way*, Vol. 8, No. 12, December 1975, 25, 27.

46. Jennifer Dunning, "Riverside Marks 17 Years of Dance," *New York Times*, January 5, 1983, C14.

47. Agnes de Mille, *America Dances* (New York: Macmillan, 1980), 16–19.

48. Gibert Seldes, *The 7 Lively Arts* (New York: Sagamore Press, 1957), 240.

ACT II. INTERMISSION. *THE BLACK CROOK*

1. The libretto for *The Black Crook* was not published until fairly recently; the outline of the plot is derived from Charles M. Barras's original manuscript in the Harvard University Theatre Collection and the prompt copy in The Players Club, New York.

2. *The New York Tribune*, September 17, 1866; the *Tribune* review is contained in George Freedley, "The Black Crook and the White Fawn," *Chronicles of the American Dance*, ed. Paul Magriel (New York: Henry Holt, 1948), 69–71.

3. Ibid., 65; Joseph Whitton, *Inside History of "The Black Crook,"* (Philadelphia, 1897), 10.

4. Julian Mates, *The American Musical Stage Before 1800* (New Brunswick, N.J.: Rutgers University Press, 1962), 161–162.

5. George C. D. Odell, *Shakespeare from Betterton to Irving*, 2 vols. (New York: Columbia University Press, 1920), 1:36, 189.

6. Mates, *The American Musical*, 177–179.

7. R. J. Broadbent, *A History of Pantomime* (London, 1901), 144, 180.

8. Richard Moody, *America Takes the Stage* (Bloomington: Indiana University Press, 1955), 206.

9. Clifford E. Hamar, "Scenery on the Early American Stage," *The Theatre Annual*, Vol. 7, 1948–1949, 84.

10. Gerald Bordman, *American Musical Theatre, A Chronicle* (New York: Oxford University Press, 1978), 14.

11. Deane L. Root, *American Popular Stage Music 1860–1880* (Ann Arbor, Mich.: UMI Research Press, 1981), 66–75.

12. *The New York World* review, September 17, 1866, is contained in Joseph Kaye, "Famous First Nights: The Black Crook," *Theatre Magazine*, July 1929, 38, 52, 64; *The New York Clipper*, September 22, 1866; *The New York Tribune*, September 17, 1866.

13. Donald Saddler, "The Black Crook," *Dance*, October 1941, 17.

14. Mates, *The American Musical*, 166, 168–169, 170.

15. Bill cited in Mates; *The American Musical*, 171.

16. Ibid., 172.

17. Quoted in Edward B. Marks, *They All Had Glamour, from the Swedish Nightingale to the Naked Lady* (New York: Julian Messner, 1944), 1.

18. Freedley, "The Black Crook and the White Fawn," 66.

19. Review cited in article on *The Black Crook* in *The Boston Sunday Herald*, June 24, 1917.

20. Richard Grant White, "The Age of Burlesque," *The Galaxy*, August 1869, 259.

21. *Appleton's Journal of Literature, Science, and Art*, July 3, 1869, 440.

22. From a scrapbook of clippings concerning *The Black Crook*, in the New York Public Library Theatre Collection, Lincoln Center, undated.

23. *The New York Clipper*, September 29, 1866.

24. Kaye, "Famous First Nights," 38; and 1929 clippings about *The Black Crook* in the New York Public Library.

25. George C.D. Odell, *Annals of the New York Stage*, 15 vols. (New York: Columbia University Press, 1936), III:313; Marks, *They All Had Glamour*, 227, 236, 251.

26. Marks, *They All Had Glamour*, 7; *The Boston Sunday Herald*, June 24, 1917; Playbill for Whitman's Continental Theatre, Boston (in Players Club, New York, as are subsequent playbills unless otherwise specified).

27. Mates, *The American Musical*, 140–153.

28. Saddler, "The Black Crook," *They All Had Glamour*, 12–13; *The Boston Sunday Herald*, June 24, 1917; New York Public Library clippings.

29. Whitton, *Inside History*, 5–10; Freedley, "The Black Crook and the White Fawn," 65.

30. *The New York Clipper*, September 29, 1866; Kaye, "Famous First Nights," 38; Whitton, *Inside History*, 32; New York Public Library clippings.

31. Whitton, *Inside History*, 18ff.

32. Cited in Marks, *They All Had Glamour*, 7.

33. *The Boston Sunday Herald*, June 24, 1917; Marks, *They All Had Glamour*, 7, 12, 13, 15; Newark Theatre bill; notes in *The Black Crook* prompt book; clipping in New York Public Library.

34. Available in the New York Public Library.

35. Available in the New York Public Library.

36. Charles M. Barras, *The Black Crook* (Philadelphia: Barclay & Co., 1873).

37. New York Public Library manuscript prompt book and clippings.

38. Constance Rourke, *American Humor* (New York: Anchor, 1953), 231.

ACT II. SCENE 4. BURLESQUE, REVUE, AND VAUDEVILLE

1. Bernard Sobel, *A Pictorial History of Burlesque* (New York: G. P. Putnam's Sons, 1956), 12.

2. Mat Fields's burlesques are in manuscript in the Harvard University Theatre Collection's Ludlow Collection.

3. Sol. Smith, *The Theatrical Journey-Work and Anecdotal Recollections of Sol. Smith* (Philadelphia: T. B. Peterson and Bros., 1854), 105.

4. Sol. Smith, *Theatrical Management in the West and South for Thirty Years* (New York: Harper and Bros., 1868), 160–161.

5. Lester Wallach, *Memories of Fifty years* (New York: Charles Scribner's Sons, 1889), 105.

6. Walter H. Draper, *George L. Fox, Comedian in Pantomime and Travesty* (Ph.D. dissertation, University of Illinois, 1957), 19; Walter H. Draper, "George L. Fox's Burlesque-*Hamlet*," *Quarterly Journal of Speech*, Vol. 50, No. 4, December 1964, 283.

7. Claudia Johnson, "Burlesques of Shakespeare: The Democratic American's 'Light Artillery,' " *Theatre Survey*, Vol. 21, No. 1, May 1980, 50–51, 56, 58.

8. Walter H. Draper, "George L. Fox's Burlesque-*Hamlet*," 381–382.

9. Richard Moody, ed., *Dramas from the American Theatre 1762–1909* (Cleveland and New York: The World Publishing Co., 1966), 402, 418.

10. *Appleton's Journal of Literature, Science, and Arts* (New York: D. Appleton & Co., 1869), Vol. 1, Nos. 1–20, 440.

11. Jack W. McCullough, "Edward Kilanyi and American Tableaux Vivants," *Theatre Survey*, Vol. XVI, No. 1, May 1975, 26.

12. Allen Lesser, *Enchanting Rebel: The Secret of Ada Isaacs Menken* (Philadelphia: Jewish Book League, 1947), 76, 79, 75; Paul Lewis, *Queen of the Plaza, A Biography of Adah Isaacs Menken* (New York: Funk & Wagnalls, 1964), 6.

13. Joseph Kaye, "Famous First Nights: The Black Crook," *Theatre Magazine*, July 1929, 38.

14. William Greene, "Strippers and Coochers—the Quintessence of American Burlesque," *Western Popular Theatre*, ed., David Mayer and

Kenneth Richards (New York and London: Methuen, 1977), 157, 161; Frank Luther Mott, *History of American Magazines* (Cambridge, Mass.: Harvard University Press, 1957), 3 (1865–1885): 206.

15. Olive Logan, *Before the Footlights and Behind the Scenes* (Philadelphia: Parmelee and Co., 1870), 138, 564, 586.

16. Ralph G. Allen, "Our Native Theatre: Honky-Tonk, Minstrel Shows, Burlesque," *The American Theatre: A Sum of Its Parts*, ed. Henry B. Williams (New York: Samuel French, Inc., 1971), 275, 278.

17. Irving Zeidman, *The American Burlesque Show* (New York: Hawthorne Books, Inc., 1967), 29, 34, 56–57, 93; Robert C. Toll, *On with the Show: The First Century of Show Business in America* (New York: Oxford University Press, 1976), 225, 231.

18. William Green, "The Audiences of the American Burlesque Show of the Minsky Era (ca. 1920–40) in New York," *Das Theater und sein Publikum*, 1977, 236, 226.

19. Zeidman, *The American Burlesque Show*, 142.

20. Ann Corio with Joseph Di Mona, *This Was Burlesque* (New York: Grosset and Dunlap, 1968), 144.

21. Zeidman, *The American Burlesque Show*, 95–105, 168.

22. Julian Mates, *The American Musical Stage Before 1800* (New Brunswick, N.J.: Rutgers University Press, 1962), 179, 200; John Tasker Howard, *Our American Music* 3d ed. (New York: Thomas Y. Crowell, 1946), 92; Glenn Hughes, *A History of the American Theatre 1700–1950* (New York: Samuel French, 1951), 107.

23. Allardyce Nicoll, *English Drama 1900–1930* (Cambridge: Cambridge University Press, 1973), 169.

24. David Ewen, *The Story of America's Musical Theatre* (Philadelphia and New York: Chilton Co., 1961), 58–59.

25. Donald Oliver, comp. and ed., *The Greatest Revue Sketches* (New York: Avon Books, 1982), xi, xii.

26. Norman Clarke, *The Mighty Hippodrome* (South Brunswick, N.J., and New York: A. S. Barnes and Co., 1968), 22, 62, 31.

27. Allen Churchill, *The Great White Way* (New York: E. P. Dutton, 1962), 113.

28. Charles Higham, *Ziegfeld* (Chicago: Henry Regnery, 1972), 63–64, 78, 178; Marjorie Fransworth, *The Ziegfeld Follies* (New York: Bonanza Books, 1956), 31; Robert Baral, *Revue* (New York: Fleet Publishing Co., 1962), 14.

29. *Broadside*, Vol. 10, No. 3, Winter 1982–1983, N.S., 3.

30. Baral, *Revue*, 101–102; Raymond Mander and Joe Mitchenson, *Revue*, foreward by Noel Coward (New York: Taplinger Publishing Co., 1971), viii.

31. Garff B. Wilson, *Three Hundred Years of American Drama and Theatre* (Englewood Cliffs, N.J.: Prentice-Hall, 1973), 373.

32. Eckert Goodman, "Richard Rodgers: Composer Without a Key," *Harper's*, August 1953, 63; John Tasker Howard, *Our American Music*, 3d ed. (New York: Thomas Y. Crowell Co., 1946), 534; June Smith, "Cole Porter in the American Musical Theatre," *Themes in Drama: Drama, Dance in Music*, ed. James Redmond (Cambridge: Cambridge University Press, 1981), 49; Abel Green and Joe Laurie, Jr., *Show Biz from Vaude to Video* (New York: Henry Holt and Co., 1951), 179.

33. Baral, *Revue*, 50.

34. Ken Murray, *The Body Merchant, the Story of Earl Carroll* (Pasadena, CA: Ward Ritchie Press, 1976), 44; Baral, *Revue*, 27, 80, 94.

35. Ibid., 123–130.

36. Russel Nye, *The Unembarrassed Muse: The Popular Arts in America* (New York: The Dial Press, 1970), 177.

37. Baral, *Revue*, 198–211.

38. Nye, *The Unembarrassed Muse*, 146.

39. John E. DiMeglio, *Vaudeville U.S.A.* (Bowling Green, Ohio: Bowling Green University Press, 1973), 19.

40. Oscar G. Sonneck, *Early Opera in America* (New York: G. Schirmer, 1915), 81.

41. Joe Laurie, Jr., *Vaudeville: From the Honkey-Tonks to the Palace* (Port Washington, N.Y.: Kennikat Press, 1972), 12; Hughes, *History of the American Theatre*, 185.

42. Milton Gerald Hehr, *Musical Activities in Salem, Massachusetts: 1783–1823* (Boston: Boston University Ph.D. dissertation, 1963), 168–169; Robert Franklin Eggers, *A History of Theatre in Boise, Idaho, from 1863 to 1963* (M.A. thesis, University of Oregon, 1963), 1; Eugene Clinton Elliott, *A History of Variety-Vaudeville in Seattle, from the Beginning to 1914* (Seattle: University of Washington Press, 1944), 10.

43. Parker Zellers, *Tony Pastor: Dean of the Vaudeville Stage* (Ypsilanti: Eastern Michigan University Press, 1971), xiv; Douglas Gilbert, *American Vaudeville: Its Life and Times* (New York: McGraw-Hill, 1940), 4.

44. Bernard Sobel, *A Pictorial History of Vaudeville* (New York: The Citadel Press, 1961), 20–26.

45. Zellers, *Tony Pastor*, 26, 35–36, 50, 57, 93, 109; Myron Matlaw, "Pastor and his Flock," *Theatre Arts*, Vol. 42, August 1958, 20–21; Myron Matlaw, "Tony the Trouper: Pastor's Early Years," *The Theatre Annual*, Vol. 24, 1968, 83, 85.

46. Charles Hamm, *Music in the New World* (New York: W. W. Norton, 1983), 258.

47. Albert F. McLean, Jr., *American Vaudeville As Ritual* (Lexington, KY: University of Kentucky Press, 1965), 17–18.

48. Charles and Louise Samuels, *Once Upon a Stage: The Merry World of Vaudeville* (New York: Dodd, Mead and Co., 1974), 24–29, 31–32, 34, 41–44, 248, 285, 8–9, 22, 50–52.

49. Clifford Ashby, "Folk Theatre in a Tent," *National History*, Vol. 92, No. 3, 1983, 8, 12, 20; Neil E. Schaffner with Vance Johnson, *The Fabulous Toby and Me* (Englewood Cliffs, N.J.: Prentice-Hall, 1968), v, vi, 82.

50. Robert C. Toll, *On with the Show: The First Century of Show Business in America* (New York: Oxford University Press, 1976), 277.

51. DiMeglio, *Vaudeville U.S.A.*, 8–9.

52. Joe Laurie, Jr., *Vaudeville*, 74.

53. Charles and Louise Samuels, *Once Upon a Stage*, 50.

54. Marian Spitzer, *The Palace*, (New York: Atheneum, 1969), 4, 96.

ACT II. SCENE 5. MUSICAL COMEDY

1. Charles Hamm, *Music in the New World* (New York, London: W. W. Norton, 1983), 195.

2. Gerald Bordman, *American Musical Theatre: A Chronicle* (New York: Oxford University Press, 1978), 8.

3. Bordman, *American Musical Theatre*, 7, 16.

4. Deane L. Root, *American Popular Stage Music 1860–1880* (Ann Arbor, MI: UMI Research Press, 1981), 69, 70, 50–54; Roger Allan Hall, *Nate Salsbury and his Troubadours: Popular American Farce and Musical Comedy* (Ph.D. dissertation, Ohio State University, 1974, 9–11; Cecil Smith and Glenn Litton, *Musical Comedy in America* (New York: Theatre Arts Books, 1981), 32.

5. Edmond M. Gagey, *The San Francisco Stage: A History* (New York: Columbia University Press, 1950), 127.

6. Bordman, *American Musical Theatre*, 28.

7. Richard Moody, ed., *Drama from the American Theatre 1762– 1909* (Cleveland and New York: World Publishing Co., 1966), 535, 538, 539.

8. Richard Moody, *Ned Harrigan from Corlear's Hook to Herald Square* (Chicago: Nelson-Hall, 1980), 155.

9. Cited in E. J. Kahn, Jr., *The Merry Partners: The Age and Stage of Harrigan and Hart* (New York: Random House, 1955), 4; also see 152, 14.

10. Richard Moody, *Ned Harrigan*, 47.

11. Smith and Litton, *Musical Comedy in America*, 36.

12. Bordman, *American Musical Theatre*, 76, 79, 113–115.

13. Agnes de Mille, *America Dances* (New York: Macmillan, 1980), 120.

14. Douglas L. Hunt, ed., *Five Plays* by Charles H. Hoyt, in Barrett H. Clark, ed., *America's Lost Plays*, 10 vols. (Bloomington: Indiana University Press, 1964), 9: x, xiv, xv, 106; George C. D. Odell, *Annals of the New York Stage*, 15 vols. (New York: Columbia University Press, 1928), XIV:58, XV:39–40.

15. Douglas L. Hunt, ibid., xv.

16. Allen Churchill, *The Great White Way* (New York: E. P. Dutton, 1962), 3.

17. Jervis Anderson, "That Was New York (Harlem—Part 1)," *The New Yorker*, June 29, 1981, 60–61.

18. James Weldon Johnson, *Black Manhattan* (New York, 1940: reprinted New York: Arno Press, 1968), 95, 102, 109.

19. Anderson, "That Was New York," 64.

20. *In Dahomey*, copyright 1902, Will M. Cook.

21. Henry T. Sampson, *Blacks in Blackface* (Metuchen, N.J.: Scarecrow Press, 1980), 9, 25, 20, 131; Ann Charters, *Nobody: The Story of Bert Williams* (New York: Macmillan, 1970), 25–26, 74–75, 9.

22. Henry T. Sampson, ibid., 20.

23. Robert Kimball, liner notes to *Shuffle Along*, copyright 1976, Recorded Anthology of American Music, Inc., 1–4.

24. George M. Cohan, *Twenty Years on Broadway*, (New York: Harper and Bros., 1925), 184–185.

25. Ibid., 262; Ward Morehouse, *George M. Cohan, Prince of the American Theatre* (Philadelphia: J. B. Lippincott, 1943), 235ff; John McCabe, *George M. Cohan: The Man Who Owned Broadway* (New York: Doubleday, 1973), 51, 127, 280ff; Arthur Hobson Quinn, *A History of the American Drama, from the Civil War to the Present Day* (New York: Appleton-Century-Crofts, 1936), 115.

26. Irene Smith, "Cole Porter in the American Musical Theatre," in *Themes in Drama: Drama, Dance in Music*, ed. James Redmond (Cambridge: Cambridge University Press, 1981), 50.

27. Stanley Green, *Encyclopedia of the Musical Theatre* (New York: Da Capo Press, 1976), 341–342.

28. P. G. Wodehouse and Guy Bolton, *Bring on the Girls* (New York: Simon and Schuster, 1953), 5.

29. Ibid., 7.

30. Stanley Green, Appendix ("Musical Productions and Discography"), *The World of Musical Comedy* (New York: Grosset and Dunlop, 1962), 319ff.

31. Miles Kreuger, *Show Boat: The Story of a Classic American Musical* (New York: Oxford University Press, 1970), 28–64.

32. Stanley Green, *Ring Bells! Sing Songs! Broadway Musicals of the 1930's* (New York: Galahad Books, 1971), 12–13.

33. Ethan Mordden, *Better Foot Forward: The History of American Musical Theatre* (New York: Grossman Publishers, 1976), 137–139.

34. Arthur Jackson, *The Best Musicals From Show Boat to A Chorus Line* (New York: Crown, 1977), 45.

35. Agnes de Mille, *Dance to the Piper* (Boston: Little, Brown and Co., 1952), 214, 240.

36. Stanley Richards, ed., *Great Musicals of the American Theatre* (Radnor, Penna.: Chilton Book Co., 1973), 1: 586, 588, 593.

37. Charles Willard, "Life's 'Progress': *Love Life* Revisited," *Kurt Weill Newsletter*, Vol. 2, No. 2, Fall 1984, 5.

38. *The Dramatists Guild Quarterly*, Vol. 20, No. 1, Spring 1983, 17, 20.

39. Lehman Engel, Lecture, April 2, 1981, at the Musical Theatre in America Conference, C.W. Post Campus of Long Island University.

40. Jerome Robbins, "Knockout Numbers," *Vanity Fair*, December 1984, 114.

41. Sondheim quoted in Craig Zadan, *Sondheim & Co.* (New York: Avon, 1974), 139, 220.

42. Frank Rich, "A Musical Theater Breakthrough," *The New York Times Magazine*, October 21, 1984, 53, 71.

43. Paul Wittke, review of "American Musical Theatre" section of *The New Grove*, in *The Musical Quarterly*, Vol. 68, No. 2, April 1982, 282.

Bibliographical Essay

The notes for each chapter not only list all the works used but also give complete publishing information. The following sections do not by any means attempt a complete bibliography but only indicate the most useful books and sometimes the most useful approaches to a study of America's musical stage.

TEXTS OF MUSICALS

Only a few books include more than one text of an American musical. Ten musicals are included in volume 1 of Stanley Richards, *Great Musicals of the American Theatre* (Radnor, Penna., 1973), ranging from *Of Thee I Sing* to *Company*; volume 2 (1976) includes book and lyrics for ten more musicals. The same editor has brought out *Great Rock Musicals* (New York, 1979), containing eight rock musicals. Occasionally, the collected works of a librettist are brought together, as in *Six Plays by Rodgers and Hammerstein* (New York, n.d.). Aside from these collections, most twentieth-century American musicals tend to be published in separate volumes for the general public and in acting editions by such houses as Samuel French and Tams Witmark.

The most useful collection for the nineteenth century is *America's Lost Plays*, originally in 20 volumes and reissued by Indiana University Press (Bloomington, 1963), with Barrett H. Clark as general editor. Here are some melodramas and some musicals (for example, Charles Hoyt's *A Trip to Chinatown*). William Dunlap's musicals of the eighteenth and nineteenth centuries were collected by Julian Mates, in *Musical Works of William Dunlap* (Delmar, N.Y., 1980). A particularly useful anthology, not only because of its musicals but especially because of its essays and introductions is Richard Moody's *Dramas from the American Theatre 1762–1909* (Cleveland and New York, 1966). Many individual plays were used, and these provide insight available in no other way—for example, T. D. Rice's *Othello* (in manuscript in New York Public Library's Performing Arts Library at Lincoln Center), *Cherry and Fair Star* in special collections at the University of Chicago library, and *La Forêt Noire* in its eighteenth-century original edition in the University of Pennsylvania.

Some anthologies are especially useful for offering a selection of plays in a particular area: Michael Booth's *Hiss the Villain: Six American and English Melodramas* (New York, 1964), for example, or Gary D. Engle's *This Grotesque Essence: Plays from the American Minstrel Stage* (Baton Rouge, LA, and London, 1978), or Donald Oliver's *The Greatest Revue Sketches* (New York, 1982).

BIOGRAPHIES AND DIARIES

In every period, biographies and autobiographies give helpful information, though frequently no more than a paragraph or two in the standard "as told to" actor's autobiography of the twentieth century. Still, a paragraph or fact here or there all helped to pull together the various strands which make up this volume. Particularly helpful were the *Diary of William Dunlap (1766–1839)* in three volumes (New York, 1929, 1930, 1931) and John Bernard, *Retrospections of America: 1797–1811* (New York, 1887); both works give the sort of insights for the eighteenth century available only to men actively engaged in the theatre. To them must be added *The Memoir of John Durang, American Actor, 1785–1816*, edited by Alan S. Downer (Pittsburgh, Penna., 1966); Durang was the first American-born actor-dancer. Other managers and performers than Dunlap and Durang put their experiences on paper, and here again we are able to judge the repertory and fit the musical into our early theatres both financially and artistically. Especially helpful are William B. Wood's *Personal Recollections of the Stage* (Philadelphia, 1855) and William Warren's *Journals* (1796–1831, original in Howard University, microfilm in Temple University).

In the nineteenth century, two of the most helpful publishers of their own reminiscences were the managers Sol. Smith and his partner and, later, enemy Noah Ludlow. Smith's volumes are more anecdotal, but he is extremely helpful on touring, on stock companies, and on the pertinent anecdote that illuminates an entire period. Especially recommended is his *Theatrical Management in the West and South for Thirty Years* (New York, 1868). Ludlow seems humorless but is master of details, and his memoir is obviously drawn from books kept over a long period of time. His *Dramatic Life As I Found It* (St. Louis, Mo., 1880, reprinted New York, 1966) remains the place to go to find an actor, a singer, a dancer, a troupe—and to note their conditions of employment along with some analysis of their worth.

Fortunately, most important figures of the late nineteenth and early twentieth centuries have their biographers, so that detailed information about, say, Weber and Fields can be found in Felix Isman's biography (New York, 1924), about Henry Clay Barnabee in his *My Wanderings* (Boston, 1913), or Tony Pastor in the biographies of Parker Zellers (Ypsilanti, Mich., 1971) and Myron Matlaw ("Tony the Trouper: Pastor's Early Years," *The Theatre Annual*, 1968). Sometimes the diary of someone unconnected to the theatre but with a love of the musical stage can provide more information than the professional artist; such a book is *The Diary of Philip Hone, 1828–1851* (New York, 1936). Sometimes the biography is more concerned with the profession than with the biography—for example, the best single work on the minstrel show hides under the guise of a biography: Hans Nathan's *Dan Emmett and the Rise of Early Negro Minstrelsy* (Norman, Okla., 1962).

Occasionally, the best sort of insight about an artist may be obtained when both an autobiography and biographies exist for the same person. George M. Cohan, for example, wrote *Twenty Years on Broadway And the Years it took to get there* (New York and London, 1925); this volume is complemented, facts straightened, and extensive background supplied by Ward Morehouse, *George M. Cohan* (Philadelphia and New York, 1943) and John McCabe, *George M. Cohan: The Man Who Owned Broadway* (New York, 1973). Two other complementary biographies are E. J. Kahn's *The Merry Partners, The Age and Stage of Harrigan and Hart* (New York, 1955) and Richard Moody's *Ned Harrigan From Corlear's Hook to Herald Square* (Chicago, 1980).

Some twentieth-century lives extend beyond themselves in much the same way that Nathan's book on Emmett did—for example, the Toby show is made clear thanks to Neil E. Schaffner and Vance Johnson's *The Fabulous Toby and Me* (Englewood Cliffs, N.J., 1968) or the autobiographies of Agnes de Mille, *Dance to the Piper* (Boston, 1952) and *And Promenade Home* (Boston, 1956).

Obviously, many other biographies exist of figures from all aspects of the American musical, some from eighteenth- and nineteenth-century figures, and a flood from the twentieth century. It is worth noting, however, that all major composers of the twentieth century have been treated to at least one biography, and many to two or three. Certainly, no picture of the American musical of this century is complete without looking into some biographies of Sondheim, Gershwin, Youmans, Porter, Berlin, Rodgers, and Kern, at the very least.

HISTORIES

Two types of histories were used throughout. The first and most extensive involved local theatre histories. No generalization was possible about the repertory, the movement of theatre, indeed the very nature of American theatre without local histories. And it was precisely the similarity of patterns throughout the United States which made possible the view of the centrality of musical theatre. Probably the single most useful of these histories is the multi-volume *Annals of the New York Stage* by George C. D. Odell (New York, 1927ff). Also especially helpful were William G. B. Carson's two volumes: *Managers in Distress, the St. Louis Stage, 1840–1844* (St. Louis, Mo., 1949) and *The Theatre on the Frontier, The Early Years of the St. Louis Stage*, 2d ed. (New York, 1965). Regional histories or histories of a particular city are well represented by Joseph Gallegly, *Footlights on the Border: The Galveston and Houston Stage Before 1900* (The Hague, 1962); Edmund M. Gagey, *The San Francisco Stage* (New York, 1950); Margaret G. Watson, *Silver Theatre, Amusements of the Mining Frontier in Early Nevada 1850–1864* (Glendale, Calif., 1964); George O. Willard, *History of the Providence Stage 1762–1891* (Providence, R.I., 1891); W. Stanley Hoole, *The Ante-Bellum Charleston Theatre* (University, Ala., 1946); Reese Davis James, *Cradle of Culture, 1800–1810, The Philadelphia Stage* (Philadelphia, 1957); and William W. Clapp, Jr., *A Record of the Boston Stage* (1853; reprinted New York, 1968).

A second approach to local theatre histories was through unpublished work, theses, and dissertations which, through local records, newspapers, and diaries make clear the origins of theatre in a specific locale. The list, again, is too long to mention here, but especially helpful were Harold Calvin Tedford *A Study of Theatrical Entertainments in Northwest Arkansas from their Beginning through 1889* (Ph.D. dissertation, Louisiana State Univeristy, 1965), and Joseph Miller Free, *The Theatre of Southwestern Mississippi to 1840*, 2 vols. (Ph.D. dissertation, State University of Iowa, 1941); other graduate studies were also helpful—by Edward Gladstone Baynham (Pittsburgh), Russell James Grandstaff (Cincinnati), William George Burbick (Columbus, Ohio), Larry Robert Wolz (Texas), and Robert Franklin Eggers (Boise, Idaho), among many others.

The second type of history was of the musical itself. Here, the indispensable work is Gerald Bordman's *American Musical Theatre, A Chronicle* (New York, 1978). Year by year, from the eighteenth century through the 1970s, Bordman lists all American musicals, with some information about each production. Other histories tend to handle the twentieth century with only a passing nod at earlier years. These include David Ewen, *The Story of America's Musical Theatre* (Philadelphia and New York, 1961); Ethan Mordden, *Better Foot Forward, The History of American Musical Theatre* (New York, 1976); Cecil Smith, *Musical Comedy in America* (brought up to date by Glenn Litton, New York, 1981); Stanley Green, *The World of Musical Comedy*, 4th ed. (New York, 1984); Lehman Engel, *The American Musical Theater: A Consideration* (New York, 1967), Arthur Jackson, *The Best Musicals from Show Boat to A Chorus Line* (New York, 1977); Martin Gottfried, *Broadway Musicals* (New York, 1979); Abe Loufe, *Broadway's Greatest Musicals* (New York, 1973); Gerald Bordman, *American Musical Comedy* (New York, 1982), and *American Operetta* (New York, 1981).

Some histories of the musical are more special in their approaches. Here we have Julian Mates, *The American Musical Stage before 1800* (New Brunswick, N.J., 1962); Deane L. Root, *American Popular Stage Music 1860–1880* (Ann Arbor, Mich., 1981); Stanley Green, *Ring Bells! Sing Songs! Broadway Musicals of the 1930's* (New York, 1971); Miles Kreuger, *Show Boat: The Story of a Classic American Musical* (New York, 1977).

TRAVEL

In every period of American history, travelers to America were fascinated with the New World and felt the need to write about it. Frequently, the traveler's lucubrations resulted in a work which seriously analyzed the country and all its ways, including the drama. Alexis de Tocqueville's *Democracy in America* (Paris, 1835 and 1840; reprinted New York, 1954) is not, of course, essentially a travel book, but his keen eye saw the direction the stage must take in a democracy. Of the dozen or so travel books perused for this study, the most useful in their comments about the theatre were Frances Trollope, *Domestic Manners of the Americans* (1832; reprinted New York, 1960); Donald Raymond Henry, *The American Theatre as Viewed by 19th Century British Travellers, 1860–1900* (Ph.D. dissertation, University of Wisconsin, 1964); Blanche Muldrow, *The American Theatre as Seen by British Travellers 1790–1860* (Ph.D. dissertation, University of Wisconsin, 1953).

SPECIAL STUDIES

Each type of musical theatre has its own chroniclers, although some are more fully chronicled than others. For example, only one book (Philip Graham, *Showboats, The History of an American Institution*, Austin, Texas, and London, 1951) and a few articles concerned themselves with the showboat, and also there is very little about burlesque, the best being Irving Zeidman, *The American Burlesque Show* (New York, 1967) and Bernard Sobel, *A Pictorial History of Burlesque* (New York, 1956). Even less has been written about the tent show—Clifford Ashby, "Folk Theatre in a Tent," *Natural History*, Vol. 92, Nos. 3, 1983, and Schaffner's *The Fabulous Toby and Me* (see above) are good examples. Yet other forms of musical theatre have had more than their share—melodrama, for example (though almost nothing touches on its music; Alan J. Downer, "Players and Painted Stage, Nineteenth Century Acting," *PMLA*, Vol. 61, No. 2, June 1946, does an excellent job, however, in pointing up its dance). Vaudeville increasingly finds writers anxious to move it from entertainment to myth: see especially Douglas Gilbert, *American Vaudeville, Its Life and Times* (New York, 1940); John E. DiMeglio, *Vaudeville U.S.A.* (Bowling Green, Ohio, 1973); and Albert F. McLean, Jr., *American Vaudeville as Ritual* (Lexington: University of Kentucky, 1965). The revue, particularly Ziegfeld's, is fairly adequately documented in a variety of books; I have found Robert Baral's *Revue* (New York, 1962) and Marjorie Farnsworth's *The Ziegfeld Follies* (New York, 1956) especially helpful. Much has been written about the circus, and increasingly works are dealing with the early American circus; I have found all of them most helpful, though I was especially dependent on the fine work done by George L. Chindahl in his *A History of the Circus in America* (Caldwell, 1959).

Some works not mentioned in either text or notes yet which offer different approaches to the minstrel show include James Weldon Johnson, *Black Manhattan* (1930; reprinted New York, 1968); Robert C. Toll, *Blacking Up, The Minstrel Show in Nineteenth-Century America* (New York, 1974); Constance Rourke, *American Humor, A Study of the National Character* (1931; reprinted New York: 1953); Alexander Saxton, "Minstrelsy as Political Institution," *American Quarterly*, Vol. 27, 3–28.

PLAYBILLS, PROGRAMS, PHOTOGRAPHS, NEWSPAPERS

Here serendipity plays a large part. The Harvard University Theatre Collection's enormous range of minstrel show playbills, for example, reveals not only the history of the minstrel show but its attempt to provide accurate portrayals in its early years, and its early educational thrust. Reviews of eighteenth- and nineteenth-century performances, so necessary in order to be able to envision productions accurately, may be found in large early American newspaper collections in the New-York Historical Society and the Library of Congress. Drawings and photographs are available in large quantities in the Museum of the City of New York for America's early years, even as the New York Public Library's Performing Arts Library at Lincoln Center provides an excellent range for more recent times.

DISCOGRAPHY

Most works on America's musicals include a discography, some annotated. Other books list available music on records exclusively: Gordon W. Hodgins, *The Broadway Musical, A Complete L.P. Discography* (Metuchen, N.J., and London, 1980), and the much more complete book by Jack Raymond, *Show Music on Record from the 1890s to the 1980s* (New York, 1982). Individual songs going back to the eighteenth century have emerged, and re-creations of many nineteenth-century songs, minstrel shows, and even musicals are now available. The best source for many of these is the large number of discs issued by New World Records.

Index

About the Author

JULIAN MATES is University Dean of the Faculty of Visual and Performing Arts, Long Island University. He is the author of *Renaissance Culture: A New Sense of Order*, *The American Musical Stage before 1800*, and articles in *American Music*, *Theatre Survey*, and *The Shakespeare Newsletter*.

American musical theatre has developed as an indigenous art form, with a long history, amazing vitality, and a variety of expression. Julian Mates is the first to show the musical stage in all its guises—from burlesque to musical comedy to grand opera—from its beginnings in pre-Revolutionary America to the present day. In addition, his book is the first to explore the relationships between the various forms of musical theatre.

Mates sensitively deals with the recurrent aesthetic question of popular versus highbrow art, noting that some of the best American composers and performers have contributed to the popular musical stage. He also looks at critical reactions to popular theatrical forms of musical entertainment. In his account of the history of the musical stage, he introduces the reader to various types of theatrical companies, the changing repertory, and the many kinds of musical performers who have animated the stage. Mates focuses on the creative relationships between the different forms of opera, the minstrel show and circus, melodrama and dance, burlesque, revue, vaudeville, and musical comedy.

This book is an entertaining illustrated guide for the musical theatre buff as well as students of drama, music, or American culture.